BRYAN CARRAWAY

SPIRITUAL GIFTS

BRYAN CARRAWAY

SPIRITUAL GIFTS

THEIR PURPOSE & POWER

Pleasant Word
A Division of WINEPRESS PUBLISHING

Printed in the United States of America

Packaged by Pleasant Word, a division of WinePress Publishing, PO Box 428, Enumclaw, WA 98022. The views expressed or implied in this work do not necessarily reflect those of Pleasant Word, a division of WinePress Publishing. Ultimate design, content, and editorial accuracy of this work are the responsibilities of the author.

Unless otherwise noted, all Scriptures are taken from the New American Standard Bible, © 1960, 1963, 1968, 1971, 1972, 1973, 1975, 1977 by The Lockman Foundation. Used by permission.

Scripture references marked KJV are taken from the King James Version of the Bible.

ISBN 1-4141-0336-0
Library of Congress Catalog Card Number: 2004099624

Christian Leaders are Praising Spiritual Gifts: Their Purpose & Power

Bryan Carraway has written a book on spiritual gifts that should be read by every Christian! He has moved aside all theological, denominational, and cultural biases, including his own, and has given us a clear treatise from the Word of God. This book on gifts is a gift to the church. I predict that God is going to use it to open minds on both sides of the charismatic/cessationist debate so that we can overcome our petty differences and unite in order to advance the kingdom in these end times.

Dr. Vic Simpson, Senior Pastor
Emmanuel Baptist Church
Huntington, MD

This book, *Spiritual Gifts: Their Purpose & Power*, by Bryan Carraway, is a concise, warm, and popular answer to the questions most often asked about the gifts of the Spirit. I recommend it to anyone who is open and seeking a deeper understanding of the work of the Holy Spirit in our day.

Dr. Vinson Synan, Dean
School of Divinity, Regent University
Virginia Beach, VA

It is essential that all Christians be equipped to use their spiritual gifts so that the church can be successful today. Bryan Carraway has helped take us past the excuses and uncertainty and challenged all of us to activate God's supernatural power in our lives. Thank you, Bryan.

Dr. Tim Hamon, CEO
Christian International Ministries Network
Santa Rosa Beach, FL

I especially appreciate Carraway's extensive treatment of the gift of tongues. If you have been confused about this gift, or others, be so no longer! You will enjoy Carraway's engaging and personal style and his easy-to-understand everyday examples. A must read for anyone serious about understanding, identifying, and putting their spiritual gifts to use!

Rev. Robert A. Buchanan, Pastor
Evangelical Presbyterian Church
Elkton, VA

Bryan has attempted to approach the discussion of spiritual gifts in an objective manner, showing great respect for those in all the "camps" that exist in the traditional church structures of today. His book is an excellent basic explanation for those who want to be introduced to this subject.

Dr. Ralph Neighbour, Jr., Pastoral Team
TOUCH Family Church
www.touchfamily.com
Houston, TX

In his own unique way, Bryan Carraway produces a readable and balanced view of spiritual gifts. His book is deeply intellectual and spiritually insightful and brings clarity to much of the confusion surrounding spiritual gifts. This is a well-researched and well-written book that can be used in the classroom or for personal devotions by those who seek God's plan for their lives.

Dr. Dwarka Ramphal, President
Heritage Bible College
Dunn, NC

Spiritual Gifts: Their Purpose & Power presents a refreshing and balanced view of the gifts within the church today. Bryan addresses giftings within the body that have been overlooked in many circles. The awareness of these giftings will encourage and give focus to individuals to fulfill their God-given destinies.

Eunice L. Barruel, International Director
New Strength International Ministries
Virginia Beach, VA

Theology void of experience has a hollow sound. When spiritual truth collides with experience, our hearts are set on fire. Bryan Carraway's book on spiritual gifts does just that—it connects the reality of the Spirit with the searching mind. I highly recommend this book. It connects.

John Miller, Senior Pastor
Church on the Rock
Texarkana, TX

Table of Contents

Discovering and Growing in the Gifts

Helps and Appendices

Spiritual Gifts Directory

This book contains detailed teaching on thirty different spiritual gifts. In order to go directly to the section that deals with each particular gift, see the directory below. For additional references regarding a specific gift, consult the index at the back of the book.

Preface

Why another book on spiritual gifts? Primarily for two reasons. I began a serious study of spiritual gifts in 1994 and was always frustrated about a couple of things. First, there were few truly balanced books on the subject. Authors seemed to fall into one of two fallacies. Either they would overglorify the role and importance of the miraculous "sign" gifts like tongues, healing, and prophecy, or they would, out of fear and denominational prejudice, ignore the sign gifts completely—or worse, attribute them to the workings of the devil or psychological hysteria. Obviously, the New Testament would not endorse either of these views.

Secondly, I was frustrated that in order to find good teaching about the gifts one would have to acquire two or three different books because many authors would only teach about the so-called motivational gifts found in Romans 12:6-8 while others focused on the "manifestational" gifts of 1 Corinthians 12:8-10. The books I found that did cover them all in one book, would still leave out the gifts mentioned in the Old Testament such as the gifts of worship and interpretation of dreams.

It was my desire, therefore, to write a balanced book on the subject and to include a comprehensive treatment of some thirty spiritual gifts found in the Bible. I'm able to approach the subject of balance because I've experienced both sides of the theological debate about the gifts of the Spirit. I was raised, and later licensed to preach, in non-charismatic churches that were skeptical about the miraculous gifts. The last ten years of my life I've ministered mainly in churches that could be described as "charismatic," where the gifts of the Spirit were encouraged in our congregational life.

So which group follows the Word of God more accurately? In my opinion, both. It depends on the issue. Therefore, there will be times in this book where I am critical and corrective of both charismatic and non-charismatic teachings, because no one group in Christendom has a monopoly on doctrinal truth.

I have many dear friends and ministry partners on both sides of this issue. Disagreements on the spiritual gifts are not something the body of Christ should divide over, and I am very encouraged to see that the historical divide between both groups has been steadily eroding for years. Our Lord Jesus' high priestly prayer in John 17:21 that the church would one day all "be one" is slowly coming to fruition. As brothers and sisters in Christ, we are all thankful for that.

In this book I've limited my use of theological terms in favor of a popular style, which is more enjoyable to read, at least for me. Therefore, this is not an academic or scholarly treatment of the gifts, but one that is, however, thoroughly researched and uses proper hermeneutics and sound exegesis (sorry, a momentary relapse). I was told by a wise seminary professor once that we must be careful as teachers not to stray from the orthodox teachings of the Bible, for there are two things one never wants to see being made: theology and sausage. I've attempted to do neither in this work.

The purpose of this book is to get Christians excited about the many wonderful gifts of the Spirit that God has given to His church. If this work causes believers to more passionately seek their gifts and use them in their ministry to bless others, then I will be profoundly fulfilled and happy. God bless you as you seek a greater understanding of these graces of God. May you continue to grow in the grace and knowledge of our Lord and Savior Jesus Christ (2 Peter 3:18).

Bryan Carraway
Virginia Beach, Virginia
June 2005

Acknowledgments

Writing a book is rarely a solo project. Mine is no exception. I would like to thank Athena Dean at Pleasant Word publishing for her vision of getting aspiring authors into print. Many thanks are owed to Robert B. Haslam, my editor. I also thank Julie Fraser and Janice Ward for proofreading the work.

I want to recognize a good friend and spiritual mentor, Dr. Vic Simpson, for his encouragement throughout the project and for his insights and critique of the book that made it a better work. I wish to also express appreciation for my review committee that read the completed manuscript and offered many valuable suggestions for its improvement. These friends are: Jennifer Bekemeier, Justin Eastwood, Ernest Gravatt, Jim and Sue Murray, and Scott Presson. Special thanks to Dr. Gary Roberts for conducting a statistical analysis and reliability study on the Carraway Spiritual Gifts Inventory. His evaluation and recommendations contributed greatly to the instrument's improvement.

And lastly, I would like to thank my wonderful wife, Pauline, who also read the manuscript and helped me greatly to refine my message. She also graciously put up with an absentee husband who seemed to live in the library during the final months of the project. It is to her that I dedicate this book. She is, without a doubt, God's gracious gift to me.

An Overview of the Gifts of the Spirit

CHAPTER 1

The Pattern of God

THE PATTERN OF GOD IN THE OLD TESTAMENT

From the beginning of time God has worked through human agency. In all His endeavors He seems to genuinely enjoy having people work in partnership with Him. In the beginning chapters of the book of Genesis we see God has just finished creating the most complex, beautiful creation that we know of today—the planet earth. God's will is that this magnificent planet be governed by his highest creation. Man is given the commission to tend God's creation. Adam is instructed to take dominion over the earth and subdue it.

A few chapters later the wickedness of man presents itself to the Lord and He decides to destroy the entire earth except for a remnant. How does God save the remnant? He uses a man, Noah, to proclaim God's coming judgment. It was Noah who spent 120 long years preparing an ark that would have taken the Lord God about 1/10th of a second to create. And yet it was God who wanted it to be that way. God's pattern is this: He always accomplishes His purposes through people.

We continue on to Genesis, chapter 12, and we discover God's plan to reveal Himself to all the earth. He does not cause a massive earthquake and then thunder His voice from the heavens roaring, "I am Jehovah, I am full of truth and righteousness, come to me ye blessed creation." God decided to reveal Himself through a man, Abraham. Abraham was to be the patriarch of a special people who would act as God's voice to the nations of the world. This special people, the nation of Israel, were to be, "a light of the nations, so that my salvation may reach to the end of the earth" (Isaiah 49:6).

Later as the Old Testament continues to chronicle the chosen people of God we see that there was much opposition when Israel began to take possession of the Promised Land. The indigenous peoples were not going to give up their ancestral lands without a fight.

So how did the Lord ensure that His people would in fact take possession of the land? He used the human instrument of the Israelite army. As Joshua discovered, the Lord was indeed the captain of the army, but God's plan to take the land was by using the armies of Israel. Only their first city, Jericho, was delivered to them by supernatural means. The other cities and tribes were defeated as the children of Israel trusted God to work through them. Again, God worked through human agency.

That special covenant people, Israel, had the awesome privilege of building God a tabernacle so that His glory and presence could dwell among His people. In the thirty-first chapter of Exodus we read about the specifications God required for the building of the Tabernacle. There were to be made: tables of acacia wood, lamp stands of pure gold, garments for the priests-vestments spun in purple and scarlet, gold braided chains, and sapphires and emeralds. Also to be built was the Ark of the Covenant, designed and carved with angelic statuettes and overlayed in gold.

An interesting observation is made as the narrative continues throughout chapter 31. It is recorded that to enable the people of

God to carry out the work of God, the Spirit of God specifically gifted two men, Bezalel and Oholiab. The Spirit of God gave them abilities to make beautiful artistic designs with gold, silver, and bronze. They were also given the ability to correctly cut and set precious stones. God also gave these men skills in carpentry, enabling them to work with wood and in all types of craftsmanship. The Lord wanted a place to dwell with His people so He gifted two men to construct Him a Tabernacle.

Perhaps the greatest example of God using a man for a great purpose was Moses. When God called Moses to lead His people out of the land of Egypt, it was a daunting task to say the least. Egypt was a world power with the mightiest army in the land. Moses was instructed by God to go before Pharaoh and tell him that he was about to lose two million slave laborers because God had called them to pack their bags and head out of town. Moses immediately responded to God and said, "Lord, I am not an eloquent speaker, I am a man of slow speech and I have a slow tongue."

Moses may not have been much of a public speaker, but the man could do wonders with rocks and staffs! God endowed him with the gift of miracles. His miracles authenticated to the Pharaoh and the Israelites that he was indeed the prophet of the Lord.

To carry out the task that God had for him, Moses was also gifted with the spirit of wisdom. It is interesting to note that even though Moses had the wisdom to lead the Israelites, it was still too much of a job for any one man to handle. Moses, among other things, had the onus of hearing all the matters of judgment that the Israelites brought before him. Can you imagine trying to act as the justice of the peace for over two million people?

Scripture records in Exodus 18:13 that Moses listened to the people's disputes "from the morning until the evening." Moses cries out in Numbers chapter 11 for God to send him some help in overseeing the spiritual and emotional needs of the people. God responds by commanding Moses to bring seventy elders of the tribes of Israel up to the Tabernacle. There around the Tabernacle the Bible records in verse 25, "The Lord came down in the cloud and spoke to him; and He took of the Spirit who was upon him (Moses) and placed Him upon the seventy elders. And it came about that when the Spirit rested upon them, they prophesied." Again we see the Spirit of God at work in the Old Testament filling His people to carry out the work that they are called to do.

The examples are numerous throughout the Old Testament of God placing His Spirit upon His servants and gifting them with unique abilities to accomplish His will on the earth. Whether it was through the prophetic words of Isaiah and Jeremiah or the miracles and healing through Elijah and Elisha, God was busy throughout the Old Testament accomplishing His will through His human subjects.

THE PATTERN OF GOD IN THE NEW TESTAMENT

When we get to the New Testament, it gets more exciting for all of us. Why? Because in the Old Testament God seems to have given His Spirit in limited ways to certain people for particular tasks. For instance, in the book of Judges we see God sending His Spirit upon the different judges at select moments to empower them to overcome their enemies. After their power encounters, the Spirit of God would ascend back into heaven.

We notice that throughout Israel's history there were never more than three or four prophets in any century. The gifting of God was always present when He worked through people, but it was sporadic and limited to only a few. The prophet Joel prophesied that a latter day was coming in which "I will pour out my Spirit on all mankind; and your sons and daughters will prophesy, your old men will dream dreams, your young men will see visions. And even on the male and female servants I will pour out my Spirit in those days" (Joel 2:28-29). I have some good news friends; you are living in those days.

In Old Testament times the Spirit of God came *upon* people, but in New Testament times the Spirit of God *indwells* people. The apostle Peter reports in the book of Acts that this "latter day" has now come at the advent of the church on the Day of Pentecost. We are now in the age when God will not just deposit His Spirit upon a few prophets and kings, but upon all who are His children.

The greatest example in the New Testament that God still works through His people is to consider God's plan of salvation. Think about it. God had a plan to redeem His people and it included using His human subjects to carry it out. God did not deliver Jesus to the earth by a loud explosion wherewith He suddenly appeared at the city gates of Jerusalem. The arrival of His dear Son came through a sixteen-year-old girl.[1] The context God chose for the death of His Son was through a trial court composed of men. God even sent His Son in the flesh to live among us as a man!

What is God's plan to get this message out about Jesus? The means is by accepting the gospel message through faith. Faith comes by hearing, and hearing the Word of God. Hearing the Word of God comes about as one preaches the Word of God, which is to no surprise accomplished through man. Evangelism is not accomplished by angels. It's done through us.

Throughout the gospels we observe that Jesus spent quite a bit of time dealing with demonic spirits that harassed and afflicted the people. He would heal those of diseases that were caused by spirits. He would cast spirits out of individuals who were tormented by them. And Jesus also gave that authority to His apostles and to the rest of the church because He wanted that vital ministry to continue. We read in Mark 16:17 that one of the signs that will accompany "those who have believed" is the ability to cast out demons.

We see throughout the New Testament that God poured out His Spirit and continued His pattern of gifting His people for particular tasks. During the early days of the church God used a prophet named Agabus several times to warn the church of future events that could be dangerous.

It was Agabus who warned the church "by the Spirit" (Acts 11:28) that a famine was soon to come upon the land. With this valuable warning the church prepared for the famine ahead of time to ensure that everyone would be all right. Later Agabus again warned the church by confronting the apostle Paul and telling him that the authorities would arrest him if he went to Jerusalem. Paul went anyway, feeling it to be the Lord's will, and was arrested as Agabus warned. The Lord protects His church by instructing and warning her through His human subjects.

In the New Testament, God was actively working, not just in Agabus and the apostles, but in ordinary Christians like you and me. Romans 12 and 1 Corinthians 12 contain lists of the gifts that God has given to the general body of Christ. God gifts some Christians with the ability to discover the principles and truths of the Word of God. They gather these truths and then share them with the rest of the body of Christ for everyone's mutual edification. These Christians have the gift of teaching.

God gifts some with the gift of evangelism. They seem to know when a person is ripe for harvesting and are very successful in bringing in souls to the kingdom of God. The gifts God has given to the church are varied because there are many different tasks that the Lord wants accomplished in the world. As we will soon explore, God gave a variety of gifts and abilities to the early believers so that they could accomplish His will for the church.

THE PATTERN OF GOD TODAY

It is exciting to know that God's plans and purposes for His church today are just as important to Him as His plans once were for ancient Israel or the early believers in New Testament times. God is still active today and is moving to have His sovereign plan carried out in our world. To accomplish His plans He continues to do all things through His people. His representative today is the church of the Lord Jesus Christ, made up of all who have been bought with the precious blood of Christ and have given their lives to Him.

We in the church are referred to as the body of Christ. Jesus has ascended into heaven and we are left behind to carry on His works until He returns. We then are the hands, eyes, and heart of God. We are called to represent Him to a world that does not know Him. Paul says in 2 Corinthians 5:20, "We are ambassadors for Christ, as though God were entreating through us."

Does Jesus tell others about Himself? No, we tell others about Him. Does Jesus lay hands on sick children today to heal them? No, we lay hands on sick children, through His power, to see them healed. Does Jesus teach people to love God and read their Bible to learn about His love? No, we teach people that it is important and valuable to study God's Word. Jesus physically left this earth 2,000 years ago, and now we are the "body of Christ."

By examining the explicit teachings in the New Testament we are going to see that the pattern of God does indeed continue today. He is still looking for willing men and women who seek to do His will. In chapters 6-9 we are going to look at some powerful testimonies that prove this to be true beyond a shadow of a doubt.

THE SOVEREIGNTY OF GOD

The people who receive ministry today will be determined by the obedience or disobedience of God's servants. God desires that the widows, the fatherless, and the castaways of society be loved and ministered to. But God's will for that particular situation will only be carried out if the church in that community gets to work. God's will is for the people in your community to know about His love and His plan for their lives. If no one evangelizes that community, however, God's work will not get done. Remember, God works through us to accomplish His will on the earth. Some of the problems we have in the world today are a direct consequence of the church's failure to carry out God's will.

Let me clear one matter up right here, however. God is sovereign and does not *need* man to do anything to get His will accomplished. A dangerous teaching in the church today states that God cannot act apart from man's free will. Some who espouse this view even go as far as to say that God can only act in proportion to our faith and must cooperate with us to get anything done. He wills that His kingdom be a partnership between Himself and His creation, but He is never bound by our failure to carry out any particular task.

He wills that we praise Him. If we decide not to, He can make stones cry out to Him (Luke 19:40). God wills that we evangelize the entire earth. If we decide not to evangelize the remote villages of Africa or Asia, it cannot thwart His plan. He may decide to let the inhabitants die without a witness, as was the case with the early Native Americans before Columbus arrived. Romans 2:11-16 states that some will die without ever hearing the law of God. The Lord will judge them differently based upon what revelation they did receive, however little.

The Lord may appear personally to some native tribes and witness of Himself. Missionaries today are reporting that this is happening in many parts of the world. God may call you to go to the remote villages of Africa. If you refuse, God will just send someone else and you'll answer to Him one day for disobeying Him. If no one will go, God can sovereignly help them change their mind and then they will suddenly decide that they would love to go to Tanzania! Remember, "The king's heart is like channels of water in the hand of the Lord; He turns it wherever He wishes" (Proverbs 21:1).

I signed up long ago for the "I don't understand all of God's ways club." I know this, though. There are times when God will allow certain tasks to remain unfulfilled. There are times when God will help you change your mind to get on with what He told you to do. The prophet Jonah found that out. There are also times when God will simply pass you over and get someone else to do what you refused to do.

The point is this: *Can* God accomplish His highest purposes without us? Yes. Would He *prefer* to? No. The body of Christ, then, needs to be getting about the Master's business. Our pithy review of the previous Scriptures makes it clear that God seeks to empower His people with gifts and abilities to carry out His will. We as Christians can no longer plead ignorance and stand before the Lord one day saying, "What, Lord? You expected me to minister to all those around me? Why, how could I? Little old me, what abilities did I have?"

THE NEED FOR SPIRITUAL GIFTS

A popular cartoon from the 1980s ended each episode teaching children an enlightening safety or life lesson. The character would end the program by saying, "And now you know, and knowing is half the battle." The problem we have in regard to spiritual gifts in the church today is that half of us still don't really understand spiritual gifts and the other half only understand half as much as they should!

Today, thirty years after teaching on spiritual gifts became popularized, the body of Christ is still woefully ignorant as Christian researcher George Barna pointed out in a recent poll. Of Christians polled, 21 percent said they had heard of spiritual gifts but didn't think God had given them one. Out of those who did respond, only 30 percent named gifts listed in the Bible. Others listed as their spiritual gifts among other things: a sense of humor, being likeable, drawing, and believe it or not, going to church! Barna correctly concludes from his findings, "If more believers understood the nature and potential of [God's] special empowerment, the global impact of the Christian body would be multiplied substantially."[2]

Knowing is *half* the battle, but the other half is *doing*. The apostle James reminds us to be doers of the Word and not just hearers. It is my prayer that if you do not know your unique spiritual gifts yet that you will by the time you've finished this book, or at least that you will be on the path to discovery. The time is short, the fields are ripe for harvest, and the laborers are few. The Christian church cannot afford to have only half of our body mobilized; we need 100 percent participation out of each and every child of God. That means all children of God must discover their gifts and start using them.

As you read the following chapters and continue down the road to spiritual-gifts discovery, I challenge you to ask yourself some important questions. They are: What will you be doing when our Lord returns? Have you discovered your place in God's kingdom? Have you discovered your unique calling and spiritual gifts? And most importantly, are you actively engaging in them for the advancement of His kingdom?

CHAPTER 2

The Continued Debate: Cessationism vs. Charismaticism

DIVISIONS IN THE CHRISTIAN CHURCH

There's more than one way to split a church. The last 2,000 years of church history has certainly confirmed that. Christian teaching and doctrine, like everything else, is subject to differing interpretations. During the first few centuries after the death of Christ the church began to gradually become an institutionalized organization.

Christianity was in the beginning a recognized legal religion in the Roman Empire. It was assumed to be a sect within Judaism and was thus allowed to operate without much interference from the Romans. Gradually the Romans realized that this new movement was in fact a distinctly different religion from that of the Jews. That is when the persecution began and we begin to read about the Christians being thrown to the lions.

Something drastic happened in 312 A.D., however, that forever changed the Christian faith. The Roman emperor, Constantine, adopted the Christian religion, and eventually the Christian faith became the official religion of the Roman Empire.

Now the Christian faith was not only allowed again, but was the state religion. Enter the ecclesiastical bureaucracy. The church's clergy began to be appointed by bureaucrats rather than local elders. Churches began to meet in beautiful, elaborate buildings rather than in homes, as was the custom of the early church. Gradually the church became a highly-organized system of geographical territories consisting of priests, bishops, archbishops, and headed by a pope.

Gifted people in the church were many times weeded out of leadership and replaced by the appointed ministers who were favored by the bureaucracy. Less than 200 years after Constantine's encounter with Christianity, in the year 497 A.D., the Roman Empire began to crumble. When the Empire went into decline, so did many other institutions. A few centuries later, the world began to see a decline in overall prosperity, education, the arts, and in the power of the New Testament church. The world was now in the Middle Ages.

It was during this time that the church had its first of two major splits. The church was split in 1054 over the issues of papal authority and the use of religious artifacts for veneration. The split left the Roman Catholic Church as the dominant church in the west, while the group in the east went by the name of the Eastern Orthodox Church.

Approximately 500 years later, the Catholic Church split again. This time the issue was over justification by faith. One of the leaders, Martin Luther, a Catholic monk, became convinced that salvation was by faith in Jesus and not by belonging to the church and ritually following her dogmas. Most historians use the date of 1517 to signal the start of the second split, which we all know as the Protestant Reformation.

DIVISIONS WITHIN THE PROTESTANT CHURCH

The Protestant branch of the church has been in a state of almost constant division since its inception. Modern-day Christians seem to disassociate with one another and form separate fellowships for all sorts of reasons. Protestant churches split over contemporary social issues, theological views, differing forms of church government, and a host of other reasons as well.

My roots are in the Baptist tradition. The Baptists trace their lineage back to sixteenth century Holland. Baptists formed their own churches when they refused to baptize infants, believing only those who have personally accepted Christ as Savior should experience that sacrament. A major Baptist group in the United States separated in 1845 into the Northern and Southern Baptist Conventions over the issue of slavery and the distribution of missionary funds among other things.[1]

The Apostolic Church of Jesus Christ was born in 1915 due to the fact that they only baptized people in the name of Jesus rather than in the name of the Father, the Son, and the Holy Spirit.[2] In 1906 The Disciples of Christ split over the issue of whether instrumental music should be played in the church.[3]

In the beginning of the twentieth century a new issue arose which gave the church yet another reason to choose sides and "split" over. This new issue was the Pentecostal movement. God began a sovereign release of certain gifts of the Spirit in an unprecedented way. Of course, these gifts of the Spirit had always been in existence in pockets throughout history, but now it was becoming a common experience for many Christians.

One of the most visible gifts that was manifesting during this time was the gift of *glossolalia*, or more commonly known as "speaking in tongues." This new phenomenon of speaking in other tongues was not too kindly accepted, and many of the ministers of mainline denominations who experienced this gift were asked to leave their churches. These ministers did so and they simply started new churches, which eventually birthed new denominations.

So now we see that spiritual gifts, sadly enough, have also been used by man to divide the church. Many of the more miraculous gifts of the Spirit (miracles, healing, tongues, etc.) were not as common throughout church history after the first and second century A.D. As I stated earlier I believe that the rise of the ecclesiastical bureaucracy in the fourth century A.D. may have contributed to the church's gradual loss of some of the gifts. There are certainly other possible explanations for this as well, but that is not the scope of this book.

I simply wanted to provide a brief synopsis of one possible explanation as to why the gifts may have occurred with much less frequency for a time. If indeed the church lost a doctrinal truth for a period of time only to regain it later, this would certainly not be the first time this type of thing has occurred.

"Lost" Doctrinal Truths Throughout Church History

There have been several incidences throughout history in which God's people have temporarily lost some form of spiritual truth that they possessed at an earlier time. In 2 Chronicles 34:14 Hilkiah the priest discovered part of the Law of Moses that had apparently been lost for some time! When King Josiah heard of this he was so stunned and upset that such a thing could happen that he wept and tore his clothes. He then gathered the people of Israel around for a public reading of the lost Scripture and vowed before the Lord to obey all that was written in the book.

Church history is full of periods when God, for whatever reason, chose not to allow His people to experience some form of spiritual intimacy that had previously been normative. First Samuel 3:1 records such a time and states, "Now the boy Samuel was ministering to the Lord before Eli. *And word from the Lord was rare in those days,* visions were infrequent" (italics mine).

The time period between the Old Testament book of Malachi and the Gospel of Matthew, known as the inter-testamental period, is also known as the "silent period." It has been called that because God did not seem to be speaking to any prophet or giving any recorded revelation for approximately 400 years!

I am sure there were some Jewish spiritual leaders of that day who formed a new doctrine stating that God's revelation was final and that there would never again be a time in which God would give mankind new revelation through prophetic instruments. If the Lord hasn't worked in a certain way for 400 years, He wouldn't then start doing something "new" a year later in the 401st year would He? Well, according to a man named John the Baptist who arrived on the scene one day, the Lord broke a 400-year-old precedent and He did indeed have something to say to the Roman world in the first century A.D.

Consider also how the church in a sense "lost" the doctrine of justification by faith. During the Middle Ages the Scriptures were mostly in Latin, and for literally hundreds of years the common people had no idea what the Bible taught. Only the very educated or the priests could read the Bible, and they were not teaching justification by faith. So for all practical purposes that doctrine was not known by the masses.

God used the Protestant Reformation to bring that "lost" doctrinal truth back to the church. And we now arrive at the issue of certain gifts of the Spirit being dormant or "lost" for a period of church history. Some of these gifts began returning to the church en masse in the early 1900s. God again had to restore truth to His people who had lost it.

For the individual who may just be beginning to explore the issue of the gifts of the Spirit, I want to give a very brief background on the main views concerning this issue. There are basically two views that are prevalent today, although there are shades of differences even in these two main views.

Based on what one believes about the continuity of the gifts, they are either in the cessationist camp or the charismatic camp. We will look at each view before going on into the actual teaching about the gifts that will begin in the next chapter. After giving a brief summary of the two views, I will share with you my particular beliefs. I will share with you a little of my background and history and how I came to believe that all of the gifts of the Spirit are available to the church today.

CESSATIONISM

Cessationists, and the belief known as cessationism, derive their name from the word "cease." Christians who are cessationists believe that some of the spiritual gifts listed in Scripture have ceased and are not valid for the church today. Many cessationists are also dispensationalists and therefore readily believe that God works one way during one time period, and another way during other time periods.

The gifts that they believe are no longer given are the foundational gifts of apostleship and prophet. They also do not believe that God gifts Christians with the miraculous gifts of tongues, prophecy, exorcism, miracles, and healing. Cessationists do not believe that all the gifts have been removed from the church. They heartily believe in and encourage the use of the so-called "non-supernatural" or non-miraculous gifts such as teaching, exhortation, giving, pastoring, and so on.

They base their beliefs primarily on two key concepts: Scripture and church history. First, let's look at what texts may indicate that God did not intend for all the gifts to continue. The primary texts

used to defend this belief are 1 Corinthians 13:8-10 and Ephesians
4:13.

A Look at 1 Corinthians 13:8-10

Let's examine 1 Corinthians 13:8 first. This passage is part of
the famous love chapter that we all hear read at weddings. It is really a passage on spiritual gifts and is placed between the section of
the various gifts in chapter 12 and the abuse of the gift of tongues
in chapter 14. It reads, "Love never fails; but if there are gifts of
prophecy, they will be done away; if there are tongues, they will
cease; if there is knowledge, it will be done away."

The cessationists are right about one thing, these gifts are
eventually going to cease. The problem is that the charismatics
and the cessationists cannot agree as to *when* they will cease. Does
Paul tell us when these gifts will one day cease? Yes, he does. Two
verses down, in 1 Corinthians 13:10, Paul states, "But when the
perfect comes, the partial will be done away." So Paul says that
the gift of tongues, prophecy, knowledge, and the like, will cease
when "the perfect" comes. What is "the perfect?" Cessationists say
that the perfect that Paul is speaking of is the completed canon of
Scripture.

A Look at Ephesians 4:13

The other passage that is used to support the cessationist view
is Ephesians 4:13. Again the context of the passage is spiritual
gifts. Paul lists five gifts of the Spirit in Ephesians 4:11 and then
two verses later gives us a time frame for how long they will continue. Verse 13 records that they will last, "Until we all attain to
the unity of the faith, and of the knowledge of the Son of God, to
a mature man, to the measure of the stature which belongs to the
fullness of Christ."

Cessationists believe that this time of "unity of the faith" came when the church had the completed version of the Bible. In other words, they would say that the apostle Paul is stating that once the Christian community had the completed Bible, the church would be in unity and all future members of the church would reach maturity. The last book of the Bible to be completed was the book of Revelation, and most scholars believe that it was written some time in the early to mid 90s A.D.

The Cessationist View on the Purpose of Miraculous Gifts

Cessationists believe that the primary purpose of the super-natural gifts was to authenticate the apostles as God's true representatives who were to write His Scriptures. They would argue that after the Bible was completed the supernatural gifts would be expected to fade away since their purpose was fulfilled. They argue that God wanted the early church, as well as the pagans of the day, to know beyond a shadow of a doubt that the apostles were His chosen messengers. When the world saw Peter and Paul and the other apostles raising people from the dead, pronouncing divine judgment on people, and healing all manner of sickness, it proved that the power of God was within them.

Cessationists would say the Bible itself clearly states that the purpose of miracles were to authenticate apostolic authority. They would point to verses such as 2 Corinthians 12:12 which states, "The signs of a true apostle were performed among you with all perseverance, by signs and wonders and miracles." Cessationists hold that after all the apostles died off and the Bible was completed, there was no longer a need for the miraculous gifts to continue.

The Cessationist Argument from Church History

We just briefly covered the biblical reasons why cessationists don't believe the miraculous gifts were supposed to continue. There is another reason they believe this as well, the argument from church history. Cessationists say that when you go back and study church history, you don't find the same kinds of miracles occurring in the later centuries of the church as compared to what is found in the pages of the Gospels or in the book of Acts.

Therefore, if we don't see them much in church history, then we shouldn't ever expect them to occur again because obviously God doesn't desire to work that way today. They also say that church history shows that when miraculous gifts did manifest, they were few and far between. So consequently, when we do see them it needs to be attributed to God's sovereign circumstances for that particular case and that it only reinforces that these gifts were never meant to continue day in and day out like they used to in the pages of the Bible.

These arguments seem to make logical sense. What do charismatic Christians have to say about these statements from cessationists? Some documents from church history do indeed indicate that many of the miraculous gifts occurred with much less frequency by the beginning of the second century A.D. This was also around the time that the last book of the Bible was written. So at first glance their argument seems to hold water. Cessationists argue that if the miraculous gifts of the Spirit began to fade away in the early 100s A.D., why would God bring them back after 1,800 years? Good question. They have a valid point and it deserves to be answered.

The Cessationist View on the Role of Prophecy

Before we go on to explore the charismatic position, we must briefly address one other reason why some Christians do not believe that all the gifts are given today. The issue revolves around continued revelation. Some of the gifts, such as prophecy, involve God speaking to us today apart from the Scriptures. Cessationists believe the gift of prophecy served a foundational role in the early church and that God never meant for it to continue past the first century A.D.

They believe prophecy was used to edify the early church, provide doctrinal teaching for later inclusion into the canon of Scripture, and to direct early missionaries as the gospel went forth into the known world. Cessationists would argue that if we accept the premise that God is speaking today apart from the Scriptures through contemporary prophecies, then we are lowering the importance and uniqueness of the Bible.

In effect, they argue that hypothetically if God were to speak through a prophecy today, the message given would be equal in authority to the established Holy Bible. This is a perfectly valid hesitation that cessationists hold, but it is based on a misunderstanding of the nature and purpose of extra-biblical revelation. Charismatics do believe that God speaks to us today apart from, but never in contradiction to, the Holy Scriptures.

The Christians who do not accept prophecy for today say that the idea of God speaking apart from the Bible is too subjective. How can someone trust dreams, visions, or little voices in one's head? These "revelations," they say, could be our own thoughts and not God's. These "words from God" could be the devil trying to lead us into error.

Cessationists argue that we have the Bible and that is all that God ever desired for us to have. Besides, they say the Bible even says in 2 Timothy 3:16-17, "All scripture is inspired by God and profitable for teaching, for reproof, for correction, for training in righteousness; that the man of God may be adequate, equipped for every good work." They would argue, "Let's quit putting all this emphasis on supernatural gifts and just realize that the Bible is all we need to do God's work on the earth today."

CHARISMATICISM

Charismatics get their name from the Greek word *charismata*, which is translated "gifts" in our English Bible. They are firm believers that all the gifts listed in Scripture are still being given to the church today. Of course the term "charismatic" is very broad and usually refers to a distinct movement within Christianity. Charismatics are usually Christians who: believe in all the gifts of the Spirit, prefer a very open and free worship style in their church services, believe that God can speak today apart from Scripture (though never in contradiction to it), and believe in the baptism of the Holy Spirit as a separate experience subsequent to salvation.

Believing in all the gifts of the Spirit does not necessarily make one a charismatic. There are Christians who do believe in all the gifts, but do not consider themselves "charismatics" in the broad sense of the word. Some prefer the term "continuationists" to describe their belief in all the gifts of the Spirit.

Many Christians are reluctant to identify themselves with the charismatic movement because they cannot agree with its other emphases and beliefs on other issues. Some charismatic groups can be, well let's just say… they can appear to be flaky. They can tend to be overly concerned and enamored with mystical spiritual experiences. Some charismatic groups run from city to city to encounter the newest, latest spiritual experience. These experiences may range from crowds of people laughing uncontrollably for hours, called "laughing in the Spirit" or they may run to some revival service where people are barking, hissing, or roaring like lions.

These emotional outbreaks are sometimes just silly and sometimes down right strange. These new "moves of God" usually have a half-life of two to three years and then something new comes down the pike. The latest thing I heard of a few years ago was the gold dust phenomenon. Supposedly God was showering down select congregations with gold from heaven that people were collecting on their faces, napkins, and whatever else they could find.

These types of fringe groups within the charismatic branch of the church are not representative of most Pentecostals and charismatics. In fact there are almost 300 million charismatic Christians today who are said to belong to the "Third Wave."[4] These Christians have embraced many of the beliefs of the charismatic movement such as acceptance of all of the gifts and expressive worship. But they do not believe that one must speak in tongues to be filled with the Spirit, and they tend to be more conservative on other issues as well. There is a variety of beliefs and opinions in the charismatic branch of the church just as there is within any denomination or group within Christendom.

Why do charismatics believe that all the gifts are still available to the church today? They base their belief primarily on two key concepts: Scripture and church history. You may say, "Bryan, you just gave those two concepts as the basis for the cessationist view. How can they both use the same evidence and get two totally different viewpoints?" Lord, I wish I knew.

It basically boils down to one point. Biblical interpretation can be a difficult and very subjective thing. There are many passages in Scripture that are not as clear as we would all like. There are many passages that could have two or three reasonable meanings. We all try our best to use the proper methods of hermeneutics (the science of biblical interpretation). We all try to seek the Holy Spirit's guidance, and yet we sometimes still cannot all come to a consensus as to how to interpret certain passages.

Another Look at 1 Corinthians 13:8-10

Let's re-examine the 1 Corinthians 13:8-10 passage from another perspective. Paul states that the gifts will cease when the "perfect" comes. Cessationists say that the perfect is the Bible. Now that we have God's Word we no longer need miraculous gifts, or so the argument goes. If we follow the passage down a few verses further Paul gives an illustration of his statement made in verse 10.

He writes in verse 12, "For now we see in a mirror dimly, but then face to face: now I know in part, but then I shall know fully just as I also have been fully known." I have an observation to make. It sounds to me like the "perfect" that Paul is speaking of is the appearance of the Lord Jesus Christ at the Second Coming. When Jesus comes I will know as I am known. When Jesus comes I will have full understanding. When Jesus comes no longer will my understanding of Scripture or prophecy be incomplete. Besides, when do you look at a Bible "face to face"? It sounds like to me that Paul is again making a reference to the Lord Jesus.

So Paul seems to be saying that the gifts of the Spirit will no longer be needed when Christians are in the presence of Jesus. Who needs the gifts of healing when the Great Physician is right in front of us? Who needs the gift of teaching when we are in the very presence of the Word of God? Yes, the gifts of the Spirit will one day cease. But not until the Lord Jesus returns to the earth to gather His church. Until that time we need every gift that God will give us.

Another Look at Ephesians 4:13

Let's also re-examine Ephesians 4:13 now. Paul again lists certain gifts of the Spirit and states that they are given "until we all attain to the unity of the faith, and of the knowledge of the Son of God, to a mature man, to the measure of the stature which belongs to the full-ness of Christ." When will the church come together in unity? When will we be a mature man? Cessationists say that occurred when the 66 books of the Bible were completed. But did that in fact actually happen in 397 A.D. at the Council of Carthage when the church formalized our canon of Scripture? I don't think so.

As we looked at in the beginning of this chapter, having a completed canon of Scripture didn't create more unity in the church. In actuality it gave us more reasons to disagree and split over as different groups formed differing interpretations of that completed canon of Scripture!

In Ephesians 4:13 Paul seems to be implying that these foundational gifts of apostle, prophet, evangelist, pastor, and teacher will be needed to help us get to maturity. But that maturity will never be fully realized until the return of the Lord Jesus Christ. Then the church will be in unity. Then the church will finally reach maturity.

We just looked at two verses that some say prove that certain gifts are not for today. I hope you can see that their interpretations, for several reasons, are suspect. If Scripture, therefore, does not theoretically rule out the continuation of the gifts, then the argument from history cannot rule out their possible return at a later date.

The Charismatic View on the Purpose of Miraculous Gifts

As we looked at moments ago, cessationists argue that the purpose of miracles was to authenticate apostolic authority. However, there is a fatal flaw in the cessationists' logic regarding the main reason for miracles in the New Testament. The Bible doesn't seem to indicate that the primary purpose for miracles was to authenticate apostolic authority.

In all fairness, sure, that was one reason for miracles, but certainly not the only reason, nor the primary reason. God gave the church healing gifts not just to prove that Paul and Peter were apostles, but because He is a loving God and desires to see people healed and alleviated from their suffering (James 5:13-15). God gives the miraculous gift of prophecy not just for teaching that would in the first century later become canon, but because he wishes for people in every century to be edified and comforted through prophetic words (1 Corinthians 14:31).

And what about the common charge from cessationists that the only people who performed miracles in the New Testament were apostles? It is recorded in Acts 8:12-13 that Simon the sorcerer was amazed at the miracles that God was performing through Philip. Verse 13 states, "And even Simon himself believed; and after being baptized, he continued on with Philip; and as he observed signs and great miracles taking place, he was constantly amazed." We need to remind ourselves that Philip was a deacon, not an apostle!

Scripture lists others such as Ananias in Acts 9:10-18 who saw a vision from God and then was used by the Lord to lay his hands upon Paul so that Paul regained his sight. Ananias was not an apostle either. Besides Philip and Ananias there were countless other Christians in the early church who possessed miraculous gifts as well.

1 Corinthians 12:9-10 mentions the gift of miracles and healing as regular gifts given to the body of Christ at large. Paul mentions in Galatians 3:5 that members of the church in Galatia were ministering in miracles. The reason we don't have more examples of these ordinary Christians with miraculous gifts in the New Testament is because it didn't fit the purpose of the apostolic writers to include them when they wrote their letters to the church.

Paul did not write the book of Corinthians to name off all the Christians who had the gift of miracles or healing. He wrote the book to answer specific questions that the church had about marriage, the Lord's Supper, and other issues that were on the minds of the members of the church in Corinth.

It was well known among the Christians of that day, however, that some were gifted in evangelism, some in teaching, some in healing, and so on. Paul, nor any of the other apostles ever claimed that miracles would only occur in the ministry of apostles.

The Charismatic Argument from Church History

Let's now consider the argument from history. Cessationists claim that history shows that the miraculous gifts faded away after the death of the apostles, proving, they say, that miraculous gifts were linked only with the ministry of the apostles. But is that really the case? Did the miraculous gifts "fade away" after the death of the last apostle?

As I stated earlier, cessationists are correct that during the time right after the apostles the miraculous gifts were much less common, but they certainly didn't cease. Any student of church history can prove otherwise with just a cursory review of the writings of the early church historians and the church fathers. Notable and respected men such as Irenaeus (c.130-c.200), Tertullian (c.160-c.225), and the great St. Augustine of Hippo (354-430) mention all manner of miraculous gifts such as healings, miracles, and exorcisms occurring in the churches of their day. Even before the Pentecostal movement of the early 1900s we had miraculous gifts in the ministries of men such as St. Francis of Assisi and Charles Spurgeon.

The idea that Christians do not need to concern themselves with the gifts of the Spirit does not make much sense to me. Why would a Christian want nothing to do with something that can help them serve God better? One final charge related to the history issue that many have against the gifts is the role of one's personal history or experience. Many cessationists claim that charismatics give more weight to their experiences than to Scripture in determining their doctrines. In reality cessationists help substantiate their beliefs by experience as well.

I believe the most articulate biblical defense for the continuation of the gifts today is presented in Jack Deere's book, *Surprised By the Power of the Spirit*. Dr. Deere has this to say about the role of experience in formulating one's doctrinal beliefs:

> There is one basic reason why Bible-believing Christians do not believe in miraculous gifts of the Spirit today. It is simply this: *they have not seen them.* Their tradition, of course, supports their lack of belief, but their tradition would have no chance of success if it were not coupled with their lack of *experience* of the miraculous. Let me repeat: Christians do not disbelieve in the miraculous gifts of the Spirit because the Scriptures teach these gifts have passed away. Rather they disbelieve in the miraculous gifts of the Spirit because they have not experienced them. No cessationist writer that I am aware of tries to make his case on Scripture alone. All of these writers appeal both to Scripture and to either present or past history to support their case. It often goes unnoticed that this appeal to history, either past or present, is actually an argument from *experience*, or better, an argument from the *lack of experience.*[5]

The Charismatic View on the Role of Prophecy

Finally, what about the charge from cessationists that some of the supernatural gifts like prophecy can be dangerous for the church? If we say that God is speaking today to His people apart from the Scriptures are we saying that the Bible is not the final, authoritative source for revelation? Absolutely not!

The Bible is the absolute standard by which any revelation is to be judged. God will not speak to an individual or His church in such a way that it violates His Word. Every prophecy, every revelation, every vision must line up with the infallible Word of God or it is to be treated as false prophecy and rejected. This is exactly why we have verses such as, "and let two or three prophets speak, and let the others pass judgment" (1 Corinthians 14:29). God always commands for prophecy to be judged when it is practiced in the church.

And if charismatics are correct in affirming that prophecy today is not equal to the preserved Word of God, the Bible, then what is its purpose? God speaks to us today for the same reasons He spoke to people in the Bible. Not all of the prophecies given by other Christians in the Bible made it into the canon of Scripture. Philip the evangelist had four daughters who prophesied, but their prophecies weren't considered canon (Acts 21:9). Paul mentions the use of the gift in 1 Corinthians 14:26-31 and in no way teaches that the prophecies Christians receive and share (which Paul acknowledges are truly from God) are to be treated as the same thing as sacred canon.

There is a huge difference in the established Bible and in prophecies given through the gift of prophecy today. Prophecies given today are for the personal edification and enlightenment of specific people for that particular moment. They are given by human beings who have sin natures and who can sometimes get it wrong.

That is why prophecy must be judged. Human prophecy is not infallible. The Bible, however, is infallible. And the prophecies and teachings of the Bible are not just for specific people and for certain times. The Bible's teachings are binding on all of God's people, for all times, for all cultures, and contain no errors of any kind.

God does still speak today. He speaks to us for guidance. He speaks to us to warn us. He speaks to us in order that we may be better able to minister to His children. The reasons are infinite. But He does speak today. And we have to learn to hear His voice.

My Journey

I come from a line of preachers. On my father's side of the family both my grandfather and great-grandfather were life-long Baptist pastors. I was raised in the church all my life. I gave my life to Christ at the tender age of nine years old. However, as is the case so many times, I was never discipled and taught how to really be a Christian. I went to church on Sundays and said grace at meals, but that was pretty much the extent of my formal training in the ways of the Lord. Like young Samuel, I was in a religious environment but did not yet know the Lord nor had the word of the Lord been revealed to me (1 Samuel 3:7).

My life radically changed at age sixteen, however. My family and I moved to a small town on the outskirts of the city where I had grown up. I began attending the local First Baptist Church there and was introduced to a youth group that was on fire for Jesus. These ten young people were serious about their faith and had a passion and a joy in their hearts that I wanted for myself as well.

I had never seen a group of Christians like this before. They did not just talk about the Bible and spiritual things—they lived it out. I soon began to realize that the form of Christianity that I had did not measure up to what these disciples were living and experiencing. It was not long after that I rededicated my life to the Lord Jesus and vowed that I would live for Him all the days of my life. That is where I fell in love with Jesus. Our youth pastor, and the youth group, took me in under their wings and I began to grow exponentially in my walk with the Lord.

Why Aren't My Experiences the Same as Believers in the New Testament?

Things were great at that church and I had nothing but thanksgiving in my heart for the love and nurturing that I was given. However, in those days as a young teenager I was always a little disturbed about some things. I spent hours reading my Bible every night and I eventually came to notice that many of the aspects of the Christian life that I read about in the Bible I had personally experienced. However, there were also many aspects of the Christian life recorded in the Bible that I had no experience with at all, and that disturbed me.

For example, I read in Philippians 4:7 about the peace of God that passes all understanding and I knew exactly what that meant. As I began to grow in my relationship with the Lord I became aware of a peace that would settle over me when I made decisions that honored the Lord's will for my life. I also began to recognize that the peace of God was absent from my life when I would do things that did not honor the Lord.

I would read in 1 John 2:27 about the Holy Spirit anointing us so that we could understand the Bible, and I knew what it was talking about having experienced that so many times in my own life. Before I was saved the Bible was boring and I had a very difficult time understanding it the few times I tried to read it. Now, it seemed I couldn't get enough of God's Word, and I was amazed at the insights that I received from God as I read His Word. But there were other passages in the Bible that I had no experience with and could not find any other Christian in my circle of friends who knew anything about them either.

For example, I would read in 1 Corinthians 14:24-25 about the role of prophecy in the church. Paul taught that when the church came together and someone prophesied that it could cause an unbeliever to realize that there is a God. I read in James 5:14-16 that when someone in your church is sick you are to call the elders of the church together to pray over the ill person to see them healed.

I read about the reality of demons and that believers throughout the Bible seemed to know all about them and were constantly being used by the Lord to bring deliverance to those in bondage. As a young boy full of faith and fire I longed to have all that God destined for His people. I wanted more of His presence. I wanted more of His power. I began to ask God to help me become all that

He wanted me to be. I wanted to follow every mandate I knew of in His Word. I wanted some of those gifts of the Spirit that He talked about in His Word also.

Soon after I came to the realization that biblically there was more of God's presence and power available to every Christian, I began to seek these things directly. I began to read books by charismatic authors and I prayed and asked God to be my teacher and to help me discover all that He had for me. I also asked Him to help me not to get into error, but to stay strictly in line with His Word.

The Lord tells us in Matthew 7:7, "Seek and you shall find, knock and it shall be opened to you." Consequently, the Bible also tells us in James 4:2, "You do not have because you do not ask." In many areas the Lord works on a faith principle. If we don't have the faith or desire to ask Him for something, there is a good chance that we'll never get it. My main motivation for seeking a deeper experience of Christ's presence and power was that I was troubled by the disconnect I saw in the lives of those in the Scriptures compared to my life and the lives of other Christians that I observed in my everyday world.

New Testament Christians seemed empowered to win souls. So did we. New Testament Christians seemed to be concerned with following our Lord's moral code by doing what was right and avoiding what was wrong. So were we. However, I also observed that New Testament Christians were infused with God's power and were oftentimes laying hands on the sick, casting demons out of tormented people, and ministering to people through prophetic words. In my Christian circles we were not doing any of those things and didn't seem to be much interested in pursuing any of that either. This deeply bothered me, and I instinctively knew that this was not because the Lord desired it to be so.

I soon realized in my naivety that there were entire doctrines in the Bible that churches no longer followed or taught for various reasons. It was around this time that I first learned of the theological system known as cessationism that made verse after verse, even entire chapters of the New Testament, irrelevant and non-applicable! I wanted no part of a system that made certain teachings of Jesus and the apostle Paul "illegal" and unwanted in our churches.

In my mind there seemed to be so much more power available for the Christian that many did not take part in. So in my late teens and early twenties I began to realize that the Lord did indeed wish to empower His people for service and that the primary way He did that was by bestowing various spiritual gifts upon His children. These spiritual gifts were amazingly diverse and were to be used to accomplish a full spectrum of purposes.

During this time of investigation in which I was seeking a deeper walk with the Lord I still considered myself theologically a faithful Southern Baptist, and I was still very suspicious of the charismatic movement and charismatics in general. I'm ashamed to say this, but my impression of them was that they were weird, emotionally-unstable people who were more interested in speaking in tongues than in winning souls.

I had been preaching and leading revival services in Baptist churches since I was sixteen. I would sometimes run into one of those charismatic Christians and prided myself on my ability to debate them and show them "the word of the Lord more excellently." To be young is to be prideful! I genuinely loved the Lord Jesus and I was convinced my denomination, the Southern Baptist Convention, was the group with the most accurate doctrine in all the land.

During those debates I would sometimes fantasize that right after my final brilliant point, the sky would suddenly grow dark, the clouds would part, and the Lord Jesus Himself would appear to my naysayer and speak these words, "Listen to my servant Bryan, the Baptist church is the true church and they understand My Word." I know teenage boys have fantasies, but honest to goodness, that one was mine! Well, what do you think the Lord did to correct His wayward, prideful son? Listen on.

Two Worlds Collide

It was also during this time that I attended a Fall Festival get together sponsored by my college's local Baptist Student Union. That night I saw across the crowded room the most beautiful girl I had ever laid eyes on. I found an excuse to approach her and we were introduced.

I immediately loved her personality, her spunk, and after some conversation, I discovered she was a sold-out Christian. A quick scan of her left ring finger immediately elevated that night from "good" to "real good." Just when I thought that this night could not get any better I asked her where she attended church. I was hoping she would say, "First Baptist Church of...(somewhere, I didn't care where)." Hey, I could have even handled "so and so Presbyterian church." What she told me however, floored me.

When she named her church it was the most popular and notable charismatic church in our city. Then suddenly like a bug hitting a windshield, it hit me. This girl is one of those tongues-speaking charismatics with mixed-up doctrine! Like Job, I felt that what I greatly feared had just come upon me!

After recovering from my shock I just could not get away from the fact that I wanted to get to know this girl more. You already know how this story ends, don't you? Well, you're right. We later began dating, and after many late-night doctrinal discussions, fastings, and prayer sessions later, we married! The Lord used Pauline to help me become more open to the Holy Spirit.

As I said, I was already seeking these things, but I was still a little suspicious of the charismatic movement due to the negative stereotypes I had grown up hearing. I needed someone to help me understand the gifts of the Spirit and to observe a church where these things were practiced. In time I came to realize that all the stereotypes I grew up hearing about charismatics were totally wrong.

They weren't weird, shallow people seeking mystical experiences. They were mature Christian men and women who had a passion for Jesus just like we did. They were people just like us Baptists; we all had our problems and we saw a few things differently, but we were on the same team. In the end, the Lord did a beautiful work in our hearts as Pauline and I balanced one another out in a complementary fashion.

I hope my story doesn't make it seem like all Baptists are hard-nosed Christians who think they have a monopoly on biblical truth, because that is not the case. Southern Baptists are some of the finest Christians I have ever met and I am proud to have been raised one, and when invited, am proud to minister in their churches today. My spirit of exclusivity was my own problem.

As Pauline and I dated and later married, we belonged to churches of various denominations that were open to the gifts of the Holy Spirit. In those churches I had numerous opportunities to see the gifts in operation. Time and again I witnessed very accurate prophetic ministry, and on one missions trip that Pauline was a part of, a woman was healed of blindness as the group laid hands on her and prayed for her healing. I was also later familiarized with a Southern Baptist evangelist who had a very powerful ministry of deliverance.

As I continued to grow spiritually over the next few years the Lord continually showed me instances of His modern-day power which solidified my belief that all these things I read about in the Bible were still happening today for the Christians who sought them out and were open to the Holy Spirit. During this season of my life I was growing in my particular giftings, and I also began to see God speak prophetically to me as I prayed to hear His voice and be used. These personal experiences powerfully validated the fact that God was indeed the same yesterday, today, and forever.

Some Early Experiences with Prophetic Words

While seeking God for more of His presence and power, I especially wanted to be guided by learning to hear His voice. I'll never forget the first time God unequivocally spoke to me; it changed my life and my theology forever. I was twenty-one years old and serving as a youth pastor intern in Poteau, Oklahoma. I attended Immanuel Baptist Church. This was a great church that was really making an impact in the community and had a very warm fellowship of committed believers who loved the Lord Jesus.

My supervisor, and the church's youth pastor, was a wonderful Christian man named Rick Snyder. During that summer we took our entire youth group up to the central part of Oklahoma for a weeklong youth camp. The camp was a place for other youth from all over the state to get together for fun, fellowship, and for a renewing of their faith before the start of the upcoming school year.

We had a camp speaker, but we also broke up into groups with the students for several teaching times throughout the week. One day I was responsible for the lesson and I was teaching in front of about fifteen to twenty students. After my lesson I began to transition us into a time of prayer and I asked the students if anyone had any prayer requests that they would like to share with the group. I paused for a few seconds and while waiting I got an unusually strong sense of the Lord's presence that suddenly came upon me.

I began to get a strong impression that there was someone who wanted prayer but that they were not responding in front of the group for some reason. I then began to be flooded with a series of impressions concerning the person who needed prayer; this person is a girl; this person is battling some very heavy discouragement. I continued to be flooded with more impressions; this person has just recently been saved and has a relative who is discouraging and even hindering her new desire to follow Christ. I then felt the Holy Spirit very gently say in my mind, "This person's relative is her uncle. Pray for her and encourage her that I am with her."

This all took place within seconds while waiting on prayer requests from the group. I have to say that I was amazed at the clarity that I was receiving and I wanted to minister to this young lady and reassure her that the Lord had taken notice of her stand for Him. I then thought to myself, *This is kind of unusual; what if these are just my own thoughts and God is not really saying this to me?*

I realized that I might look a little silly saying this, but I did it anyway. I then proceeded, "I feel that there is someone here who is having a hard time living the Christian life because of a family member who is discouraging you. Who is this? We would like to pray for you." Almost immediately a young teenage girl raised her hand and said, "That's me. It's my uncle." I thanked her for responding and began to pray for her asking God to strengthen her and to not allow her uncle to interfere with the plans the Lord had for her. I could tell that it made her feel encouraged to be prayed for. After prayer I dismissed the group, in awe of what the Lord had just done.

I had just experienced a prophetic word from the Lord! I remember reading about that happening to many other Christians throughout the Bible, and now it was happening to me!

Another memorable occasion when the Lord used me to minister to someone through a prophetic word involved a close friend. He called me one day in the midst of a pretty dry season in his spiritual walk. When I picked up the phone, I immediately was flooded with a series of thoughts from the Lord.

I felt the Lord say in my heart and mind, "He is about to confess that he has lost his virginity. He is very depressed and upset that he has done this. Be merciful and gentle with him...." That is all I sensed.

After just a few seconds of talking I could tell that he was not his usual perky self. There was a sad inflection in his tone of voice and I could tell that he was depressed or upset about something and that he had called because he needed a friend. I waited, wondering if what I just had flash in my mind was true. Sure enough he did not beat around the bush and in just a matter of a minute or two confessed to me that he had slept with a girl he had just recently started dating.

I realized that he knew he had committed a serious sin. He was from a family that had been in church most of his life, and he knew that God was disappointed in what he had done. He was broken and hurting at that moment. He needed to be reassured of God's love. He needed to hear that God could forgive him and restore his fellowship with Him. A time of rebuke and a serious time for discussion of how he let the situation get out of hand were to be done at another time. God had instructed me to minister compassion and gentleness to him, and that is exactly what I did. These are just a few examples of the times when God has used a fresh word from heaven to minister to others through me.

Convinced That the Gifts of the Spirit Are For Today

Around this same time in my late teens and early twenties I continued to study in depth what the Bible had to say about spiritual gifts. I read everything I could on the subject and I talked with other Christians more mature than myself to gain their wisdom and insight as well. I began asking God to show me what my giftings were. As I pressed into God and stepped out in faith, over a period of a few years I gradually became aware of what my gifts were. I also began to widen my circle of friends to include those outside of my own theological background.

I soon discovered that there were many other Christians who had similar experiences with prophetic words and that this occurred regularly in their walk with God. These Christians were from all types of denominations and backgrounds such as Southern Baptists, Methodists, and charismatics. I met other Christians I knew to be impeccable morally and ethically who experienced other supernatural power encounters such as miraculous healings and dramatic deliverances. I soon could come to no other conclusion but that God was still gifting His people with the same spiritual gifts that I read about in the Bible—even the more supernatural ones.

Those early days of my Christian journey were invaluable. I thank God for the godly men and women the Lord put in my life who mentored and taught me that there was a deeper walk available to every Christian. I have learned that God really does speak today in dreams and visions, in prophecies, and in that still small voice within our heart. I have learned that God is still in the miracle business and that He can still calm the storm and bring deliverance to those in satanic bondage.

As you can see, I have been on a journey. I have learned that God does indeed desire to equip His people for ministry. I know that God is gifting His people with powerful supernatural gifts of the Spirit. I know this because I read that it is so in the Bible. I also know that this is true because I have personally experienced this in my life. And remember, a man with an experience is never at the mercy of a man with an argument.

CHAPTER 3

New Testament Teaching on the Gifts

WHAT ARE SPIRITUAL GIFTS?

Spiritual gifts are supernatural endowments and abilities that are selectively given to every Christian by the Holy Spirit for the purposes of personal ministry and for the advancement of the kingdom of God.

Spiritual gifts are divinely given. They are not natural abilities. Spiritual gifts are supernatural abilities. Christians as well as non-Christians have natural abilities. All people have specific inclinations and predispositions toward certain behavior traits and abilities. This concept, however, of specific abilities people possess from birth is very similar to the concept of spiritual gifts.

For example, we all know of certain people who are said to be "mechanically inclined." These people always amaze me. They seem to be unintimidated by any mechanical device or new piece of technology. You call them over to look at your car, your oven, or your television and they seem to have no problem fixing anything. You ask them where they learned to repair televisions or carburetors and they reply, "Nowhere. I just tinkered around with it and discovered a way to fix it." Meanwhile, if you are like me, you thank them profusely for their help and pray as they're leaving that they don't notice your VCR that you've had for ten years is still flashing "12:00" because you never learned how to program the stupid thing!

We also know some people who are naturally sanguine in their personality. They strike up conversations with perfect strangers in church, at the mall, or in a restroom at a football game. They love people and are very easy going. We know other people who are totally different. They would never approach a stranger and begin a conversation. These examples are just natural inclinations toward behavior and natural strengths for certain abilities that are characteristic of both Christians and non-Christians.

I have always thought it fascinating when I talk to mothers about their child's personality. Mothers tell me almost invariably that the personality their child has to this day was basically identifiable in that child by the age of twelve to eighteen months. When I think about such things, my brother John often comes to mind. We came from the same womb but are very different in many ways. I'm the cerebral type that loves to read books and research issues. I am very laid back and very much a people person. I'll get depressed if I don't have people around me most of the time.

My brother is exactly the opposite. He is perfectly content staying to himself for days without interaction with others. My brother is very smart but definitely not a bookworm like me. He got all the physical strength genes. He is an avid boxer. I remember that in one match he knocked a guy out cold in the first ten seconds of round one. He is very muscular and quick. The only people I will ever intimidate in a boxing ring are small children and elderly ladies. The point is this, even though my brother and I are from the same family, we are quite different in many regards.

Just as in the natural realm with natural gifts, Christians all have supernatural gifts from the supernatural realm. Just as with newborn babies, our spiritual gifts are there from the moment of our new birth when we accept Christ as our Lord and Savior. I have found that again, just as in the natural, most Christians can begin detecting their spiritual gifts between twelve to eighteen months after their salvation experience.

In the first few months after salvation most new believers are so excited and zealous that they can sometimes seem to display all the gifts to a certain extent. But I have found that within about twelve months or so they will begin to gradually settle down into a consistent daily walk with the Lord and the gifts of the Spirit endowed to them will begin to become increasingly obvious.

Twelve months after salvation is usually a good time to begin helping a new Christian find his or her spiritual gifts. This time frame is also sufficient to allow individuals enough personal history in the faith to begin to analyze their own successes in ministry and their motivational tendencies. It is truly a loss of potential ministry for people to have been Christians for a couple of years or more having still not identified their gifts.

THE BIBLICAL LIST IS NOT COMPLETE

Spiritual gifts are mentioned several times in the New Testament. However, virtually everything we know about them is contained within only six chapters of the Bible. The Bible mentions them in Romans 12, 1 Corinthians 12-14, Ephesians 4, and 1 Peter 4. Each of these four books of the Bible gives us a list of certain spiritual gifts. The lists are contained in Romans 12:6-8, 1 Corinthians 12:8-10;28, Ephesians 4:11, and 1 Peter 4:9-11.

Scholars disagree as to how many spiritual gifts are mentioned in Scripture because the language is not explicit. When Paul and Peter wrote about spiritual gifts in their epistles they would usually name a few items as examples, call them "spiritual gifts" and then provide a little teaching about them. Each time they wrote about the gifts their lists were different. This implies that the list of gifts in the Bible was probably never meant to be exhaustive.

A student of the Bible must remember that the Bible is not written systematically. All the teaching about spiritual gifts is not found nicely compacted together in two chapters of one book of the Bible. We piece together our doctrine and understanding of spiritual gifts by studying all the passages of Scripture that speak about them. Even after doing this we are still left with a lot of questions because most of the gifts were never defined by the apostles. There is no statement in the Bible that says, "An apostle is a person who…" There is not a statement that says, "The gift of discernment is the ability to…" We must rely on the personal experiences of Christians throughout the ages to add to our understanding of the specificity of certain gifts.

For instance we know from the personal experience of Christians that some have the ability to discern things about people that the rest of us cannot seem to do. Perhaps they sense that a particular person should not be trusted because they have an ulterior motive. They may go to their pastor and say "Pastor, don't form a ministry partnership with so and so. I believe the Lord has showed me something very dangerous about him." Sure enough, six months later this potential ministry partner is found to be a charlatan and leaves the ministry in disgrace. The pastor breathes a sigh of relief and thanks God for the discerner in his congregation. We see that one of the gifts listed in Scripture is called a "discerner of Spirits" and we deduce, "Oh, that's what that is! The Bible told us that some Christians would have that ability."

Many non-charismatics will argue that we cannot definitively say that the gift of discernment allows people to receive supernatural revelatory information because the Bible does not give us a definition of this gift in 1 Corinthians 12:10. Those same people will have no problem defining in their books what the gift of administration, helps, or giving is, even though the Bible never defines those gifts either.

In other words, their logic seems to be that we can use Christian experience to define characteristics of spiritual gifts that the Bible is silent about as long as the definitions are non-supernatural. What this really boils down to is that these Christians have an anti-supernatural hermeneutic built into them that cannot allow anything supernatural to occur today. It's frustrating to me that some cessationists cannot admit to their obvious anti-supernatural bias.

Let's take a look at the lists we do have in Scripture and see what some of the gifts are that the Lord has given to the church. Below are the lists of the gifts that are taken from the four books I mentioned earlier.

Romans 12:6-8	1 Cor. 12:8-10	1 Cor. 12:28	Ephesians 4:11	1 Peter 4:9-11
prophecy	word of	apostle	apostle	hospitality
serving	wisdom	prophet	prophet	speaking
teaching	word of	teacher	evangelist	serving
exhortation	knowledge	miracles	pastor	
giving	faith	healing	teacher	
leading	healing	helps		
mercy	miracles	administration		
	prophecy	tongues		
	discernment			
	tongues			
	interpretation of			
	tongues			

If we remove the duplication of gifts that are mentioned in more than one list (for example prophecy and teaching) we arrive at twenty-two different gifts. Some like to see prophecy and prophet as the same gift, in which case the list would contain twenty-one gifts. Some see the gifts of leading and administration as the same gift called by two different names, so they arrive at twenty gifts. I see these latter two gifts as separate gifts and so I believe that our list as of now contains twenty-two distinctly mentioned spiritual gifts. In case you're counting, many scholars believe that Peter's reference to the gift of "speaking" in 1 Peter 4:11 is actually a reference to the gift of prophecy.

I believe there are other gifts given to the church today as well. I am not saying my list is exhaustive either. But certain other abilities or divinely placed motivations listed in Scripture seem to me to be spiritual gifts in the true sense of the concept. Some of these are found in other places throughout the New Testament and a few are found in the Old Testament. All of the following gifts are found in Scripture, however. We will look at these other gifts in more detail later. For now, here are the other gifts:

Old Testament	New Testament
craftsmanship	deliverance
interpretation of dreams	missionary
worship	intercession
	martyrdom
	simplicity

By combining the gifts mentioned in Romans, 1 Corinthians, Ephesians, and 1 Peter with the other gifts that are mentioned in other places in the Bible, we arrive at some thirty different gifts. Now that we have mentioned them all let's take a look at what our final list looks like:

administration	helps	missionary
apostleship	hospitality	pastoring
craftsmanship	intercession	prophecy
deliverance	interpretation of dreams	prophet
discernment	interpretation of tongues	serving
evangelism	knowledge	simplicity
exhortation	leadership	teaching
faith	martyrdom	tongues
giving	mercy	wisdom
healing	miracles	worship

As you can see, God has gifted His church with a wide variety of abilities. Now let's consider why God has given us these gifts and what purpose they serve.

GOD'S PURPOSE FOR SPIRITUAL GIFTS

Three primary purposes for the giving of spiritual gifts are mentioned in Scripture. Peter tells us in 1 Peter 4:10, "As each one has received a special gift, employ it in serving one another, as good stewards of the manifold grace of God." The gifts are given so that we may serve one another in the body of Christ. Paul echoes Peter and states in Romans 12:13 that the gifts are for "contributing to the needs of the saints."

A second purpose for the gifts is so that each child of God is able to specialize in a certain ministry area for more effective service. This purpose is stated in 1 Corinthians 12:7 where Paul says, "But the manifestation of the Spirit is given to every man to profit withal" (KJV). Our spiritual gifts make us each uniquely talented in certain areas and we are expected to profit the work of the kingdom by creatively using these gifts.

A third purpose for the gifts is mentioned as well. In Ephesians 4:11 Paul mentions five special gifts that are given "for the perfecting of the saints for the work of the ministry, for the edifying of the body of Christ" (KJV). What is stated here is that the Lord has given the five office gifts of apostles, prophets, evangelists, pastors, and teachers to "perfect" or equip the rest of the church for greater ministry service.

These five gifts are known by many names. Some call them the office gifts, others the ascension gifts; still others refer to them as the five-fold ministry gifts. I prefer the term "foundational gifts" which is taken from the text itself where Paul mentions in Ephesians 2:20 that the prophetic gift and apostleship are the foundation of the church. These foundational gifts are especially given to help mature and guide the rest of the church. They are gifts that are governmental; authoritative in nature.

No Excuses

Some Christians have mistakenly believed that if they are not gifted with a particular gift, then they are excused from that particular function altogether. Nothing could be further from the truth. Just because you do not have the gift of evangelism, you are not excused from the mandate to tell others about Jesus. The Lord commands every believer to witness (Matthew 28:19-20). Just because you may not have the gift of serving that does not imply that you never have to serve others. All Christians are commanded to humbly serve one another (John 13:14-15).

Every Christian is commanded to show mercy, serve others, evangelize, and teach. Every Christian can pray for the sick, cast out demons, or be used by God to perform a miracle. Again, even though some don't have a certain spiritual gift, they are still expected to fulfill the roles associated with that gift as the Lord provides opportunities. However, God specifically gifts some Christians with a specific anointing to evangelize, to show mercy, to cast out demons, or to heal the sick, etc. The truth is that those who are specifically gifted in certain areas will have much more success in those ministries than the average Christian. That is because they have a supernatural anointing for that ministry.

This is perhaps one of the greatest errors we have to guard against when teaching Christians about spiritual gifts. Can you imagine what a football coach would say if one of his receivers didn't take the opportunity to block an opposing player who was headed straight for the team's running back? I can hear the player now, "Coach, I'm not a tackle, I'm a receiver. It wasn't my job to block that guy, so I let him run by me."

Or can you imagine if two plays later that same receiver fumbles the ball and it wobbles right past the team's center who just stares at it as it's swooped up into the arms of the opposing team? Can you imagine the center on the sideline telling his coach, "Sorry, coach, once I snap the ball my responsibility to this team is over, that dumb receiver should have picked up his own dropped ball!" The coach would be well within his rights to scream like a drunken madman, "Yes, you've all got certain positions on this team, but good grief, guys, use some common sense! Help this team out when the times call for it, even if it's outside of your official position description!"

So in essence, we ought to spend 80 percent of our time and energies in the ministry areas where we are gifted, but we need to also realize that we will all from time to time function in some of the roles associated with other gifts. Also, every Christian will one day appear before the judgment seat of Christ to give an account of what they did with the gifts and talents that God gave them.

I personally believe that we will be judged more strictly by God in the ministry areas that relate to our particular spiritual gift. For example, I believe that I will be held more accountable than the average Christian for the teaching I did, or did not do, because God specifically gave me that gift and He expects me to use it properly to bless others and to further His kingdom.

THE GIFTS ARE GIVEN BY THE HOLY SPIRIT

The Bible indicates that although there is perfect unity and equality in the Godhead, there is a division of roles found within each member. God the Father is the ultimate authority and the originator of the Trinity's sovereign plan for all things. God the Son is the redeemer of mankind and the head of the church. God the Holy Spirit is He who indwells all believers upon salvation and empowers us for Christian service.

The language of 1 Corinthians 12:4-6 is a deliberate attempt by the apostle Paul to include all three members of the Trinity in his teaching on spiritual gifts. However, verse 7 of chapter 12 states, "But to each one is given the manifestation of the Spirit for the common good." I believe that Paul stresses in verses 7-11 that it is the Holy Spirit who is most associated with imparting gifts to us.

Some teachers like to classify certain gifts as being gifts of the Spirit (1 Corinthians 12:7-10), gifts of God (Romans 12:3b-8), and gifts of the Son (Ephesians 4:7-11). I view all the gifts as being given by the Spirit. The biblical writers frequently use a crossover reference when describing the various roles performed by certain members of the Trinity.

For example, we all know the Bible teaches in numerous places that it is the Holy Spirit who indwells believers upon salvation, and yet in John 14:23 the apostle John quotes Jesus as saying that He and the Father will make their home within the believer. While the verse literally says that Jesus will make his home with the believer, other verses clarify that He does this, but it is *through the person of the Holy Spirit* that this is accomplished (John 14:17, Romans 8:9, 1 Corinthians 3:16).

There is also another problem with the view that different members of the Trinity assign different gifts. The gift of prophecy, which is said to be a "gift of God" in Romans 12:6, is also mentioned in 1 Corinthians 12:10 in the list of so-called "gifts of the Spirit." The gift of teaching appears in Ephesians 4:11 as a so-called gift of Christ, but it also appears in Paul's list in Romans 12:7 as a gift given by God the Father! Paul purposely mixes these gifts all together when speaking of them because he is specifically not making rigid distinctions between the gifts! The definitive biblical teaching on the *charismata* appears in Paul's letter to the Corinthians where he makes it clear that ultimately, spiritual gifts are given by the Holy Spirit.

THE GIFTS ARE NOT THE FRUIT

Another important truth we need to realize is that the gifts of the Spirit are not to be confused with the fruit of the Spirit that are mentioned in Galatians 5:22-23. The gifts of the Spirit are distributed selectively throughout the body of Christ and no Christian is expected by God to manifest all of the gifts. The fruit of the Spirit are concerned with inward works of the heart that all Christians are expected to manifest in their lives. Perhaps a table would be helpful at this point.

Gifts of the Spirit	Fruit of the Spirit
• Have to do with motivations and abilities	• Have to do with inward character
• Help us do the works of Jesus	• Help us become like Jesus
• Are temporary	• Are eternal
• Produce gifted Christians	• Produce godly Christians
• Christians are not expected to manifest all of them	• Christians are expected to manifest all of them

VARIETY IN OUR LEVEL OF GIFTEDNESS

Lastly, another important truth concerning spiritual gifts is the fact that not all of God's people are equally gifted. Every Christian has at least one spiritual gift. In fact, in my years of studying the gifts, I have come to realize that most Christians have two or three primary gifts that they operate fluently in, accompanied by one or two support gifts. Some Christians have four or five primary gifts. And in rare cases, some Christians may have six or more gifts that are regularly manifested in their life. God does not distribute the gifts of the Spirit any more equally than He does anything else.

Another pattern we observe in studying Scripture is that God loves variety and He always assigns differing levels of authority and glory to every sphere of creation. He doesn't seem to be too concerned with being "fair" in the sense that everyone gets exactly the same thing as everyone else. The account of creation in Genesis states that God made the greater light, the sun, to rule the day, and created a lesser light, the moon, to rule the night. He gave a greater glory to the sun and a lesser glory to the moon.

The animal kingdom is another demonstration of this concept. God made some animals fast while others are slow. Some are weak and some are strong. God made some animals to swim, some to fly, and some to walk upon the earth. Some, like the duck, can do all three. God gives a great variety even in the life span of His animal kingdom. Of the animals that He made, He designed the common fruit fly to live about thirty-seven days and then it dies, while the giant tortoise can live 200 years.

In the angelic order God created an innumerable host of angels consisting of two classes, the cherubim and the seraphim. Apparently, only the seraphim are allowed close access to the throne room of God (Isaiah 6:2-3). In the creation of the family God gave the husband a greater authority than the wife. In the church God gives a greater authority to the apostles and prophets than He does the rest of the church. And in regard to spiritual gifts we read in 1 Corinthians 12:11 that the Holy Spirit assigns the spiritual gifts sovereignly as He wills. Every Christian gets a spiritual gift. Some Christians get several.

However, we must remember the words of Jesus who said, "To whom much is given, much is required." The more gifts you have, the greater the accountability you have before God. Jesus explains this concept in Matthew 25:14-30 in the parable of the talents. Not every servant received an equal amount of the master's money. But whatever amount they did receive they were responsible for turning a profit on. It is much less stressful to be in charge of investing $100 rather than $100,000.

This concept is especially true for those with very powerful offices within the church such as prophets. Prophets have a great influence over the church (over the parts of the church that recognize that office). Because they are entrusted to such a high level office, their margin for sin and error is much less than yours or mine. A person with a highly-developed prophetic gift that is used very visibly in the church can be killed by God for sins that you and I could get away with.[1] This is because the threshold for error is less and less the higher up in leadership we are in God's kingdom.

Although on one occasion the Lord was even willing to forgive the Israelites for dancing naked in a sexual orgy, that same degree of tolerance and mercy was not extended to Moses. The Lord met Moses on a road one night to kill him just because he had not circumcised his child (Exodus 4:24). If you have several spiritual gifts there is no reason to get proud. Rather you ought to be extremely humble and seek to do everything you can to not waste the talent that the Lord has given you. And remember, if you serve the Lord faithfully and use the gifts He has given you, there is a very good chance He will give you others later on in your spiritual walk. Remember the parable; our Father rewards faithfulness.

The spiritual gifts are not given on merit or intelligence or holiness or any other factor. They are given by the will of the Spirit. The most gifted people in the church are not always the most godly. In fact, if I see one trend in some churches that disturbs me, it's the accolades that are given to some because of their high level of giftedness. It is very easy to become enamored by someone who has a very highly developed prophetic gift or is used greatly in healing. We tend to sometimes place more honor and recognition upon these people. In reality we ought to honor and seek to imitate those who live a holy and consecrated life before the Lord.

There is nothing wrong with being proud and excited about one's spiritual gift. I love the spiritual gifts the Lord has given me, and I thank Him for them regularly. It is a great privilege to see God work through me to minister to other people. We must keep this all in perspective, however, and realize that it is only by the grace of God that we have them.

As the apostle Paul so aptly said in 1 Corinthians 4:7, "What do you have that you did not receive?" All glory belongs to God because He is the source of all things. Giftedness is not the epitome of spirituality in the Christian faith. Holiness and humility are the signs of a truly great man or woman of God.

CHAPTER 4

A Closer Look at 1 Corinthians 12-14

DON'T BE IGNORANT

"Now concerning spiritual gifts brethren, *I would not have you ignorant* (KJV)." This is how the apostle Paul starts out his extensive teaching on the gifts of the Spirit in 1 Corinthians 12:1. This is a phrase that Paul uses very sparingly in his letters to alert his readers that he is about to discuss something of extreme significance. A few of the other times in which the apostle uses this little phrase is in relation to the divine mystery of the election of Israel and when he teaches about the resurrection of believers at the Second Coming of Christ.[1] As you can see, the apostle Paul apparently felt that the issue of spiritual gifts was one that every Christian should be well informed about.

There are many things in life that I don't know much about. My brother-in-law bought me an answering machine for Christmas a few years ago that I still don't have a clue how to operate. This thing has fourteen buttons on it, each with its own function! Where are the good ol' days when a man could actually use his own answering machine?

This contraption records messages, records entire phone calls, allows you to leave memos to yourself, can be checked from any touch-tone phone, and I believe I read somewhere in the owner's manual that you can raise up independent nations with this particular model. Peter thought that this would be a great gift idea for Pauline and me because he loves high-tech gadgets. He once bought a super state-of-the-art vacuum cleaner for $3,000.00! Please pause for a moment right now and pray for him.

My point is, there are things in life that you can be ignorant about and it probably won't affect you too much. There are things in the Bible that you can be ignorant about without much consequence as well. I know Christians who don't entirely understand the whole "third heaven" experience the apostle Paul talks about in 2 Corinthians 12:2, and they seem to be doing OK. Who really totally understands the doctrine of election? Or how about the Trinity for that matter?

But that is not the case with spiritual gifts at all. This is a subject in Scripture that will reap consequences for you spiritually if you do not get a hold of this. This is because your spiritual gifting is a partial indicator of the will of God for your life. If you are ignorant about your spiritual gifts, then you are not fulfilling part of the calling and destiny that God has for your life. Trust the apostle Paul on this one. Decide that you are not going to be ignorant about your spiritual gifts.

THREE DIFFERENT VIEWS ON HOW SPIRITUAL GIFTS OPERATE

Some slight difference of opinion exists among teachers in the church over whether Christians actually possess certain spiritual gifts over a lifetime or whether they just manifest different gifts at different times as need arises. Some of the men and women whom I greatly admire hold a different view from me on this issue, so it is with the utmost respect for them that I offer you my alternative view.

Those who teach that all Christians receive a gift or gifts by the Spirit that they retain possession of throughout their lifetime are said to hold the "constitutional view." Those who teach that we don't retain ownership of any gifts, but rather simply manifest whatever gifts are needed for each situation, hold the "manifestational view." Besides these two views, the most popular view in the church today is a hybrid of the first two views. I call it the "motivational view," and Bill Gothard popularized it in the 1970s.

Other popular authors adopted the motivational view such as Don and Katie Fortune, as explained in their excellent book, *Discover Your God Given Gifts,* and soon it became the dominant view regarding the gifts.[2] The motivational view holds that the gifts listed in Romans 12:6-8 are given to God's people as permanent possessions and that every Christian has at least one of the seven gifts listed there.

The gifts of 1 Corinthians 12:8-10 are seen as manifestational in nature and are therefore not given as permanent gifts. This view sees those gifts as being resident in the Holy Spirit and only manifested through believers for limited amounts of time and for specific occasions as determined by the Spirit. Lastly, this view sees the spiritual gifts listed in Ephesians 4:11, not as spiritual gifts per se, but as "gifts of people" given to the universal church.

Paul's Language When Describing Spiritual Gifts

The basic reasoning for the motivational view originates from the fact that the apostle Paul used three different Greek words to describe the gifts when he mentioned them in Romans 12:6-8, 1 Corinthians 12:8-10, and Ephesians 4:11. I don't believe Paul was trying to make rigid distinctions or highlight three separate classes of gifts just because he used three different words for the gifts. As a matter of fact, technically speaking, Paul actually used five Greek words interchangeably in his writings to describe the gifts. No teacher that I am aware of, however, suggests that there should now be five classes of spiritual gifts based on the five Greek words used.

Paul had various reasons for using different words to describe the gifts. These reasons ranged from using terms preferred by others (*pneumatikon*), using an Old Testament term (*domata*), using a term he actually preferred (*charismata*), and using the most common word in the Greek language of his day for "gift" (*dorea*).

In the book of 1 Corinthians Paul is answering a series of questions put to him by the church at Corinth. One of the questions concerned what a faction of the church was calling *pneumatikon* ("spiritual things" or "spirituals"). Our English Bible correctly translates this word "spiritual gifts." Paul starts off in 1 Corinthians 12:1 talking about these *pneumatikon* and tries to correct the Corinthians who are using the gifts as signs of how spiritual they must be because they're able to prophecy, speak in tongues, and perform miracles.

Paul validates their experiences but introduces a corrective by renaming these endowments *charismata* (gifts of grace) because he wants to emphasize that the gifts are given by God's grace, not by man's inherent spirituality. He also emphasizes that these gifts the Corinthians are so excited about (tongues, prophecy, miracles, etc.) are actually a manifestation (*phanerosis*) of the Spirit, not a manifestation of their own spirituality! It is due to Paul's use of this term *"phanerosis"* (manifestation) in 1 Corinthians 12:7 that some teachers see the gifts listed here as a separate class of gifts that they call "manifestational gifts" and which are believed to be different from those listed in Romans 12:6-8 where the gifts are called *charismata*. However it is often not noted that right after Paul speaks of these "manifestations" he also begins using the term *charismata* throughout the rest of 1 Corinthians chapter 12; the same term he later uses exclusively in Romans 12:6-8!

Years later when Paul was teaching the Ephesian Christians about spiritual gifts, for the sake of variety in Ephesians 4:7 he used the common Greek word for gift, the word "*dorea*." And in Ephesians 4:8 Paul quotes the Old Testament book of Psalms and uses yet another word for "gift," *domata*, because that is the word used in Psalms 68:18. Therefore in summary, Paul used five words in the New Testament for what we call "spiritual gifts." Those words were *pneumatikon, phanerosis, charismata, dorea,* and *domata.* These words were used for specific reasons but were never used by Paul to highlight distinct classes or types of gifts.

Did Paul Teach There Were "Motivational" and "Manifestational" Gifts?

Another fact to consider is that when Paul spoke of spiritual gifts in his letters, he would always name off a few and then present a little teaching about them. Each time he wrote about the gifts he mixed them altogether and in no way attempted to confine them to "manifestational gifts" and "motivational gifts." For example, he lists "prophecy" in Romans 12:6 and calls it a *charisma* while naming that same gift among the *phanerosis* in 1 Corinthians 12:10. Likewise, he lists the gift of "teaching" in Romans 12:7 as a *charisma*, and then lists the "teacher" among the *domata* of Ephesians 4:11.

The motivational view is so named because the gifts of Romans 12 are said to produce motivating tendencies for ministry within the believer. I wholeheartedly agree. But isn't this true for all spiritual gifts, not just those in Romans 12:6-8? For those who have the gift of discernment, which is listed in the 1 Corinthians 12:8-10 list, is there not a motivational urge within them to carefully evaluate the spiritual state of things? What about the gift of evangelism listed in Ephesians 4:11? A primary characteristic of someone with that gift is a strong urging to share the gospel that very much motivates and colors everything they do. The same can be said for the gift of intercession, helps, etc.

Lastly, are the gifts given in 1 Corinthians 12 really manifestational in nature, not residing within us? Take the gift of tongues for example. Believers who have the gift of tongues don't just speak in tongues in occasional manifestations, but rather can exercise that gift anytime they want as a volitional act of their will, as the apostle Paul confirms in 1 Corinthians 14:27-28.

This is because this gift is resident within them. Those who are endowed with the word of wisdom are given that anointing all of their life. Paul assumes that after time, people in the church know who those folks are and that others should bring their disagreements to them because they are known to "possess" that gift (see 1 Corinthians 6:5).

There have been many in the church who were widely known to possess other so-called "manifestational" gifts like the gift of healing in such people as Kathryn Kuhlman and John Wimber in times past, or Francis McNutt today. These individuals had a resident anointing that was within them all their life, not a manifestational, occasional experience. The same could be said with all of the gifts listed in 1 Corinthians 12:8-10.

Experience aside, I think the most convincing argument for the constitutional view is Scripture itself. When the apostle Paul is discussing the gifts in 1 Corinthians 12, he uses an analogy of a human body to illustrate his point. He instructs the Corinthian believers that although they all have different gifts (as symbolically represented by body parts) they are to all have the same respect and love for one another.

He states in verse 21, "and the eye cannot say to the hand, I have no need of you: or again the head to the feet, I have no need of you." Paul did not say, "Quit being jealous church, you may be an eye today, but tomorrow you may manifest as a foot. Oh head, do not be proud for you may cease to be a head and turn into a toe tomorrow." As a matter of fact, a few verses down in verse 28 Paul states that we are all to accept our place where God has *appointed* us. He then starts a series of rhetorical questions in which the implied answer to each is "no!" These questions are to illustrate that God assigns each Christian certain spiritual gifts that we possess for our whole life and that it is not to be expected that we will ever all have the same gift.

The very analogy of permanent body parts that Paul appeals to makes no sense if gifts constantly fluctuate from part to part. And where does Paul choose to employ the body part illustration? Not in Romans 12:6-8, but in 1 Corinthians 12, in the direct context of the so-called "manifestational" gifts! Paul seemed to be heavily implying here that each Christian has his or her own gifts and that they need to accept where the Lord has placed them within the body of Christ.

THE DANGERS OF GIFT PROJECTION

Before we go any further I want to caution you about the danger of what C. Peter Wagner calls "gift projection."[3] Actually this caution was first given to us by the apostle Paul in 1 Corinthians 12:12-27. Paul tells the Corinthian church to not think differently about other Christians just because they are not manifesting certain gifts that one segment of the community highly values. In the case of the Corinthian church, that gift was primarily the gift of tongues. That error was what necessitated the apostle having to write an entire section regulating that one gift and giving proper instruction about its use and function.

Some Christians, who are ignorant about spiritual gifts, will mistakenly try to project their gift on everyone else around them. They may attempt to reprove you for not acting like them or doing what they do in their service for God. In most cases this stems from them not understanding that a big reason for why they do what they do is because of the gifting of God within them.

They may not realize that not everyone has the same ability and anointing from God that they do. If you are on the receiving end of people projecting their gifts, it can cause you to become insecure or discouraged. You feel this way because you realize that you cannot match those persons' ability and you become frustrated. Sometimes people project their gifts and don't realize it.

Although any gift can be projected, I have found that there are four gifts that are commonly projected by those who have them. They are the gifts of tongues, evangelism, faith, and simplicity (some call the simplicity gift "voluntary poverty"). Let's first of all consider the gift of tongues. Many in the charismatic branch of the church have tried to force this one gift on the entire body of Christ even though the Bible clearly states that not all will speak in tongues (1 Corinthians 12:30).

The result has been division and discouragement on the part of many. Some Christians desperately want to fit in with their circle of Christian friends, so they pretend to speak in tongues or begin to convince themselves that they have this gift by just repeating certain sounds and syllables over and over. The result doesn't hurt anyone or do any real damage; it just leaves us with lots of Christians throughout the world who don't really have the gift of tongues. They just speak gibberish when they get in a crowd of others who really have this gift.

I have found that when you place a new Christian in a church that believes everyone must speak in tongues, the result is that eight out of ten of those people will be "speaking in tongues" within a few months. Spiritual peer pressure is a very real phenomenon. When you place a new Christian in a church where tongues is just taught to be one of the many gifts, with no particular glory attached to it, the chances that the new convert will speak in tongues will dramatically decrease.

Typically those with the gift of evangelism have a tendency to project their gift as well. They witness to people all the time. They witness in grocery stores, at the ball game, and maybe even door-to-door. They sometimes look at the rest of us and say, "What's the matter with the rest of you? This isn't hard, get on with it!"

One of my favorite preachers has a very strong evangelism gift. He leads people to Christ sometimes on a weekly basis. When he tells the latest story of who he led to Christ that week, I get very excited, and then I get very depressed. I look at my own life and realize that I usually only lead two or three people to Christ every few years. Compared to him I sometimes feel like a failure. I have to remind myself that I am who I am. I need to be thankful to God for the few souls I have had the privilege of leading to Christ.

The gift of faith is commonly projected as well. My wife believes that many in the Word-Faith movement are really just Christians with the gift of faith who are trying to project that gift on the entire body of Christ. Haven't you heard preachers tell their awesome stories of faith about how God provided for their needs or how He led them to do a great work for the kingdom that to everyone else looked impossible? Then they told you that, "Every Christian can do what I do, bless God! Every Christian has faith!"

That's not entirely true. Every Christian does have faith, but not every Christian has the special gift of faith. These Christians have an extra anointing of faith that the rest of us do not have. Those with this gift ought to be encouraging the rest of us, not making us feel as if something is wrong or lacking in us if we are not like them.

Lastly, the simplicity gift is often projected as well. Those with this gift live a very simplified lifestyle and give much of their material possessions and money away to others less fortunate than themselves. Some with this gift can tend to look down on other Christians as being "materialistic" and "selfish" because they do not bless the poor and needy with their abundance.

Again, every Christian should be a generous giver and seek for ways to bless and help others who don't have as much as they do. The early church in the book of Acts certainly left us a good example that we in the western church need to get a hold of. But there are certain Christians who are called to this ministry. They should be sensitive to the rest of us and not judge us. Don't project your gifts on others. Don't look down on other Christians who are different from you. "As each one has received a special gift, employ it in serving one another, as good stewards of the manifold grace of God" (1 Peter 4:10).

ALL THE GIFTS ARE NEEDED

1 Corinthians 12:17 states, "If the whole body were an eye, where would the hearing be? If the whole were hearing, where would the sense of smell be?" God has placed within His church a perfect mix of gifts that, when all are operational, produces a powerful church that can fully carry out all that the Lord God desires to do on the earth today.

We need all of the gifts for the church to be healthy and fully functional. When we begin to see certain gifts as not being of value, then we are beginning to move into error and ultimately we are not pleasing God. Every gift is needed in the church. We need the pastors and the teachers. We need those gifted in service and mercy. And we need those gifted in discernment and deliverance. When we neglect certain gifts then by design there are certain ministries that just will not be accomplished.

Matthew 17:14-21 tells the story of a father who had a demon-possessed son. He brought the son to Jesus' disciples in hopes that they could cure the boy. Sadly, these commissioned ambassadors of God were impotent when facing the powers of darkness that haunted this poor boy.

Thankfully, Jesus was still on the earth at this time and the distraught father found our Lord and approached him. "Lord, have mercy on my son: for he is a lunatic, and is very ill; for he often falls into the fire, and often into the water. And I brought him to your disciples and they could not cure him."

Friends, that is one of the saddest stories in the Bible. If there is one institution, if there is one people among all that live upon the earth that should be able to help, it ought to be the servants of the most high God. And yet the same thing happens in our churches everyday. Those churches that do not allow the operation of certain gifts to occur in their fellowship are impotent in the face of some problems that can only be dealt with using certain gifts.

The end result is that those churches often appear virtually powerless in times of great crises. When a great crisis comes into the life of some members of these churches they are forced to seek ministry from outside churches that do practice all of the gifts. Other members in these situations have no faith or belief that anything can change and so they simply accept whatever has happened to them as being the "will of God."

Many times this may be true. But often the case is that Satan has attacked a family member with sickness or oppression and God in no way wills for that situation to remain as it is. But remember, God operates by faith. If we don't ask Him for something, there is a very good chance that we will never get it. Every week, Sunday after Sunday, there are people in our congregations with family members possessed by spirits and there are people with sickness and disease. There are people who desperately need a prophetic word from God. They come to the church and they leave, because the church cannot help them. My friends, these things ought not to be.

God did not design His church to just be a place for great oratory, fellowship groups, and Bible studies. His church is also to be a place where the power of God is displayed to this lost world; where healings occur, demonic strongholds are broken, and the prophetic word of the Lord is proclaimed. The kingdom of God is not just word, but also power (1 Corinthians 4:20).

The supernatural gifts such as deliverance, miracles, and healing are not the panacea to the church's problems, however. You see, God meant for all of the gifts of the Spirit to be in operation. The apostle Paul tells the story in 1 Corinthians chapter 5 of a young man that was involved in a sexual affair with a woman who was probably his stepmother. He was rightfully cast out of the church for his unrepentant sin. But apparently this young man fully repented later and wanted back into the fellowship of the church.

Paul exhorted the church in 2 Corinthians 2:5-8 to restore this man by loving him and forgiving him. At that moment in his life, this man didn't need a bunch of Christians surrounding him who could supernaturally prophesy over him all night. What he needed were some Spirit-filled saints gifted in mercy to wrap their arms around him, cry with him, and love him back into the fellowship.

You see, we need all the gifts. The church has been divided many times along gift lines. Those who highly value the sign gifts all get together and form associations of churches. Those who particularly value teaching form their own little associations where the greatest goal is the acquisition of biblical knowledge. Those with serving and simplicity gifts gather together to care for the outcast and oppressed. And before we know it a schism exists that the apostle Paul tried to warn us about.

There is a better, biblical way to exist as the body of Christ. That is to realize that all of the gifts are important and that we should not be dividing over them. And we should remember that every Christian in our church is uniquely gifted and has something of value to contribute to the body life of the fellowship.

DIVERSITY OF OPERATIONS

1 Corinthians 12:4-7 is a key section of the apostle's teaching about the gifts. Paul states in this section,

"Now there are *varieties of gifts*, but the same Spirit. And there are *varieties of ministries*, and the same Lord. And there are *varieties of effects*, but the same God who works all things in all persons.

But to each one is given the manifestation of the Spirit for the common good."

The apostle is making a key point here that you do not want to miss. What is the key word that Paul is trying to stress here? Yes, the word "variety," of course. First he states that there are a variety of gifts or *charismata*. Some of the gifts are revelatory in nature such as prophecy or tongues. Some are service-oriented, such as serving and helps. Others are extremely impressive and supernatural such as healing and miracles.

Paul also states in verse 5 that there are varieties of ministries or *diakoniai*. The meaning of this word is literally "services." In other words, Paul is stating that not only is there variety in the gifts themselves, but there is a variety of ways that each gift can be expressed.

For instance, just because individuals have the gift of pastoring, it does not mean that they will necessarily be involved in pastoring an entire congregation on a full-time basis. One can use that gift to pastor a smaller group in the church such as a cell group. That person may be involved in a discipleship ministry, regularly discipling small groups of new believers in the church. Wise is the pastor who finds members within his flock who are also gifted by the Spirit to pastor. Those members will have a natural shepherding instinct for the people of God and can be used greatly to help care for the congregation.

Another example would be to look at the gift of exhortation. This gift can be expressed in numerous ways. Exhorters make excellent counselors or altar workers. And if your church has a greeting ministry that welcomes guests when they first arrive, consider using greeters who are gifted in exhortation. They are a natural for that ministry.

Those with teaching gifts may be able to write curriculum as well as they can teach. A pastor may want to utilize their ministry skills in writing training manuals for the church's various ministries. The combinations are endless. Every one of the gifts can be used in many different ways to accomplish many different services.

Lastly in this section Paul states in verse 6 that there are varieties of effects or *energemata*. This word literally means "energy" or "power." That is, there is a variety even in the outworking of God's power within each gift that is different in each person. This is exciting because Paul tells us here that when we are exercising our spiritual gifts we are not operating in our own power. We are literally conduits of the power of God!

This phrase is rich in meaning. God's power works in Christians in different ways. Therefore, there is variety in the way people operate in their gifts even if they have the same gift. God takes His power and pours it out through His human vessels who have unique personalities, experiences, and backgrounds. The result is a wonderful variety in the way each Christian's gift operates.

I would like to make one other point about this word. I believe that this word also implies a sovereign range in the power of the gift that we have. This idea is similar to what Paul taught in Romans 12:6 where he states, "And since we have gifts that differ according to the grace given to us, let us exercise each accordingly: if prophecy, according to the proportion of his faith."

Even though two Christians may share the same gift, one may be more highly developed in that gift than the other. For example, not every Christian gifted in evangelism has the same level of anointing as Billy Graham. One person may lead several people to Christ every time they share the gospel or get a chance to preach. Billy Graham, however, evokes thousands of decisions for Christ in almost every public service in which he preaches, no matter what the culture is. Billy Graham has probably led more people to Christ than the apostle Paul.

Think about the prophetic gift as well. I know Christians that I would say are prophetic. They receive supernatural revelation from God quite often, especially when they minister publicly. This revelation is usually very general, however. Perhaps they sense certain illnesses that God wants to heal that night. They may get a picture in their mind of a young child that needs prayer and they may describe this child's approximate age and name the illness.

In the church we also have more seasoned and highly developed prophets such as a Bill Hamon or a Cindy Jacobs. The prophetic words that these individuals give are much more specific than are those given by most of the prophetic people that I know. The point is, God gives variety in our level of giftedness. And I truly believe that most of us are nowhere near our potential.

THE GIFT OF TONGUES

Of all the gifts listed in Scripture, the one that usually receives the most attention and scrutiny is the gift of tongues. This gift has been the topic of debate and disagreement between Christians for 2,000 years. It is interesting to note that while some gifts receive nothing more than one verse in the Bible, the gift of tongues receives an entire chapter of specific teaching by the apostle Paul. It's also interesting that the most controversial gift in the early church is still the most controversial gift today. One would think that the detailed teaching that the apostle left us would have been enough for future Christians to build a consensus around, but such has not been the case.

The gift of tongues is a unique gift. Unlike most of the other gifts, it has no Old Testament precedent. It is an entirely New Testament phenomenon. It is also the only gift that has as one of its purposes the judgment of others. We'll take a look at that role in a moment. The only reason I am singling out this gift for specific mention is because the apostle Paul did so and because I believe the church has yet to properly understand this gift today. Let me start off by saying that I personally do not have this gift and have never spoken in tongues.

The gift of tongues is a powerful gift. Those who have it describe an intensity and an intimacy with God that is enviable. The ability to speak mysteries and praises to God in a heavenly language is a moving experience. This gift rejuvenates and builds up the faith of those who have it. The ability to intercede and to pray in the perfect will of God are powerful tools in the Christian's arsenal. And that is why God gave this gift. It does all these things.

But because this gift involves in one sense a deeper intimacy in one's prayer life, it can lead to pride. Apparently this is what began to happen at the church in Corinth. Some members who had this gift were beginning to make those who didn't have it feel like second-class Christians. Some who had the gift were so over zealous about it that they wanted to practice this gift at all times, even in front of non-believers who would not know what to think about it or be directly helped by it.

A schism began to develop in the church at Corinth over this and the other miraculous gifts. The apostle Paul therefore took the time to write the church in an attempt to correct the problems that were occurring. His advice is recorded for us in 1 Corinthians 12-14 and it is required reading for every Christian. Regardless of how you feel about the gift of tongues, as a Christian you are bound to follow the Word of God's teaching concerning this particular gift.

We have to be careful about misguided loyalty. We are ultimately Christians, not Lutherans, Methodists, Baptists, or charismatics. When the group we have decided to associate with holds beliefs that run contrary to the Word of God, then the Word of God must win our loyalty.

I know churches that flat out refuse to allow speaking in tongues in their congregations, even though the Bible clearly states in 1 Corinthians 14:39, "Do not forbid speaking in tongues." These churches have simply ignored this clear command from the Word of God, and like the Pharisees they have put their particular denominational tradition above the teaching of Scripture (Matthew 15:3). That is very, very dangerous.

I know that many churches forbid speaking in tongues because the gift can be misused and lead to disorderliness. This does sometimes happen. I have been in a few church services where the meeting was completely out of order. However, we do not stop practicing a doctrine just because it can be abused.

I happen to believe very strongly in the eternal security of the believer. That doctrine can be very abused. Christians that hold to it can believe, mistakenly, that their sin really has no consequences. They can tend to say, "Praise the Lord brother, once saved always saved!" Just because a teaching in the Bible can be abused it does not give us a right to no longer follow the teaching. We simply must correct the abuses while still following the teaching.

One reason that the gift has been so divisive is because those who possess it have had a tendency historically to equate it with superspirituality. In a sense they feel they have arrived at a new, higher level of intimacy with God. Logically, those who have not experienced this gift are looked at as not having attained that level. Of course, I am speaking in very broad generalizations and I am in no way saying that all people with the gift of tongues today are guilty of this. I am simply giving the general historical background to this issue.

In fact, I have been ministering in charismatic churches for the last ten years and can count on one hand the times anyone with this gift has displayed a condescending attitude toward me. On the contrary, I have always been immediately loved and totally accepted by those in the charismatic community.

The "Prayer Language" and the Gift of Tongues: Two Separate Gifts?

Still today, however, there are many who teach that you must speak in tongues to truly be baptized in the Spirit. This is exactly the kind of thinking that the apostle Paul tried to correct in the book of 1 Corinthians. He even stated in 1 Corinthians 12:30, "All do not speak with tongues, do they?" Of course the implied answer to his rhetorical question is a resounding, "No!"

The problem is further propagated today with some charismatics trying to get around that verse by stating that in that verse the apostle was only talking about the "gift of tongues" and not the "prayer language," or common tongues, that every believer receives when they are baptized in the Spirit. I have only one problem with that belief... It's not in the Bible. Nowhere in Scripture does Paul teach that there is a gift of tongues that some Christians receive as their spiritual gift and a second type of tongues that every Christian is supposed to receive at some time later in their Christian walk. Paul refers to one phenomenon in the Scripture—the gift of tongues. Some have this gift and some do not.

It has been said that the "gift of tongues" is for public proclamation while our "prayer language" is for our private use. Again, that doesn't seem to hold water in Paul's writings. First Corinthians 14:27-28 shows that tongues can be used publicly in a worship service if someone is present with the gift of interpretation. If no one is present with that gift, then Paul states that the person gifted in tongues is to use his or her gift in a devotional, private way and just "speak to himself." Paul never teaches that there are two different gifts because there are two different uses. He teaches about a gift that has two uses, namely public and private expressions, and gives instructions on it.

Are Tongues the Sign of a Second Blessing?

Some may still say, "Aren't there lots of Christians in the book of Acts who later received a second blessing from the Holy Spirit as evidenced by speaking in tongues? Doesn't that heavily imply that this is a special sign that is given to Christians when they encounter the Holy Sprit in a deeper way?" Well, there are a few problems with that assertion, so let's take a closer look at this issue.

First of all, the individuals who received the gift of tongues in the book of Acts were not previously saved Christians who received a second blessing evidenced by tongues. In every case except one, the individuals who received the gift of tongues in Acts were brand new, born again Christians who happened to receive the gift of tongues at their conversion.[4] They were not previously saved individuals who were now getting something from the Holy Spirit that they had not previously received from Him, i.e. a special prayer language.

In the book of Acts twenty-five salvation experiences are recorded of single individuals or groups. In every case except one, those who are saved immediately receive the baptism of the Holy Spirit and upon their newfound salvation are also gifted by the Holy Spirit with a gift or gifts. The regular pattern in the book of Acts does not portray previously-saved individuals coming back to the apostles to receive something they did not receive from the Holy Spirit the first time. And yet many of my charismatic brothers and sisters use two passages in Acts as proof texts to teach that all Christians should speak in tongues. Perhaps a couple of tables would be helpful at this point.

Conversions in the Book of Acts

Biblical Text	Locale and Description	Convert/s Recorded as Speaking in Tongues
Acts 2:41	Jerusalem: 3,000 unnamed converts	no
Acts 4:4	Jerusalem: 5,000 unnamed converts	no
Acts 5:14	Jerusalem: multitudes of men & women	no
Acts 6:7	Jerusalem: some Jewish priests	no
Acts 8:12	Samaria: some unnamed converts	no
Acts 8:38	Gaza: Ethiopian eunuch	no
Acts 9:18	Damascus: Saul of Tarsus	no
Acts 9:35	Lydda & Sharon: some unnamed converts	no
Acts 9:42	Joppa: some unnamed converts	no
Acts 10:47	Caesarea: Cornelius & his family	YES
Acts 11:21	Antioch: a large number of unnamed converts	no
Acts 13:12	Salamis: Sergius Paulus	no
Acts 13:43	Perga: many Jews & God-fearers	no
Acts 13:48	Perga: some unnamed Gentiles	no
Acts 14:1	Iconium: a great number of Jews & Gentiles	no
Acts 14:21	Derbe: some unnamed converts	no
Acts 16:14	Philippi: Lydia and her family	no
Acts 16:33	Philippi: a prison guard and his family	no
Acts 17:4	Thessalonica: a multitude of God-fearers	no
Acts 17:12	Berea: some prominent Greek men & women	no
Acts 17:34	Athens: Dionysius, Damaris, and others	no
Acts 18:8	Corinth: Crispus and his family	no
Acts 19:5	Ephesus: disciples of John the Baptist	YES
Acts 19:18	Ephesus: many unnamed converts	no
Acts 28:24	Rome: some unnamed converts	no

As one can see, from the twenty-five recorded conversions of individuals or groups, the mention that anyone spoke in tongues occurs in only two of them, or 8 percent of the time. We know from his later epistles that the apostle Paul also spoke in tongues, so that changes our figure to 12 percent. If there is a pattern to be found in Acts, it's this: most Christians back then, as well as most Christians today, were not given the gift of tongues! Those who would teach that the "normal" pattern in Acts portrays Christians as speaking in tongues either at conversion or at a latter time through a second blessing, or baptism in the Spirit, are hard-pressed to prove that from the Scriptures.

In all fairness we shouldn't include all twenty-five examples above to discover what Luke is trying to portray as the normal pattern of salvation-spirit baptism-water baptism. It could be argued that he wouldn't necessarily mention people being baptized in the Spirit (with the so-called "evidence" of speaking in tongues) in every occasion as sometimes he just wants to quickly emphasize the fact that some group or groups received Christ along the way on Peter and Paul's missionary journeys. I would agree with that argument as well.

To see the pattern Luke records for salvation-spirit baptism-water baptism, it is only fair to consider the nine passages in Acts in which he gives us detailed salvation accounts and includes such things as the city, situation in which the convert was saved, their evangelist, their baptism, etc. By observing these, we can see what patterns there are, if any, in the book of Acts regarding people speaking in tongues. Let's take a look.

DETAILED SALVATION ACCOUNTS IN THE BOOK OF ACTS

	Person accepts Christ; receives the Holy Spirit at the moment of salvation	Person is water baptized; (sometimes various spiritual gifts at salvation are mentioned)	That person later returns to receive from the Spirit something not given at the moment of salvation
Acts 2:37-41 3,000 on Day of Pentecost	Yes	Yes	No Record
Acts 8:12-17 The Samaritans	No	Yes	Yes[5]
Acts 8:26-39 Ethiopian eunuch	Yes (implied)	Yes	No Record
Acts 9:1-19 Saul of Tarsus	Yes	Yes	No Record
Acts 10:1-48 Cornelius & family	Yes	Yes	No Record
Acts 16:14-15 Lydia & family	Yes (implied)	Yes	No Record
Acts 16:22-34 Prison guard & family	Yes (implied)	Yes	No Record
Acts 18:8-11 Crispus & family	Yes (implied)	Yes	No Record
Acts 19:1-7 Disciples of John the Baptist	Yes	Yes	No Record[6]

As you can see, the individuals in these passages received from the Holy Spirit at the moment of their new birth. Of these nine accounts listed in Acts, only two cases (Acts 10, Acts 19) involved speaking in tongues. That is two out of nine, or 22 percent of the cases. Again, if we include the apostle Paul then the figure is 33 percent.

In these cases where these early Christians received the ability to speak in tongues it is nowhere stated that this is anything other than the "gift" of tongues. Paul never mentions in any of his epistles that all Christians can speak in tongues even if they do not have the "gift" of tongues. To try to use the two passages above to make the argument that all Christians should speak in tongues is, in my opinion, not exegetically justifiable.

THE PURPOSE OF TONGUES

One other issue I want to mention before we go on is the purpose of the gift of tongues. Of course it is used as a means for praise, intercession, and building up one's faith. But there is also another purpose for the gift. Many times, in the charismatic branch of the church, we have used it as an indicator to one another to prove that we are Spirit-filled. We say to each other, "Praise God brother, are you baptized in the Holy Ghost with the evidence of speaking in tongues!" Of course when I'm asked that question I always have to reply, "Hey, you got twenty minutes? I have a couple of charts I want to show you."

Mistakenly, what some of us have done is to try to use the gift of tongues to perform a role that it was never designed for. Namely, we have tried to use it as a sign to one another in the church to "prove" that we are Spirit filled. Interestingly, Scripture states that its secondary purpose is just the opposite. Paul says in 1 Corinthians

14:22, "So then tongues are for a sign, *not to those who believe*, but to unbelievers..." (italics mine).

Paul previously states in verse 21 that, "In the Law it is written, by men of strange tongues and by the lips of strangers I will speak to this people, and even so they will not listen to me." Paul is referencing Isaiah 28:11, a passage of Scripture in which God pronounces judgment against Israel for its sin.

God is stating that one day Israel will be so apostate that she will no longer even be able to hear the voice of Yahweh. Instead she will one day observe another group communicating with God (the new Israel, i.e., the church) and will be so distant from God that the communication will be unintelligible and sound like babble in Israel's ears. This is very similar to what the prophet Amos prophesied in Amos 8:11, "Behold, the days are coming, declares the Lord God, when I will send a famine on the land, not a famine for bread or a thirst for water, but rather for hearing the words of the Lord."

Throughout Scripture there is a direct correlation between our relationship with God and our ability to hear His voice. Consider a few examples of this truth. In the beginning before the fall of man, Adam enjoyed an intimate relationship with God that included face-to-face walks in the garden in which they would fellowship with one another.

Think of Moses, who was probably the closest man to God in the entire Bible. The Lord said of Moses in Numbers 12:6-8, "Hear now my words: if there is a prophet among you, I the Lord shall make Myself known to him in a vision. I shall speak with him in a dream. Not so with Moses, he is faithful in all my household; with him I speak mouth to mouth, even openly and not in dark sayings." Compare that with the revelation that Pharaoh received when he wanted to just know the name of the Israelites' God. Moses was told to just tell him that "I am who I am" had spoken.

In John 12:28-31 God the Father spoke audibly from the heavens and only some of the crowd could hear! The rest only thought that they heard some thunder in the background. In your own life have you not noticed that when you begin to backslide spiritually you begin to have difficulty hearing clearly from God?

So we see that this New Testament phenomenon of speaking in tongues is not a sign for believers. It is a sign of judgment on unbelieving Israel and the unbelieving lost world at large. When unsaved people hear Christians speaking in tongues, it is actually a symbolic picture pointing to the fact that they are cut off from that revelation. That is heavenly communication that is only to be shared between God and His people. To the rest of the world it's supposed to sound like babble. That's its purpose. How true it is that, "… a natural man (unsaved man) does not accept the things of the Spirit of God; for they are foolishness to him, and he cannot understand them, because they are spiritually appraised" (1 Corinthians 2:14).

Well I'm glad that after 2,000 years of disagreement on this doctrine I was finally able to set the issue straight! No, seriously, I know that Christians still disagree about this issue. I have many dear friends I work with in ministry who would disagree with me on this issue, and that is OK. This is not something the church of the Lord Jesus Christ needs to divide over.

If you have the gift of tongues you ought to thank God often. It is a powerful supernatural gift of the Spirit that will do wonders for you and helps build the kingdom of God as well. If you have never spoken in tongues there is absolutely no reason for you to feel inferior at all. That just means God has given you some of the other 29 gifts of the Spirit! No matter what gift we have, let us use it to glorify the name of Jesus and see the kingdom of God expand across the earth.

THE MOTIVATION BEHIND THE GIFTS

This discussion on the gift of tongues leads perfectly into what is taught in 1 Corinthians 13. This has often been called the "love chapter" and rightly so. The Lord tells us what our motivation should be when practicing the gifts of the Spirit. Our motivation should be love. We are never to be arrogant or look down at another Christian because they are not manifesting certain gifts.

In the church we are told to esteem each other as being better than ourselves. Jesus washed the feet of His disciples to leave us an example of how to honor and prefer one another. If there is one thing that causes righteous indignation within me, it's seeing people minister in an arrogant manner and who exercise their spiritual giftings in such a way as to draw attention to themselves rather than to the Son of God. The closer you are to God the more humble you ought to be and the more willing you ought to be to associate with someone of perceived lesser status than yourself. Pride, self-preoccupation, and insensitivity towards others have no place in the kingdom of God.

As you develop your unique spiritual gifts, you will naturally be superior to other Christians in certain areas because of your gifting. But if you are not careful, Satan will tempt you to think more highly of yourself than you ought in order to make you fall. You must always guard against this. When exercising our gifts we must always do so as an act of service and blessing to others and as a way to glorify Jesus.

As Christians we must daily come before the Father and say, "Search me O God and know my heart, try me and know my thoughts: and see if there be any wicked way in me, and lead me in the way of everlasting" (Psalms 139:23-24, KJV). We have to keep a constant watch on our attitudes and actions. True Spirit-filled Christians look for ways to build up other Christians. They do not make others feel inferior and less important because they are not manifesting certain gifts.

CHAPTER 5

The Classification & Implementation of the Gifts

CLASSIFYING THE GIFTS

We now come to the issue of classifying the gifts into different groupings. A wide variety of opinion exists as to how these gifts should be organized. The most common classification used today divides the gifts into three groupings based upon the different lists of the gifts as found in Romans 12, 1 Corinthians 12, and Ephesians 4 respectively. This is the classification system used by those who hold to the motivational view as mentioned in chapter four.

Some like to divide the gifts into two primary categories, those that revolve around speaking/proclamation and those that revolve around serving/ministering. That classification system would look something like this:

Gifts of Speech	Gifts of Service
prophet	(The remaining 22 gifts)
prophecy	
word of knowledge	
word of wisdom	
teaching	
tongues	
interpretation of tongues	
evangelism	

Others like to divide the gifts into those they believe were temporary versus those they believe are to continue throughout the church age. This classification system is used by cessationists. They sub-divide the "permanent" gifts into various groupings. Their list would look like this:

Temporary Gifts 33 A.D.- c.95 A.D.	Permanent Gifts 33 A.D.- Return of Christ
apostleship prophet prophecy healing miracles tongues deliverance	(The remaining 23 gifts)

There are lots of other ways in which we can classify these gifts, but I think you get the point. I don't believe there is a right or wrong way to classify them. You may have a better way to organize them than I have listed here. I have seen many different classifications used.

I personally classify the gifts into three main groupings based upon the overarching criteria of, "What is the main purpose of these particular gifts?" I have found three groupings that satisfy me well enough, and this is how we'll look at the gifts in the next four chapters. I see three primary purposes for the gifts. Therefore my classification system looks like this:

Sign Gifts	Ministry Gifts		Foundational Gifts
healing	administration	int. of tongues	apostleship
miracles	craftsmanship	knowledge	prophet
deliverance	discernment	leadership	evangelism
tongues	exhortation	mercy	pastoring
prophecy	faith	missionary	teaching
martyrdom	giving	serving	
	helps	simplicity	
	hospitality	wisdom	
	intercession	worship	
	int. of dreams		

The sign gifts are so called because they serve as signs to each generation that the kingdom of God has arrived and is advancing upon the earth. These gifts demonstrate the awesome power of God to both the church and the lost world. Martyrdom is included in this grouping because it is a gift that serves as a sign to the world. The persecution of God's saints is a sign of the unregenerate, evil heart of man. It's a vivid symbol that we are still on the other side of paradise and this great spiritual war that we are involved in is not yet over. The Lord uses martyrs to seed a nation with the gospel and to break up the hard ground so that later evangelistic efforts will be successful.

The second grouping I call ministry gifts. The ministry gifts are extremely varied and help to accomplish a wide variety of tasks in the church. Their use in the body of Christ ensures that the necessary "work of the ministry" can be accomplished.

And finally, the foundational gifts are used to build up and expand the universal church. Apostles laid the foundation of the church, prophets provide prophetic insight and direction to the church, and evangelists ensure that the church enjoys steady growth and stays on target with our most important function of winning souls to Christ. Pastors and teachers are given to nurture, instruct, and lead local congregations so that each of God's individual flocks is loved and taken care of by a God-appointed, Spirit-anointed local shepherd. These five gifts, in particular, make up the foundational elements needed for the body of Christ to grow to maturity.

THE FIVE-FOLD PURPOSE OF THE NEW TESTAMENT CHURCH

Now that we have looked at the primary classification for these gifts, we need to see them in relation to one other element as well.

We need to look at the gifts of the Spirit in relation to the overall purpose that God has for His church. What is the overall purpose of the church of Jesus Christ? The answer to that question is vital. It will determine the direction a church takes. It will determine what activities and ministries a church involves itself in. It will determine how the church spends its money, hires staff, and trains its members.

Thankfully, the Scriptures reveal to us what the primary purpose of the local and universal church should be. It is a five-fold purpose and we see it in Acts 2:42-47. Those verses of Scripture give us a summary listing of the activities of the first century church. Luke records in verse 42, "And they [the church] were continually devoting themselves to the apostles teaching and to fellowship, to the breaking of bread and to prayer." Verse 47 adds, "And the Lord was adding to their number day by day those who were being saved."

The church is called the bride of Christ. In essence, in a spiritual sense, we are His wife. We can use this acronym, WIFES, to help us remember this five-fold purpose. It is: Worship (*breaking of bread*), Instruction (*apostles' doctrine*), Fellowship (*fellowship*), Evangelism (*the Lord was adding*), and Service (*prayer*). Prayer is of course just one representative act of service or "ministry" that should characterize the work of the church toward its own members and toward the world at large. Virtually any ministry activity, prayer included, can logically fall under the fifth purpose of "service." Everything the early church did fell under one of these five purposes. Every command in the New Testament that God gives us falls under one of these categories as well. I challenge you to find an exception.

Everything a church does ought to fall under one of these five purposes. These five purposes should determine your church's priorities, ministries, and energies. God's plan for the church is rather simple wouldn't you say? He wants us to be a community of worshipers who exalt His holy name and who live lives of holiness. He wants the church to be about the business of instructing and equipping others to become disciples. He wants the church to live in community and experience true fellowship with Him and with one another.

He wants the church to be about spreading the glorious gospel to every man, woman, and child upon the face of the earth. And finally, the church is to also be a place of ministry and serving. We must be about doing the same works that Jesus did. We need to feed the poor, bind up the brokenhearted, teach the masses, heal the sick, and deliver those in oppression.

And do you know what is so exciting? Every one of the spiritual gifts God has given His people helps us directly fulfill one or more of these eternal purposes! Your gift is not unimportant in the kingdom of God! The local church you belong to desperately needs to grasp this concept so you can help that church fulfill all God desires to do in your community.

You are a vital link in the health of your church. Your church will never be everything it was destined to be unless you take up your place of divinely appointed service. Without you, your church may be 95 percent of what it was supposed to be, but it will never be 100 percent of what it was destined to be.

Even if your gift is serving, and all you ever do is serve meals at your church's soup kitchen for the poor and needy, doesn't that help fulfill one of the five-fold purposes of the church? Of course it does. Somebody has to remember the poor and needy and serve them. If Jesus were physically on the earth today, that would be an important ministry in His mind, as it was when He walked the earth 2,000 years ago. Every gift in the body of Christ is needed. God is calling all Christians to discover their gifts and then use them to accomplish the purposes He has for His church.

So another way of looking at the many different gifts is to try to discover which of the five-fold purposes they best help to fulfill.

Let's take a look at just a sample of the different tasks and ministries that could logically fall under the five purposes. As you look these over, think about which gift or gifts would be especially suited for that particular task or ministry.

The Five-Fold Purpose of the New Testament Church
W-I-F-E-S (Acts 2:42-47)

Worship	Instruction	Fellowship	Evangelism	Service
praise & worship	preaching	ministry projects	city-wide outreach	prayer ministry
communion	teaching	weekend retreats	prison ministry	benevolence
holy living	equipping	agape meals	visitation	various ministries
tithing	Sunday School	testimonials	missions	counseling
drama ministry	ministry training	youth trips	task groups	ushers
cell groups	cell groups	cell groups	cell groups	cell groups

Implementing the Gifts in the Local Church

Christian Schwarz in his book, *Natural Church Development: A Guide to Eight Essential Qualities of Healthy Churches*, lists the eight quality characteristics of healthy, growing churches. He conducted extensive studies and interviews of numerous churches. He also talked with hundreds of church members, staffs, and pastors to arrive at his conclusions. In his findings, the number two quality characteristic of successful churches was that they implemented a "gift-oriented ministry." That is, the members were involved with ministries in the church that matched their particular spiritual gifts. Schwarz had this to say about this important concept:

> When Christians serve in their area of giftedness, they generally function less in their own strength and more in the power of the Holy Spirit…An interesting corollary result of our research was the discovery that probably no factor influences the contentedness of Christians more than whether they are utilizing their gifts or not. Our data demonstrated a highly significant relationship between "gift-orientation" ("My personal ministry involvements match my gifts") and "joy in living" ("I consider myself to be a happy, contented person"). None of the eight quality characteristics showed nearly as much influence on both personal and church life as "gift-oriented ministry."[1]

The above comments represent a paradigm shift that has occurred in much of the church in the last thirty years. Traditional pastors still see themselves as the primary "minister" of the church who is expected to be the expert evangelist, counselor, administrator, preacher, exhorter, and deliverer. The truth is that the pastor is there to equip the rest of the congregation to do the actual work of the ministry. It may be difficult for some pastors to come to terms with, but there are people in his congregation who are more highly gifted at soul winning, praying, teaching, etc., than he is.

I believe that one of the most destructive beliefs we have in the church today is the concept of the clergy and the laity. This artificial distinction separates the body of Christ into two groups, the "real" ministers and the "volunteer" ministers. This concept has absolutely no biblical basis and has mistakenly led many Christians to believe that the responsibility for ministry rests mainly on the paid staff of their local church. The truth is that every Christian is a minister of the gospel. All Christians (not just pastors and famous evangelists) have been given specific gifts by the Holy Spirit to enable them to do their part in "the work of the ministry." If you have been called to be saved, then you're called to serve.

More and more pastors are finally realizing that their primary calling is to equip the members of their congregation to do "the work of the ministry." A giant starting point in doing this is to find out what giftings are present in each local church. The giftedness of each particular church will determine the quality of ministry that takes place. As Schwarz stated, the churches that have figured this out are experiencing the blessings that naturally flow from following what is the biblical paradigm, that is, every member is a minister.

There are many ways a church can transition to gift-based ministry rather than pastoral-based ministry. Some churches incorporate spiritual gift tests into their membership seminars. Once they discover new members' unique gifts, they try to get them plugged into ministries commensurate with those gifts. Other churches cultivate a non-threatening atmosphere in their congregations in which members are encouraged to try their hand at several ministries until they find one they feel comfortable with and successful in.

For pastors reading this book, let me encourage you to really think about this concept and take it before the Lord in prayer. It is the responsibility of a pastor to make sure the members of his congregation know their spiritual gifts. As God gives a vision to pastors for their churches, they need to break down all of the church's goals and ministries into sub categories and place them under one of the five-fold purposes.

Every church ought to have both a short-term (1-5 years) and long-term (5+ years) strategic plan in place. This strategic plan is what declares the distinctiveness of the church. It lists the vision, goals, and strategies that God has for that church in that particular community. Goals need to be set in place and particular ministries (both current and future ministries) need to be defined and agreed upon. Then the leadership of the church needs to figure out ways to match as closely as possible the ministries of the church with the spiritual gifts of the people.

There is an untapped diamond mine of talent and passion in the pews of every local church. It is the job of the pastor to find these folks and to refine them with teaching, ministry opportunities, encouragement, and affirmation. Once found and refined, these Christians will do amazing things for the kingdom of God. It's a win-win opportunity. The overworked pastor actually gets help in doing the work of the ministry. The average church member finds out he is needed, appreciated, and valuable in God's kingdom.

THE BENEFITS OF A GIFT-BASED MINISTRY PARADIGM

If churches will adopt a gift-based ministry paradigm, they'll notice several benefits. Church leaders especially need to take this to heart. These benefits include:

1. *Greater Effectiveness in Your Church's Ministry Programs* – every ministry in the church will be stronger, more effective, and will achieve greater results when staffed by Christians who have gifts that match their ministry involvements. Move the "volunteers" out of the way and make room for Spirit-anointed folks who are called to that ministry.
2. *Decrease the Burn-Out/Drop-Out Rate of Your Members* – People grow weary when they serve in areas where they are not happy or effective. Consequently, you can't pull people away when they serve in areas where they see God blessing, lives being changed, and ministry fruit occurring!
3. *Increase the Confidence and Self Worth of Your Members* – When Christians discover their unique gifts, it leads to

feelings of joy, thankfulness, and confidence. It tends to lead to well-adjusted Christians who have balanced egos, who know what they are and what they're not.

4. *Increase the Retention Rate of Your Church* – People drop out of church for lots of reasons, including not feeling needed or appreciated by anyone. When Christians are courted for ministry positions and the church genuinely recognizes the valuable contributions they are making, people feel part of a team and want to stay in such an environment.

FORMAT FOR CHAPTERS 6–9

I want to encourage you to be in a spirit of prayer as you begin to read over the nature and characteristics of these different spiritual gifts. If you are a Christian, God has given one or more of these gifts to you. Discovering and using your gifts will unleash a fresh passion for ministry within you. We will look at the gifts in relation to the three groupings we discovered earlier. Immediately following each gift will be the original Greek word used in the New Testament to describe this gift. This is to give you an idea of what is the literal essence of each gift. A definition will then follow as well as some additional discussion and insight on what makes each gift unique.

Also with each gift I have placed an example of some Christian who greatly demonstrates this gift. Some of the examples will come from the Scriptures, some from contemporary Christians, and some will be historical examples. I think it helps to have a flesh-and-blood example to solidify the teaching. Some of the gifts will receive a lengthier treatment as compared to others simply because some gifts have other peripheral issues that I would like to discuss or because there are some gifts that I feel the body of Christ is particularly uninformed about. One of these is the gift of apostleship, as we will now explore.

THE GIFTS OF THE
HOLY SPIRIT

CHAPTER 6

The Foundational Gifts

APOSTLESHIP

The unique, God-given ability to exercise strategic leadership and spiritual authority over large segments of the body of Christ for the purpose of greatly increasing the church's impact in its work for the kingdom of God. Ephesians 4:11, 2 Corinthians 12:12

The New Testament has more than eighty occurrences of the Greek word *apostolos* from which we get our English word "apostle." It is a derivative of the common Greek word *apostello* which means, "to send." In secular Greek writings after the fifth century B.C. it is usually translated "fleet," as in a fleet of ships. It is sometimes even translated "admiral," as one in command of a fleet of ships.[1]

Some scholars believe the word is similar to the Hebrew word *saliah*, which can mean "sent man." This word has with it the idea of an envoy who is dispatched by a religious authority or ruler to represent them and act on their behalf.[2] The word is used with some variety throughout the New Testament, so biblical scholars are not in agreement as to its precise definition. However, most will agree with the general meaning of "one who is sent."

There is today a renewed interest and debate as to whether God is restoring this gift to the church. While the gift of tongues may have been the most controversial gift in the past, many consider this gift to be the new dividing line in the church. There is a growing movement in the church to expect and accept that God is restoring the gift of apostleship today. This makes many other Christians feel very uncomfortable.

Many in the charismatic branch of the church are now embracing the belief that God is restoring the apostolic office. This has only begun to be popularized and somewhat accepted within the last ten years. I began to notice a significant change of mood in the mid-1990s regarding this gift. As I read through the pages of Christian magazines such as *Charisma*, I would come across advertisements for upcoming conferences in which the main speakers would be "Pastor so and so" and special guest "Apostle so and so." I would sometimes visit churches where the special speaker that evening was "Apostle Adi Gallia" or something such as that.

I am certainly not against the idea that God could restore the apostolic gift today, but I do think that we need to be careful about using that term too loosely. What I have found is that we are currently making the mistake of calling certain people apostles who simply have ministries that may be *apostolic* in nature. I mean to take nothing away from some of these men of God who are doing wonderful things for the kingdom. We should recognize them for who they are; they are godly pastors, evangelists, or other Christian leaders who have apostolic ministries, but they are not themselves apostles.

Upon closer inspection, the individuals I am aware of who are now being called apostles do not meet the criteria to be what the Bible would call an apostle. I personally believe that we must not water down what is the biblical definition of an apostle. To avoid confusion and for the sake of respect for that great office we should only call those apostles who are apostles indeed.

There is much confusion in Christian circles today as to who apostles are and what it is they do. Many mistakenly believe that apostles are simply missionaries. It is true that some apostolic ministry is similar to that of a missionary, but the biblical function and role of the apostles involved much more than simply planting churches in foreign fields.

Others believe that apostles are just those who have translocal influence over a group of churches. This is certainly an apostolic characteristic, but again it takes much more than that to be an actual apostle. The early church would have called those individuals bishops, as in the Bishop of Rome or the Bishop of Ephesus. For the purposes of our brief study we will examine what the Bible states concerning the function, requirements, and signs of apostleship. After examining that, I want to address the false arguments that are now being given as to why the gift of apostleship could not be for today.

The Basic Functions of an Apostle

The roles of an apostle in the New Testament can be classified under four broad headings. The apostles were: special ambassadors of Jesus, the foundational leaders of the church, they were the conduits of divine revelation, and they established the basic preaching message of the early church.

First and foremost, the apostles were special ambassadors or representatives of Jesus. He gave them unique authority and power to act as His special witnesses. Their arrival and the signs and wonders they performed signified the coming of the kingdom of God. These men were sent to announce to Israel that the long-awaited Messiah had finally arrived. To validate their message they were given the authority to cast out demons, heal the sick, raise the dead, and perform all manner of supernatural deeds.

A second function of the apostles was that they were the foundational leaders of the early church. When Paul evangelized the cities that he traveled through, one of the things he would do was appoint elders in every church (Acts 14:23). The apostles did not directly oversee the churches they founded, but they did install the new church's first generation of leaders.

In the apostle Paul's case he would act as a senior overseer who would answer theological questions, render judgments, and pass on instructions via his personal letters to the churches. The day-to-day operations of the church were taken care of by local elders. We see an excellent example of apostolic leadership in Acts 15 with the whole Judaizing controversy. Certain Jews were requiring and teaching that new converts still had to be circumcised and follow the Law of Moses to be saved. Acts 15:2 states that it was the "apostles and elders" who decided this question and passed on their ruling to all the other churches.

This authority over doctrinal issues and church government was not the only area in which the apostles exercised their leadership. They also had the leadership authority to correct individual Christians and churches as well. Paul actually commands that one member of the Corinthian church is to be "handed over to Satan for the destruction of the flesh" (1 Corinthians 5:5). Acts 11:13 recounts the story of Paul pronouncing blindness upon Elymas the sorcerer. The apostle Peter pronounces divine judgment upon two church members, Anaias and Sapphira, for lying about a financial contribution that they had given to the church (Acts 5:1-11). Instances such as this illustrate the awesome power and authority that an apostle had entrusted to him.

A third function that we see in the apostles was revelatory in nature. God gave the apostles divine insight into the mysteries of the faith. The apostle Paul had special insight into the mystery of the church (Ephesians 3:1-6) and the election of Israel (Romans 11:25-32). He even received revelation that he was not permitted to share with the rest of the church (2 Corinthians 12:1-4).

This revelation of the "deeper truths" was not all the apostles received and communicated. They taught the early church the practical, foundational doctrines that formed the core of our Christian doctrine today. Acts 2:42 records that the early church continued daily in "the apostles' doctrine." Ephesians 4:14 states that God gave the apostles such revelation and had them pass it along in their teaching ministry so that His church would not be carried away with every new wind of doctrine. The apostles laid a sure foundation of teaching that has served the church well and kept us on course for the last 2,000 years.

A fourth function the apostles were known for in the early church was that they were the carriers of the salvation message throughout the known world. It was their function to personally testify about the resurrected Jesus as ones divinely sent. This involved their missionary/church-planting role. Paul was assigned to the Gentile peoples while Peter was divinely instructed to minister among the Jews. Other apostles were sent to various other geographical areas to spread the gospel and establish churches.

The basic message of the apostles wherever they went included that the Old Testament Scriptures are fulfilled in Christ, the crucifixion and resurrection of Jesus is a historical fact, and that all men must repent and turn to Christ in faith for salvation. In essence the apostles gave us the basic gospel message that continues to be proclaimed today.

The Requirements for Apostleship

The actual requirements for apostleship were rather simple. All apostles had to have received their commission from the Lord Jesus personally and all apostles had to have seen the resurrected

Christ. For members of the original Twelve there was one additional requirement; they had to have been with Jesus throughout his earthly ministry specifically since the baptism of John the Baptist (Acts 1:21-26).

Jesus called the biblical apostles personally with a simple "follow me." Paul, of course, had a personal call in Acts 9:2-7 where Jesus appeared to him and commissioned him for apostolic ministry. We see in 1 Corinthians 15:7 that James, the Lord's brother, was also given a personal invitation as an apostle. Secondly, all the apostles experienced a sighting of the risen Christ. The original Twelve saw the risen Lord in Matthew 28:16-17. The apostle James (the Lord's brother) is said to have been visited by the risen Lord in 1 Corinthians 15:7. Paul, of course, saw the risen Lord on the road to Damascus.

Paul seems to consider this as a true requirement for one's claim to apostleship. He states in 1 Corinthians 9:1, "Am I not free? Am I not an apostle? Have I not *seen* Jesus our Lord?" It is this seeing the resurrected Lord that makes the apostolic preaching set apart from any other. The apostles have seen the resurrected Lord. There is an authority and certainty their preaching contains that cannot be duplicated by any other.

There were other apostles besides the Twelve, however. This in itself is a type of proof that would indicate that God desired to give the church other apostles besides the Twelve. The Twelve are a unique group as compared to others in the New Testament who are later called apostles. The original twelve apostles' names are engraved in the twelve foundations of the walls in heaven (Revelation 21:14).

Jesus says in Matthew 19:28 that the Twelve will sit on twelve thrones in heaven judging the twelve tribes of Israel. They are a special group. Paul himself in 1 Corinthians 15:5 calls this group "the Twelve," realizing that even he is not a member of that sacred circle. The Twelve were unique. They alone were personally mentored and groomed for ministry by Jesus Himself. Because of this, later biblical apostles still could not claim the experiences and intimacy with Jesus that the Twelve had. Their brand of apostleship cannot be repeated.

However, the Scriptures are clear that God personally appeared to and commissioned others to be apostles besides the original twelve. The twelfth member of the original twelve was Matthias who replaced Judas Iscariot the traitor (Acts 1:26). Paul is clearly called an apostle in Acts 14:14. Paul affirms Barnabas as an apostle in 1 Corinthians 9:5-6. He infers the same in a comparison of 1 Thessalonians 1:1 with 1 Thessalonians 2:6 that Timothy and Silas were apostles. The other apostles all recognized James, the Lord's brother, as a genuine apostle as well (Galatians 1:19).

In 2 Corinthians 11:13 Paul has to warn the church of "false apostles," which would have been pointless if such an office were confined to the Twelve only. In summary, the Bible never teaches that after the original twelve pass away there could never be other apostles. On the contrary, the Bible calls some seventeen individuals "apostles."

The Signs of an Apostle

The biblical data show four confirming signs that helped the early church to determine true apostles. These four signs were: a shepherd's heart for the people of God, proven apostolic ministry fruit, signs and wonders, and a life marked by suffering and opposition.

I am omitting for obvious reasons the number one characteristic that should mark all ministers of the gospel. That of course is a godly lifestyle of morality and integrity. Anyone claiming to be an apostle today will be someone whose life is in order morally and financially. Concerning anyone who would work in ministry, our

Lord told us that we would know them by their fruit (Matthew 12:33).

Just like their master, Jesus, the apostles all had a sacrificial shepherd-type love for the people of God. Paul prayed "night and day" for the Thessalonian church desiring to see them and wanting to perfect their faith. In 2 Corinthians 12:14 he refers to the church as his "children" and himself as their "parent." The apostle John in his epistles also refers to those under his care as his "children." The apostles did not lord their authority over the church as power-hungry tyrants. They displayed a Christlike love and sacrifice toward all those they ministered to.

Secondly, those who claimed to be apostles could point to the fruit of their ministries as a type of proof to their claim. Paul states in 1 Corinthians 9:2 that the Corinthian church and the great work that he started there is his "seal of apostleship." The apostolic anointing on the preaching and teaching ministry of the apostles was hard to compete with. As a result of just two of Peter's sermons the church increased by 8,000 people!

Entire cities were transformed by the power and ministry of the apostles. When they entered a city, things did not stay the same for long. The Jews of Thessalonica had this to say when they heard that some of the apostles had arrived in their city, "These that have turned the world upside down are come hither also" (Acts 17:6, kjv). Under this select group the church spread like wildfire all over Judea, Asia Minor, and the uttermost parts of the earth. Apparently if one called himself an apostle there would be plenty of ministry fruit to back up that claim.

A third sign of a true apostle were the signs and wonders that followed their ministry. Paul explicitly states this as a sign of apostleship in 2 Corinthians 12:12 when he stated, "The signs of a true apostle were performed among you with all perseverance, by signs and wonders and miracles." A modern equivalent today would *not* be the ability to have mass numbers of people "slain in the Spirit" at your meetings. True apostolic signs and wonders are a little more difficult to counterfeit.

The shadow of Peter walking by someone could bring healing (Acts 5:15). Handkerchiefs and other articles of clothing taken from the apostle Paul could drive out evil spirits from people (Acts 19:11-12). Apostles were used by God to raise the dead even as Jesus did (Acts 9:36-40). And as we mentioned earlier, apostles could pronounce acts of judgment upon people, both Christian and non-Christian.

A fourth and final sign that the Bible seems to indicate was that hardship and opposition were very much a part of the apostles' lot in life. Because of their very high level office within the church, Satan and his demonic forces were constantly harassing these men and trying to stop their work in expanding the kingdom of God. Paul stated in 1 Thessalonians 2:18 that Satan would sometimes succeed in preventing him from carrying out his mission in regard to the churches.

Paul also briefly confides to the church in 2 Corinthians 12:7 that God has allowed a demonic presence to continually harass him as a strategy to keep him humble and dependent upon God because of the great revelations he had received. We see throughout the Bible that the apostles were often beaten, imprisoned, slandered, and generally opposed by the secular and religious establishments of the day.

Perhaps in the modern era the persecution would not be as severe in countries that allow the free exercise of religion, but I still believe that modern apostles would be a lightning rod for criticism and ostracism. The world system does not accept the message and authority of God, and it does not accept His representatives. Jesus warned us to not be surprised about our reception with this present evil world system. He told us in John 15:18, "If the world hates you, you know that it has hated Me before it hated you."

False Arguments Against Apostleship for Today

We now need to briefly look at three common arguments that are offered when attempting to prove that the gift of apostleship cannot be given today.

#1. Apostles wrote Scripture. If we entertain the idea that apostles were given today, we would have to open up the canon and allow for new revelation and new books of the Bible to be written by latter day apostles.

Nowhere in the Bible is Scripture writing considered to be a requirement for apostleship at all. Only five out of the seventeen apostles mentioned in Scripture wrote any books of our Bible. When one considers that the books of Mark, Luke, Acts, Hebrews, and Jude were written by non-apostles, this idea is only reinforced. Those five books (based on word count) make up 51 percent of our New Testament![3]

Therefore, any modern apostle today should not be expected to write Scripture or add to it in anyway. I am in perfect agreement with the Word of God and with conservative Christianity in that our canon of sacred Scripture is closed and represents the full and final revelation of God. It alone is sufficient for the church. Any modern apostle who would attempt to introduce some new revelation that contradicted the Scriptures should immediately be declared a false apostle by the church.

#2. Ephesians 2:20 states that the apostles were part of the "foundation" of the church. Since the word foundation implies a one-time base that is to be built upon, the office must logically be historically limited to the first-century apostles.

Upon closer scrutiny this apparent problem withers. Verse 20 also includes Christ as being foundational, and in verse 22 the "you" refers to the early church believers as being part of that foundation and building. Clearly this language is metaphorical and applies to every generation. Every generation experiences Christ (not just first century Christians); every generation has believers (not just first century Christians); and every generation can (theoretically) have apostles and prophets.

#3. Since Jesus physically left the earth over 2,000 years ago, no person today can meet the biblical requirements of apostleship, i.e. to be with Jesus since the baptism of John, to be personally called by Jesus, and to have actually seen the resurrected Lord.

As we looked at already, only the original Twelve had to have been with Jesus since John's baptism. The other two criteria could be met today through a personal visitation by our Lord. As a charismatic Christian I have no problem with the idea of God doing such a thing. There is certainly no biblical reason to suggest that such an encounter would be impossible. However, merely viewing a Christophany (experiencing a manifestation of Jesus) would not make one an apostle. There would have to be a specific call to apostleship, and the signs of an apostle would need to be there also to verify that individual as an apostle.

Are Apostles Given Today?

After weighing the biblical evidence I have come to the conclusion that the Bible does not rule out the possibility that apostles could be given to subsequent generations of believers. I can think of a few in church history that I feel comfortable applying the label to. I think a strong argument can be made for St. Patrick of Ireland (c.389-c.461).

St. Patrick was used mightily by God to turn Ireland from a land of Druid worshipers into a Christian nation within thirty years. Under his ministry thousands were saved and hundreds of churches were established. Like the apostle Paul, he discipled, and then appointed as overseers, priests and bishops all over the nation. He had a spiritual authority that was recognized by the whole nation.

The reports of his miraculous deeds are too numerous to list, but suffice it to say that over thirty raisings from the dead were attributed to him as well.[4] Beginning in the late eighteenth and early nineteenth century God did begin to release in a fresh new way an outpouring of His Spirit which is unprecedented in church history. In the last few centuries the church has again recognized the office of evangelist and the office of prophet. Why should it surprise us if in these last days the Lord gives the church apostles again as well?

If God chooses to activate this office again in our century, we have in place the biblical information necessary to recognize these men. They would be men who have translocal influence over a certain locale. They would be men of holiness and integrity who have demonstrated over time that their ministry bears much fruit for the kingdom. We can expect that they would have significantly strengthened local churches and greatly expanded the church in certain geographic territories.

They would correct, and at times discipline the church as God gives them the discernment and ability. Signs and wonders would be a regular part of their ministry as a further confirmation of their apostolic calling. But most of all these men would have a sacrificial love for our Savior and a love for His people, the church. They would not be power-hungry, ego-driven ministers who lorded their authority over the churches that submitted to them.

They would accept peer accountability from other apostles. They would lead by example and be men of humility. They would weep often, pray for long hours, and serve as fathers in the faith for those who would follow them. They would endure persecution as good soldiers of Jesus Christ, and they would be willing to die for the gospel of their Lord if necessary. Will God give us apostles today? I don't know. But let all who aspire to such an office know its roots and never tarnish that sacred record.

Prophet

The unique, God-given ability to receive special revelations from God and to then serve as a messenger, delivering those communications to those whom God directs. Ephesians 4:11, Acts 21:9-12

Since the beginning of time God has chosen in each generation a select group of people to serve as His special messengers. These men and women are known as prophets. The Greek word used to describe these messengers is *prophetes* and it means, "one who proclaims." The related verb would be *prophemi*, which means, "to speak forth." Therefore, prophets speak forth the word of the Lord on behalf of God.

In the New Testament era their importance to the foundation of the church is second only to apostles (1 Corinthians 12:28). All prophets are gifted with the gift of prophecy, but not all who have the gift of prophecy are also called to the office of prophet. For this reason, I believe it's accurate for us to distinguish between the two and to treat them as two separate spiritual gifts given to the church.

Both Peter and Paul taught that prophecy was liberally given throughout the body of Christ as a sign of God's anointing upon the church in the last days. That's why we have verses such as Acts 2:16-18 and 1 Corinthians 14:1 speaking of the whole body's ability to prophesy. The democratization of prophecy therefore occurs in the end times enabling all of God's people to experience this phenomenon from time to time.

However, Paul does teach in several of his epistles that some have an extra anointing of prophecy in the form of a distinct spiritual gift. These are those who have prophetic abilities to a much greater degree than the average Christian. And Scripture also shows that some have such a degree of the gift, along with a God-recognized authority by the rest of the church, that they are referred to with the noun, "prophet."

Agabus in the book of Acts is such a person. The entire church recognized the mantle of authority he held, and when he spoke the church listened and obeyed. We'll look at the general gift of prophecy in chapter nine. For now we will focus on the gift and office of the prophet.

Since the primary role of a prophet (or prophetess) is to serve as a special messenger of God, the question that naturally comes up is, "What kind of messages do prophets give?" Are they messages about God's will? Are they predictive messages about the future?

There is much debate in theological circles as to whether the Bible presents prophets as primarily forth tellers (declarers of God's truth) or foretellers (declarers of the future). I've always refused to take sides in this debate. The very question is akin to asking whether a husband's role in regards to his wife is primarily that of protector and spiritual head *or* that of lover and best friend. To choose one over the other is silly. Obviously Scripture commands him to be both! And so it is with prophets. The Bible portrays Old and New Testament prophets as both forth tellers and foretellers.

In their forth telling role, God used the Old Testament prophets to call Israel back to her covenantal standards when she strayed. In those days the prophet's messages revolved around common themes of holiness, justice, and repentance from the ways of the world (see Micah 6:8 or Isaiah 1:16 for example). New Testament prophets also called people back to a relationship with God and warned of backsliding as did their Old Testament counterparts. Revelation 1:9-3:22 is an example of this.

The prophets of today have this same message for God's people. Therefore a foundational characteristic of a true prophet is a zealousness for God's laws and God's will that goes beyond that of the average Christian. The heart of God for holiness, justice, and mercy is burned into the heart of the prophet by the Holy Spirit. Sin grieves them. Society's lack of respect for God's standards deeply disturbs the heart of a prophet.

The second characteristic of prophets is that they receive supernatural revelation from God quite regularly. Amos 3:7 states, "Surely the Lord God does nothing unless He reveals His secret counsel to His servants the prophets." This revelation comes in many ways. The most common way is through deep inner impressions. God also speaks to prophets commonly in dreams and visions (Numbers 12:6), audible voices (1 Samuel 3:1-9), and through common observations of everyday life (Jeremiah 18:1-6). God uses prophets to give messages to individuals, churches, and even nations. They are used to encourage, confirm, correct, and even rebuke depending on the will of the Lord at the moment.

A third characteristic of a prophet or prophetess is a divinely-given authority that is recognized by the church. The Lord grants upon his prophets this mantle so that the church will respect the message and the messenger. Of course this respect must be earned as well, but by the very nature of the gifting, it is one that causes one to be somewhat in awe of the power of God being displayed.

I'll never forget the first time I came into contact with a prophet who was ministering in our church as a guest. He had a word from the Lord for many people that night, and Pauline and I were called out as well. He fixed his eyes on us and immediately began making declarations and observations over us that literally stunned me.

Among the things he declared that the Lord had not forgotten was a private prayer I had been praying for some time (now suddenly made public!), a covenant Pauline had made with the Lord regarding something in her personal life, and he accurately prophesied a year in advance that a new ministry opportunity would open for us requiring a move out of our current church and city.

The prophet reminded me that I have a tendency to struggle with pride and therefore encouraged me to continue to be submissive and learn from the mentors God had placed over me. He shared a few other things, and by the end of it I was on the verge of bawling like a baby. How I held it in I'll never know. At that moment all doubt died forever. Of all the billions and billions of people on the planet, the Lord God actually knew me personally.

He knew and heard the private prayers I offered up to Him in my walks at night. He was already strategically planning ministry moves for us years in advance. And the Lord had just revealed some of these things to another mortal man a few feet away from me via a special gift that Bible calls "prophecy."

That was the first time I really understood what the apostle Paul meant in 1 Corinthians 14:25 when he spoke of prophetic ministry as revealing "the secrets of the heart." Paul stated that when this gift operates, it causes unbelievers to declare, "God is truly among you!" It is my heart's desire that all children of God would receive a prophetic message at least once in their lifetime. It is a blessing and encouragement beyond words.

Yes indeed, prophets are a great blessing, but because this gift is so powerful, its misuse can be especially damaging to the church. Because of this fact the apostle Paul gives some special regulations concerning it in 1 Corinthians 14 most important of which is that all prophecy must be "judged" to make sure it is in line with God's established Word. This directive is for protection against false prophets sent in by the enemy to confuse the church. Paul also reminds the church in 1 Thessalonians 5:19-22 to not disallow prophecy, but to carefully weigh it so that the church is protected against manipulation caused by prideful or immature prophets.

Before moving on, let's consider one of the greatest prophets in the Bible, the prophet Isaiah. Isaiah ministered in the eighth century B.C. during the reign of four Judean kings. His wife was also a prophetess and ministered alongside her husband. God called Isaiah during a time in which Israel's heart had grown cold toward God.

Isaiah spent over fifty years preaching a basic message of trust in God, repentance from sin, and of warning the nation that her strength comes from God not from forming pagan alliances with other nations. Besides a constant cry for a return to holiness, Isaiah was also used by God to deliver amazing prophetic revelations to the nation regarding the consequences of her corporate sin.

Isaiah accurately foretold 150 years in advance that the nation would ultimately be destroyed by Babylon (which at the time was not even a world power) and later released under a ruler whose heart God would stir. Isaiah even named the ruler as "Cyrus" which history records was exactly who later did release the Jews from captivity. Isaiah accurately prophesied the judgment of various nations of his day including Assyria, Philistia, Ethiopia, Egypt, and Tyre.

And most importantly, Isaiah gave some of the most specific prophecies concerning Christ some 700 years before His birth! He prophesied his virgin birth (Isaiah 7:14), his ministry (Isaiah 61:1-2), and his crucifixion (Isaiah 53:5). Prophets today, like Isaiah, have a burning desire to call God's people back to their first love. Like Isaiah, they are voices of conscience, which whisper in our ears, "This is the way, walk in it."

EVANGELISM

The unique, God-given ability to cause others to be aware of their need for Christ and to then present the gospel in such a way that others believe it and accept it. Ephesians 4:11, 2 Timothy 4:5

While all Christians are expected to share their faith, God has given some a special anointing to do so. These Christians are much more successful in bringing souls into the kingdom than are the rest of us. The apostle Paul explains in 1 Corinthians 3:6-8 that some plant the Word, some water, and some get to bring in the harvest. These harvesters are the evangelists.

Only one individual in Scripture, Philip, is called an evangelist (Acts 21:8). Philip was one of the seven deacons of the Jerusalem church. We see him ministering out of his gifting throughout the Scripture. Acts 8:5 records, "And Philip went down to the city of Samaria and began proclaiming Christ to them." We know he truly possessed an evangelistic gift because many people were being added to the kingdom because of his preaching. Verse 12 of Acts 8 continues, "But when they believed Philip preaching the good news about the kingdom of God and the name of Jesus Christ, they were being baptized, men and women alike."

It was Philip who led a high governmental official of Ethiopia to Christ in Acts 8:25-39. Scripture goes on to record that he preached Christ powerfully and convincingly throughout all the cities of Judea, Samaria, and Caesarea.

The life of Philip illustrates perfectly the three primary characteristics of those with the gift of evangelism. That is, those with this gift possess a strong desire to proclaim the gospel, a boldness in doing so, and an extraordinary effectiveness when they do so.

The word "evangelists" (euangelistes) is derived from the Greek word, euangelizo, which means, "to proclaim, to bring a good report." The word for "gospel" is euangelion, which means, "good news." Therefore an evangelist is one who proclaims or announces the good news of salvation that is found in Jesus Christ. This is the primary characteristic of an evangelist. They have a burning desire to share the gospel with everyone they meet. They are very concerned about the eternal souls of people.

Commensurate with this gift is a special boldness that God gives as well. Evangelists are usually not timid, shy people. They have no problem talking to strangers and often are the first to speak when meeting someone new. They don't seem to possess the hesitancy that other Christians have when talking to others about

Christ. Evangelists are like Philip in Acts 8 when he witnessed to the Ethiopian official. Philip boldly went up to this total stranger and began to dialog with him. Verse 35 records, "Philip opened his mouth…and preached Jesus to him." This is a classic picture of an evangelist. They approach you, attempt to establish some rapport with you, but sooner or later the conversation is going to end up being about Jesus!

A third characteristic of those gifted in evangelism is that they regularly lead people to salvation in Christ. Those gifted in evangelism are a great blessing to the church. They help build the church by continually bringing in new souls to the kingdom. Those gifted in evangelism also have an ability to adapt to the different types of people God brings across their path.

They seem to know how to be all things to all people, and in doing so are very skilled in appealing to a wide variety of people. Evangelists instinctively know how to witness to shy people, boisterous people, open people, and closed people. They skillfully know when to use Scripture, or when to make an appeal from experience while speaking to someone about the Christian faith. However, one thing is common to them all. They all preach Jesus unapologetically as the answer to all of mankind's problems. Evangelists are not ashamed of their Lord or His gospel, and with a passion they live to tell others about Him. This passion to tell others about Jesus can be seen in the life of one particular man.

Dwight was just a teenager when he first began to show an aptitude for business. He left home at the age of seventeen to become a successful and wealthy businessman. He had a personal goal to accumulate a fortune of $100,000 during his lifetime.[5] This was quite a considerable sum considering it was 1854. He was well on his way to achieving his dream; he was saving money, working hard, and earning high commissions as an aggressive shoe salesman in the bustling city of Boston.

He had a natural knack for business and for making money. After working awhile for his uncle in Boston, he later moved to Chicago where business prospects seemed even better. He once wrote home boasting that he now made more in one week in Chicago than he used to make in one month back in Boston. He even bragged that he had money to spare and was putting it to good use, loaning it out for 17 percent interest.[6]

Young Dwight was well on his way to becoming what so many Americans aspire to today. He wanted to make money, and lots of it. If something hadn't changed, his life would have consisted of accumulating wealth, acquiring numerous material possessions, and then dying with the world no better because of his brief existence. However, that's not the way this story ended.

Dwight promised his uncle that when he arrived in Boston he would attend church. This was one promise that would be easy to keep. He probably thought it would help his sales and increase his contacts if he attended. Good churchgoers needed shoes also, didn't they? Dwight soon settled on the Mount Vernon Congregational Church. While there, his Sunday school teacher, Edward Kimball, took an interest in him. Kimball was concerned about Dwight's spiritual condition and dropped by to see him at the shoe store one day. There he began to talk to Dwight about Christ. The young man listened intently as the message of God's love pierced his heart. Upon hearing the gospel young Dwight made Christ his Savior right there during business hours at the shoe store.

It was not long after his conversion that Dwight joined Plymouth Church and continued to grow in the Lord. Soon thereafter Dwight began to notice that his desire for wealth and affluence began to wane. In its place was a new desire to see others experience the love of Christ as he had.

Not knowing anything about spiritual gifts, he simply began to act on the inner impulses and desires within his heart. He began inviting friends and co-workers to church. His passion for souls continued to increase and he soon began to go out on the streets looking for anyone, vagabonds, street children, even perfect strangers so he could witness to them about the love of Christ. He was soon filling up four entire pews each Sunday with people he had invited to church![7]

It was soon after this that another divine contact came into his life. Another Sunday school teacher from the church came by to visit Dwight and was very down in spirit. He related to Dwight how he had been unable to lead any of the girls in his Sunday school class to Christ. Dwight suggested that they make a visit to each of the girls personally. At the first house the teacher tried once again to lead one of the young girls to Christ. This time upon hearing him the young girl began to tear up. Dwight then prayed right there, out loud, that she would give her heart to Christ and she did! They went to the next house, and the next, and the next, until within the span of ten days the entire class had given their lives to Christ! Later this eventually famous evangelist said of that episode that, "God has kindled a fire in my soul that has never gone out."

You may have figured out the identity of this evangelist by now. It was the great Dwight L. Moody (1837-1899). D. L. Moody discovered early on in his Christian life that he had a "gift" for evangelism. And because he yielded to that call on his life, God used him mightily. D. L. Moody eventually became the greatest evangelist of the nineteenth century. He held mass evangelistic crusades throughout all the major cities of America and England. He preached to well over 100 million people during his lifetime. Out of those, hundreds of thousands (possibly millions) came to Christ.

The evangelistic fire within him never stopped burning while he lived. In addition to the church and three Bible schools he started, he was also responsible for helping to organize the Student Volunteer Movement. This was a missions movement that mobilized tens of thousands of college students for overseas missions.

By looking in the natural, Moody should never have been able to do such things. After all, this was an unordained "layman" who never went to a Bible school or seminary. He was the sixth of nine children, the son of a bricklayer. And, oh yes, Moody never made it past the sixth grade.

What D. L. Moody did have was the spiritual gift of evangelism, and spiritual gifts aren't dependent upon background, educational level, or status as the world sees it. Ah how true it is, "For consider your calling brethren, that there were not many wise according to the flesh, not many mighty, not many noble; but God has chosen the foolish things of the world to shame the wise, and God has chosen the weak things of the world to shame the things which are strong" (1 Corinthians 1: 26-27).

PASTORING

The unique, God-given ability to nurture, protect, and to help bring to maturity, a group of Christians. Ephesians 4:11, 1 Timothy 3:1

The Greek word used in Ephesians 4:11 is *poimen* which means "shepherd." Many refer to this gift as the gift of shepherding and perhaps it is better to call it that because to say "pastor" or "pastoring" usually has a connotation in our culture of a seminary-trained, professional minister. The fact of the matter is that there are lots of individuals pastoring churches today who do not have this gift. They are, however, performing the role and function of a pastor.

Consequently, there are millions of church members sitting in congregations who never plan to attend seminary and yet they do indeed possess the spiritual gift of pastoring or shepherding. We have wrongly tied this gift to those who are in full-time ministry while not realizing that this gift can be exercised very effectively by Christians who are not called to full-time vocational service.

Denominations that forbid women from serving as pastors need to understand that God gives this gift to both men and women and that serving as a senior pastor over a congregation is just one of the many ways this gift can be used. Those churches that forbid women from the office of pastor need to provide other ministry outlets for their women who possess the gift. To do otherwise would be to waste precious talent that God has blessed a congregation with.

God has given this gift to the body of Christ to ensure that His children are cared for and brought up to spiritual maturity. Like a mother who instinctively and unselfishly loves her children, so do those with this gift instinctively and unselfishly love the people of God.

Those with shepherding gifts usually are well-developed people emotionally. They can give and receive love easily. Since their gift is primarily relational they tend not to be task oriented, but rather people oriented. The gift manifests itself primarily in three areas: nurturing, protecting, and instructing. I believe the apostle Paul had a very strong pastoring gift that can easily be seen throughout the pages of the New Testament. Let's take a look at how the apostle demonstrated these traits in his ministry.

To the churches he planted, Paul was known as a wise and caring leader. We can get a glimpse of his pastoral love for other Christians in 1 Thessalonians 2:8 where he writes to the church, "We were well pleased to impart to you not only the gospel of God but our own lives, because you had become very dear to us." Paul's concern for the repentant sinner in 2 Corinthians 2:4-8 is also very moving.

In typical Pauline fashion he writes about the anguish of heart he has gone through at the news that one has strayed. But in his letter when he hears the backslidden son has returned to the faith his only concern is that the church reaffirms their love for the fallen one. Paul was worried the young man would be overwhelmed with too much sorrow if he didn't sense he was forgiven and accepted back into the church. His heart of compassion broke at the thought of one of his sheep not feeling loved by the others. Throughout the epistles we see the picture of a man who wept often, prayed "night and day" for those he oversaw, and who nurtured God's people with a sacrificial love.

Those with the pastoral gift are also very much concerned with protecting God's people from that which would endanger them spiritually. In the early days of the faith Paul was especially concerned about the many false teachings that were entering the church that, if embraced, would undermine the faith of these new converts.

Luke records in Acts 20:28-31 that Paul warned the Ephesian elders "night and day" about the dangers of spiritual deception. Those with the pastoral gift have a protective instinct in regard to other Christians. They want others to embrace the things that will help them grow, and they warn them about traps that the world and the enemy may be setting for them.

Lastly, those gifted in pastoring will be natural teachers or coaches. They genuinely want to see other Christians blessed and productive in their service to God. This was constantly on the heart and mind of the apostle Paul. He wrote to the Roman church that he was eager to visit them so that he could make a spiritual impartation into their lives (Romans 1:11). In his letters to the churches we see that he could not resist imparting practical or doctrinal truth to everyone he wrote to. He took every opportunity available to teach, enlighten, and encourage other Christians. While those with the teaching gift don't always have a pastoral gift, it is very common for those whose primary gift is pastoring to also have a secondary gift of teaching.

Perhaps the most effective way to utilize the gifts of these Christians is to place them as leaders of home cell groups where they can provide nurturing and coaching to a group of ten to fifteen Christians. Another idea would be to use these Christians as deacons and deaconesses who have a certain number of families they are responsible for. They could visit those families weekly or bi-weekly and pray for them and minister to them as need arises.

It really doesn't matter what strategy a church comes up with as long as they use these God-anointed men and women in their divinely-ordained role as shepherds who care for the rest of the flock.

TEACHING

The unique, God-given ability to discover God's truths and to communicate them in such a way that others can understand them and grow spiritually. Ephesians 4:11, Acts 18:24-26

The Greek word used in Ephesians 4:11 to describe a teacher is the word *didaskalos*, which simply means "teacher." Those with the teaching gift both love to teach and have an ability to impart biblical truth to others in such a way as to bless them. This gift is one of two gifts (the other being prophecy) that was considered so important it was included in all three of the main passages that speak about spiritual gifts (Romans 12, 1 Corinthians 12, and Ephesians 4).

The prophet Hosea once observed, "My people are destroyed for lack of knowledge" (Hosea 4:6). One of the saddest things today is looking over the church and seeing so many Christians who are ignorant about the Word of God's teachings on so many issues. Christians wonder why they cannot get ahead financially, and yet according to Malachi 3:9-11 those that do not tithe are under a self-imposed financial curse.

Some can't seem to figure out why there is turmoil in their home and the whole time they are not living according to the divine plan for the family (Ephesians 5:22-6:4). I've met Christians who have been saved for twenty or thirty years and yet still did not know what their spiritual gifts were. When I hear this I often think to myself, "What have your pastor and Sunday school teachers been teaching for the last thirty years?"

Some of the blame for biblical illiteracy must be pinned on ourselves. We all know as Christians that we should be regularly reading the Word of God. But to ensure that the church does understand the truths of God, the Lord has specifically called some Christians to a ministry of teaching. These individuals can present the Bible's teachings in such a way that they are easy to understand and assimilate into one's life.

There are four characteristics that are found in those who have the gift of teaching. First of all, they hold the Word of God in high regard. Teachers love the Bible and love to read the Bible. They get very disturbed when they hear others taking verses out of context or stretching verses in an attempt to make them say more than they are actually saying. They believe strongly that all teaching should be backed up with the Bible, not personal opinions or personal experiences.

Secondly, those with the teaching gift are often very systematic in their study of the Bible. They have developed a personal system whereby they can master the rich texts of God's Word. They love to organize the Bible's teachings into dominant themes, subjects, and categories. They are very thorough when studying the Word of God. They make full use of commentaries, word studies, and Bible dictionaries. The concordance is their best friend. If their house were on fire they would retrieve their Bible, their concordance, and if time permitted, their spouse!

Thirdly, they have a burden to see God's people fully informed about the whole counsel of God. Teachers can't stand to see Christians ignorant about their calling, their spiritual gifts, the Second Coming of Christ, or anything else for that matter. Teachers have a burning desire to impart truth to God's people so that they will grow to be mature saints who can fulfill their destiny in Christ.

Fourthly, those with the teaching gift are great communicators. It is important to not confuse someone who has a vast understanding of the Bible and spiritual things with a true teacher. One may have that and yet not have the ability to impart that information to the rest of the body. That is the difference. True, Spirit-gifted teachers have an ability to communicate and impart truth to other Christians. They can present truths and teachings to a group and instinctively know how to deliver it so that everyone is edified. They are skillful readers of body language and facial expressions and can tell when they need to reroute and deliver their teaching in a different way so it can be grasped.

Those with the teaching gift may have specific anointings with certain groups. Some are excellent with children while others are more successful in teaching adults. Some are great with small groups and others do equally well with groups of one hundred or more. As with all the gifts there are different anointings and ranges within the same gift. It is interesting that research has shown that most pastors also possess the teaching gift. This makes sense because when God calls individuals to the pastorate, He usually will give them the gift of teaching as well because they need that gift to instruct the flock under their care. 1 Timothy 3:2 states that those who would desire to be pastors/elders must be "able to teach."

A problem I've noticed in many churches is people trying to teach who don't have the gift of teaching. The result is that the people in their classes are bored, confused, and not able to fully integrate the teachings of the Bible into their lives. Sometimes due to a lack of gifted members in a certain ministry area, we have to step into roles that are outside of our giftings. However, a church really needs to try to remedy that problem as soon as possible and ensure that their primary teachers do possess the gift of teaching. Both the church and the people will greatly benefit when this is done.

The teaching gift can be used in a variety of ways. One could teach a Sunday school class, teach and disciple other Christians in a one-on-one setting, write curriculum, or perhaps preach. One caution must be mentioned about this gift. James 3:1 warns those with the gift of teaching about their greater accountability before God. Because those entrusted with this gift are speaking into the lives and helping to spiritually form others, they will be judged stricter than the average Christian.

God does not want His children harmed with false teachings. This is not in the Scripture to make us so timid that we will not step out in faith and begin practicing this gift. None of us will have perfect doctrine and totally understand everything in the Word of God. Some of the most godly men and women in the faith still disagree about minor points of doctrine and secondary issues. What the Bible is warning about here is an attitude of irreverence that takes lightly the teaching of God's Word.

All who are in a teaching ministry should learn the basic rules of hermeneutics and be careful to rightly divide the Word of Truth. They should also be open to correction from others if their teaching on some point is found to be in error.

A great example of the teaching gift today can be seen in Kay Arthur. Kay had always wanted to be a missionary, but after having served only three years in the field, she and her husband had to return to the States due to a heart condition she was diagnosed with.[8] Although it appeared to be the end of a dream in God's service, the Lord had other plans with Kay through another spiritual gift He had bestowed upon her.

Kay was an avid student of the Word and had developed a powerful Bible study method known as Precept Upon Precept. What started off as small home Bible studies soon grew larger as word got out about a gifted teacher who could literally make the Bible come alive. The teaching ministry grew and eventually became Precept Ministries. The ministry produced study courses on a wide range of biblical passages and topical issues and eventually grew to become a worldwide ministry impacting over 100 nations and strengthening the faith of millions of believers.

CHAPTER 7

The Ministry Gifts, Part I

FAITH

The unique, God-given ability to discern God's will for a particular matter and to fervently pray and work toward accomplishing that end while inspiring others to do the same. 1 Corinthians 12:9, Numbers 13:30

The Greek word used to describe this gift is *pistis*, which simply means "faith." The gift of faith is a special measure of faith that only some Christians have. The Lord in His goodness allows some people to have an easier time overcoming the hindrances of their mind, their current situation, or the naysayers. These men and women simply believe whatever God tells them about something will happen. And they go to work partnering with Him to make it happen.

That is the essence of this gift. Those who possess it are the ones who emphasize the promises of Scripture. They will often be the first to quote Scripture in relation to some current problem or obstacle. They claim the Word and the Holy Spirit activates certain promises to them, and they will stand on them until the thing they are praying for comes to pass.

A second characteristic of those with the gift of faith is that they are usually positive, can-do people. Prophets often emphasize the decay of culture, the judgment of God, and can sometimes tend to be negative. Rarely are negative people gifted in faith.

Christians gifted in faith help stretch the church to believe God for greater things and they can be a great source to encourage the body when times get tough. A wonderful modern-day example of the gift of faith in action can be seen in the life and ministry of Dr. Dion Robert.

A friend of mine formed a friendship with him and ended up writing his doctoral dissertation on Pastor Dion's amazing church in the Western African nation of Cote d'Ivoire. The church basically started out as a mission in the capital city of Abidjan in 1975. The first service had three people in attendance, Dion, his wife, and their daughter. In the early years of the work growth was slow. Pastor Dion used the Four Spiritual Laws, he evangelized, he started all the right programs; however, after one year he only had twenty-five converts. That's when he cried out to God to speak to him. He did.

God gave Dion a divine plan to evangelize his city, nation, and the whole of Africa. Pastor Dion calls it the "Program of God," and it's based on seven core values, one of which is spiritual gifts. Their goal is to place 100 percent of the church membership into ministries commensurate with their spiritual gifts.

Thirty years later after instituting the program of God, Pastor Dion's church, Eglise Protestante Baptist Ouvres et Mission, now numbers over 150,000 members and has over 14,000 cell groups. Over 700 churches have been planted in one-third of the nations of Africa and also in the U.S., United Kingdom, France, Canada, Denmark, and Sweden. Pastor Dion had this to say about the vision God gave him for the church:

We must know how to listen to God, how to receive from Him, and above all, know Him. Thus I started to learn to live by the Spirit and by faith. The result was not long to come. The Lord opened my spirit and my eyes. He communicated His wisdom, which sustains everything living. I started to organize the church according to the model that He showed me, little by little.[1]

He demonstrates one who has an especially high anointing of the gift mix of faith-administration. One who can believe God for great things and can devise the most efficient systems and plans, which leads to the dreams having a chance at actually succeeding.

Those with gifts of faith are able to help the body of Christ believe God for seemingly impossible things. And even in the small matters of everyday life, these saints remind us that who God calls He equips, and what God orders He pays for. They are a great blessing and example to us all, exhorting us to believe our Lord for great things.

EXHORTATION

The unique, God-given ability to encourage, strengthen, and admonish others for the purpose of helping them to reach their God-given potential. Romans 12:8, Acts 9:26-27

Some teachers refer to this gift as the gift of encouragement. One man in the New Testament especially illustrates this gift and that is the apostle Barnabas. Interestingly, his name even means "son of encouragement." Barnabas was famous for seeing potential in people and then helping them to reach their God-given destiny.

When no one would accept the apostle Paul as a genuine believer, it was Barnabas who made a passionate defense of Paul and persuaded the other apostles and elders in Jerusalem to take Paul in as a fellow brother in Christ. Barnabas used his gift in this instance toward both groups. For Paul, he used the gift *to encourage* this relatively new and untested servant of the Lord. Toward the other apostles and elders he used the gift *to admonish* the others to not pre-judge Paul.

We also see this gift demonstrated when John Mark once abandoned Paul and Barnabas on a missionary journey and later wanted to accompany them on a second journey. Scripture doesn't tell us the back-story, so we don't know why John Mark left midway in the first journey. Perhaps the young boy was just homesick, or perhaps he didn't at that time have the maturity to stick it out when things got difficult.

At any rate in Acts chapter 15 Barnabas sees potential in the boy and recommends that they give him a second chance. Paul disagrees and they have such a heated argument that they part ways. It is easy to see why Barnabas fought for John Mark. It was because of the gifting of God within him. Exhorters believe in people and they can't turn down someone who wants another chance at serving God. If exhorters believe you are genuine they will work with you to no end to see you mature in your walk with God.

The Greek word used in Scripture to describe this gift is the word *parakaleo*. This word is used over 100 times in Scripture and can have a wide variety of meaning depending on the context. The most common meanings include, "to admonish," "to exhort," and "to comfort."

The word *parakaleo* is from the same root word used to describe the Holy Spirit Himself, *paraklete*, which means "comforter." In much the same way that the Holy Spirit's ministry to us is multifaceted in that He both guides, encourages, and rebukes us (depending on what we need at the time), so do those divinely anointed with the gift of exhortation. Exhorters are like trusted best friends who only have our best interests at heart and who yearn for us to be successful in that which we are called to do.

Those with this gift exhibit three prominent characteristics. First of all, they tend to be people-oriented, not task-oriented. They are very intuitive about the emotional state of others and can sense whether one is down, discouraged, or even backslidden. Second, exhorters yearn to see people reach their potential in Christ. When they see apathy, half-heartedness, and a spirit of defeatism in Christians, it greatly vexes their spirit. They love to encourage others and turn bad attitudes into positive attitudes. They will instinctively gravitate towards those needing their divinely-ordained "pep talks," and they will seek to genuinely bring impartation into the lives of others.

Third, exhorters are growth oriented. They have a holy urge to help others mature in their faith, and because of it they are very likely to use their gift by mentoring others for a season or by recommending books, strategies, or other advice that will result in others overcoming whatever obstacles are currently impeding their spiritual growth. Those gifted in exhortation simply will not allow you to come up with any excuse for not being closer to Jesus this year than you were last year!

INTERCESSION

The unique, God-given ability to perceive the heart of God for nations, individuals, or specific situations and to pray fervently and strategically until God's will comes to pass. Luke 2:37, Acts 12:5

I must say that this is one of the most powerful gifts of the Spirit that I know of. Although it's never specifically labeled as a spiritual gift, the Bible does portray some who had a special ministry of prayer. Those would include Daniel (Daniel 9:3) and Anna the prophetess (Luke 2:36-37). The Greek word used to describe Anna's ministry of prayer is the word *deasis*, which means "a plea, prayer, or supplication."

Of course all Christians are expected to pray as a means of cultivating their relationship with our heavenly Father. All of us can move heaven, and James 5:16 reminds us that prayer offered up by the sincere child of God can accomplish amazing things. That being said, the Bible and church history show us that some Christians feel a special calling to the ministry of prayer, and that those who do have a special anointing for prayer can literally change lives and nations.

This seems to be a rare gift in the body of Christ. C. Peter Wagner states that according to his research only about 5 percent of Christians have this gift, and there appears to be a significant gender bias in the distribution of the gift as well. According to his research, eight out of ten intercessors are women.[2] I do not yet have enough statistical research logged to feel comfortable sharing my findings on the percentages of Christians who possess each gift (I hope to do that in the future), but I will say that my findings on this gift are similar.

I don't know why the Lord gives this gift to women more than men, but it doesn't really matter. We in the church need to thank Him that He gives us this gift at all, for it is a mighty weapon in the church's mission to the world.

Ironically, my favorite intercessor of all time does happen to be a man. This man was such a prayer warrior that he was even known by the name of "Praying Hyde." John Hyde (1865-1912) was the son of a Presbyterian minister. He felt called to missions, and in 1892 sailed to India where he would serve for nineteen years until his death. He and some fellow intercessors prayed for many years for a spiritual breakthrough in India and it finally came in 1904 in northwest India in the city of Sialkot. Thirty days before a convention meeting there, Praying Hyde and two other intercessors prayed night and day for an outpouring of the Spirit, and it occurred!

Many people came to faith in Christ and the church in India was growing stronger day by day, but for Hyde it wasn't enough. As he saw those who had accepted Christ, his soul was in continual anguish for those who still hadn't come to the cross. It was then that he began to lock himself in his room for hours each day and do nothing but pray for repentance and restoration for the people of India.

Through tears and fastings he cried out, "Father, give me these souls, or I die!"[3] At first he asked God for a soul to be saved every day. This occurred, and at last he had peace in his heart and found some relief from the burden he felt. In time however, the burden began to return and he then found himself having to petition God for two souls a day in order for the burden to be lifted. Within two years from the outpouring, over eight hundred people had given their lives to Christ.[4] It was then that Hyde began praying for four souls a day. Many days he would lead up to ten or fifteen people to Christ, and on days when he didn't he stated that the burden would literally hurt his heart.[5]

His friends said he would still be praying when they retired for the evening and when they awoke in the morning, Hyde had already been up praying before the break of dawn. He sometimes would not sleep at all and would pray all night believing his mission was similar to that spoken by the prophet Isaiah, "On your walls, O Jerusalem, I have appointed watchmen: All day and all night they will never keep silent. You who remind the Lord, take no rest for yourselves; and give Him no rest until he establishes and makes Jerusalem a praise on the earth" (Isaiah 62:6-7).[6]

Not all intercessors will have the same level of anointing that Praying Hyde had, but they will all be able to bless the universal church and their individual churches through their gift. There are three traits that can be used to identify those with the gift. First of all, they feel a strong burden to pray. I've never met an intercessor who doesn't pray at least an hour or two a day. Some pray much longer than that. Prayer is not a burden to them, rather the burden to them is not making enough time to pray!

Secondly, intercessors get particular burdens about things and can't quit praying until God removes the burden from them. Oftentimes when they get a burden for a particular person or situation they accompany their prayers with symbolic acts. For instance, one may place pictures of a country all around their home or car and lay hands upon those pictures or maps as they intercede for that nation's leaders or people.

I remember one intercessor who approached me excitedly one evening in church because our city had installed some lights under the overpasses of the interstate highway that ran through our city. She energetically exclaimed, "God's placed these lights all around the city to signify that His illumination will soon envelop our city. He does this in the natural first, and then in the spiritual!" She was noticeably excited. I must say I have never seen a woman get so worked up about some overhead lights being put up. I couldn't break out into thankful, dancing adulations over that, but she sure could!

A third trait found in intercessors is that they hear clearly from the Lord about what He wants to do. In essence the intercessory gift consists of God telling the intercessor what He wants them to petition Him for. So they spend long hours doing just that. For this reason some intercessors won't even pray for certain things unless God gives them permission to do so. They are held very accountable for what they do pray and they are sensitive to pray as they are led by the Spirit, not necessarily by the needs they see in front of them.

These saints need to be identified and placed as watchmen over the church. They will help the church to breakdown strongholds and break up the ground the enemy holds so that your church can go forward in full power into your community for the glory of the Lord Jesus Christ.

HOSPITALITY

The unique, God-given ability to open one's home to others and to create such an environment of warmth and acceptance that genuine ministry occurs. 1 Peter 4:9-10, Acts 16:14-15

Ben Franklin once said, "Dead fish and visitors both stink after three days."

I think it's safe to say that brother Ben didn't have the gift of hospitality. Thankfully, however, the Lord usually puts within each church at least one person who does.

The Greek word the apostle Peter used for this gift is *philoxenos*, which literally means, "love for strangers." These Christians have a special ability to make others feel welcome and special. Specifically this gift involves the desire to use one's home as an opportunity for ministry. But in all actuality, those with this gift have an ability to project an inviting atmosphere conducive to ministry wherever they are, not solely in their homes.

Those with this gift have a strong desire to connect with people and to see them refreshed, restored, and released for ministry. A second trait of those with this gift is that they genuinely enjoy entertaining and ministering to others in their home. These men and women are usually the first to offer up their homes for visiting missionaries to stay. They often use their home as a ministry platform for those down on their luck who need a place to stay short term. Naturally these Christians make wonderful host homes for cell group meetings or home Bible studies. A third characteristic of this gift is a comfortableness with strangers. Those with hospitality gifts are drawn to people they've just met and are very open to ministering to them and getting to know them.

I remember that in one church I served there was a woman named Sherlyn Kotrla who greatly exhibited this gift. Whenever possible I tried to have our special events in her home because of the atmosphere of love and peace that exuded from the place. She was a class "A" hostess and made every guest feel welcome. It was strange, but I could tell that ministry seemed to flow much easier when we had meetings in her home.

I believe Lydia in Acts 16 had this gift also. Very soon after her conversion she welcomed the apostle Paul and his companions into her home that was later used as the base for ministry for the entire city of Philippi. If your church hasn't already identified all those with the gift of hospitality, then that needs to get corrected quickly. These saints and the ministry they offer are a great blessing to a congregation, and they need to be utilized.

LEADERSHIP

The unique, God-given ability to perceive God's ideals for a matter and to then organize, inspire, and lead others in the completion of that endeavor. Romans 12:8, Acts 15:13-20

One misconception we need to clear up is that people who serve in a leadership role must possess the spiritual gift of leadership. If that were the case, churches would really be hurting because, like all the other *charismata*, only a small percentage of Christians have this gift.

Millions of fathers successfully lead their families, and millions of pastors successfully lead their congregations without possessing this gift. One does not have to have this specific gift in order to manage affairs, delegate tasks, or cast vision for one's group. Even those without this gift can be trained and become competent in basic leadership principles. That being said, there is, however, a supernatural, Spirit-endowed, special gift of leadership that some have. These Christians are far more effective in the leadership realm as compared to the rest of us.

When I was thinking of who in the body of Christ today best represents this gift the answer was immediately obvious. There is a man today whose vision and leadership has been used by the Lord to expand the kingdom of God on a global level. Let's take a minute to hear his story.

M.G. packed up all his belongings in a little trailer and with his wife and children moved to a certain city on the eastern seaboard. The area he relocated to was just miles away from where the Jamestown settlers first arrived in North America in 1607. When these God-fearing men landed, they planted a huge wooden cross in the ground, prayed, sanctified the area, and asked God to use that place as an evangelistic beacon to the rest of the world.

M.G. believed the area was special and that God had given him a vision to help carry out that 400-year-old prophetic petition. M.G. felt led of God to buy a television station that could be used to broadcast the gospel to the surrounding area. With absolutely no background in television or programming, and with $70 in his pocket, he began inquiring about how one might purchase a local television station![7]

He later discovered that there was in fact a defunct UHF station for sale in the neighboring city. After securing some financial backing, he purchased the station. In time the programs he produced became more and more popular and he continually upgraded his facilities. He was later able to expand his broadcasting station and buy other stations. Today it is the largest Christian broadcasting organization in the world reaching tens of millions of people with the gospel with stations across the United States and in many overseas countries such as Ukraine, India, Indonesia, and many others.

After the steady success of his Christian television stations in the mid 1970s, he became burdened by the lack of godly, Bible-believing universities which could compete with the mainstream liberal educational institutions which were graduating thousands of students each year with a secular, humanistic worldview.

He felt a calling by God to establish a completely Christian graduate school. Today, twenty-five years later the university he started has become the premier Christian graduate school in America with an annual enrollment of over 3,000 students. Each May hundreds of passionate, Spirit-filled Christians go out from the school to enter such professions as law, divinity, government, business, education, and communication. The school's students take to heart the mission of the university, which is, "Christian Leadership to Change the World."

In the late 1980s Jerry Falwell's Moral Majority was all but disbanded. M.G. felt that part of the problem was that many Christian groups focused too heavily on changing our nation through direct lobbying of Washington. He felt the Lord gave him a strategy for how to mobilize Christians politically and how to see our nation return to its Christian morals and foundation.

He felt the strategy needed to be at the grassroots level and that rather than focusing strictly on the congress the energy needed to be in placing Christians in office in the local school boards, county offices, and state-wide races. He shared his vision with others. They caught the vision and created chapters in major cities across America and in all the states. What grew out of that was the Christian Coalition, the largest and most influential political action group in the nation. Since its founding in 1989, the Christian Coalition has helped elect thousands of Christian candidates to positions of authority across the nation.

Through the millions of voter guides distributed to churches each year, the result has been that hundreds of thousands of Christians now vote and are actively involved in the political process to see godly men and women elected to city, state, and nationwide offices.

In 1990 M.G. started yet another organization which would have nation-wide ramifications. He started the American Center for Law and Justice (ACLJ) to counter the liberal and atheistic American Civil Liberties Union (ACLU). While the ACLU fights to remove all vestiges of Christianity from American life, the American Center for Law and Justice fights to protect the first amendment rights of all Americans. The ACLJ offers legal services to Christians who have been discriminated against because of their faith in Christ. The ACLJ has won numerous cases before the Supreme Court of the United States, thus protecting the rights of believers in a culture that is becoming ever-increasingly anti-Christian.

I could go on and on with other examples of how this man's leadership has rallied the body of Christ to advance the rights of Christians and to expand the worldwide influence of the church but space will not permit. Have you guessed the identity of this Christian yet? It's Marion Gordon Robertson, who is better known by his nickname "Pat" Robertson.

The religious programming organization he started was the Christian Broadcasting Network (CBN) located in Virginia Beach, Virginia. CBN is best known for its most popular program, "The 700 Club" which has been running continuously for over forty years. CBN is involved in much more than religious broadcasting, however. Each year millions of people are fed through the benevolence program "Operation Blessing." Over 200 million souls have been won to the kingdom through CBN's evangelistic outreaches. The school Robertson started was Regent University. Pat Robertson has accomplished so much because he has a highly-anointed gift mix of leadership and faith.

He is able to perceive what the Lord wants to do in a situation and then can cast a vision in such a way that others rally around him and get excited about carrying it out. One reason I chose to attend seminary at Regent was because I was attracted to the worldwide vision of Dr. Robertson and I wanted to study under the anointing of a world changer.

During my time as a student there I had the pleasure of serving as class president for the School of Divinity and thus had the opportunity to interact with Dr. Robertson from time to time. He possesses a firm confidence, but it's not arrogance. He believes that when God gives him a vision for something it will become successful because the vision comes from God, not from him.

I've observed through the years that those gifted in leadership are never satisfied with the status quo. They are ever seeking to start a new endeavor, improve an existing program or structure, or to share a new insight with those around them. Pat Robertson is exactly the same way.

I recently asked him what more was there to do since he has started and established a successful Christian broadcasting company, a successful university, numerous legal and political organizations, and other Christian benevolence ministries. He didn't pause for a second but immediately stated that the vision the Lord has given him now is to see the communist nation of China won to Christ.

He says he envisions 200 to 300 million more Christians in China in the next ten years and that the nation will have a transformation. I have no doubt that this vision is from the Lord and that he will rally intercessors, evangelists, and others to see this become a reality. He is a textbook example of one with the leadership gift.

The Greek word Paul used to describe this gift in Romans 12:8 was *prohistamenos*, which is related to the verb *prohistemi*, which means, "to direct, to be at the head of, to manage." The essence of the gift is the ability to lead others into that which God establishes or desires to do. Not everyone will operate at the same level of a Pat Robertson, who has worldwide influence, but those gifted in leadership will have a natural ability to rally others for the cause of Christ.

My wife possesses this gift. It is so rewarding for Pauline to find new ways to develop a ministry or to improve the processes or programs at her workplace. She has a natural ability to see the potential in things and people and then to rally others to carry out new plans. She views everything in life through a leadership lens. In every job she has ever held this spiritual gift naturally spills out of her into the workplace where she is usually promoted very quickly or recognized by the company or organization for her ideas that help grow the company and bring in more clients and/or customers.

Those with the leadership gift possess three primary characteristics. First, they are visionaries. These Christians do not accept the status quo. They are not satisfied with the current number of Christians in their city. They are not satisfied that their church or ministry is operating at the maximum level of efficiency. They are not satisfied that the best way of doing something is how it's being done now. Leaders are dreamers. They want to accomplish great things for God and they want to see God's people accomplish great things, so they work to that end.

Second, those gifted in leadership have a greater ability to influence and rally others with their ideas as compared to others. They have an ability to know when and how to share something that will cause others to believe it can be done. They are great motivators and oftentimes great communicators.

Third, those with leadership gifts know how to lead people and organizations to reach their desired goals. They can oversee groups of people and know which action steps need to be implemented at what time to cause the group or organization to prosper. In the church those gifted in leadership make excellent elders and board members as long as they also qualify spiritually for those positions. In that capacity they will have a remarkable insight into what needs to be done to take the church to the next level of effectiveness in the community.

One thing about those gifted in leadership is that usually they don't have to be approached about getting involved in some ministry aspect of the church. Chances are they are already fulfilling ministry needs and getting others involved due to the fact that their gift will not allow them to stay idle for long.

ADMINISTRATION

The unique, God-given ability to administrate and organize people and resources in order to achieve maximum efficiency in the work of the kingdom. 1 Corinthians 12:28, Acts 6:1-6

At first glance one may be tempted to think that administration isn't a very spiritual function in and of itself. We may even question why God issues this as a spiritual gift. The answer is simple. Our God is a God of order and He allows all things, secular and sacred, to rise or fall based on their level of organization.

He blesses order and thus He gives some in the body of Christ an anointing to bring that order. A great example of one with this gift in the Old Testament was Jethro. In Exodus 18 Jethro instituted a plan to better organize the civil governmental leaders of Israel. The result was that things ran much smoother after his plan was in place and Moses got to get home a lot earlier each night. I'm sure Zipporah was appreciative.

However, to observe one of the greatest Christian administrators God ever gave the church we have to look forward to the eighteenth century. The fires of revival were flaming high during the Great Awakening of the 1730s and 40s. Thousands of people were coming to Christ and a noticeable change was occurring in the lives of the colonists and in the lives of many in England.

However, as often the case is, just as many people were dropping out of the movement after a short time and returning to a life of sin. This trend was greatly disturbing one of the prominent revival preachers of the day. He wondered if there was a better way to follow up with these new believers to ensure that intentional discipleship could take place which would cut down on the numbers of those falling away after making a profession of faith. Read for yourself his reflections on the matter:

> But as much as we endeavored to watch over each other, we soon found some that did not live in the gospel. I do not know that any hypocrites were crept in, for indeed there was no temptation; but several grew cold, and gave way to the sins which had long easily beset them…We groaned under these inconveniences long, before a remedy could be found. The people were scattered so wide in all parts of the town, from Wapping to Westminster, that I could not easily see what the behavior of each person in his own neighborhood was; so that several disorderly walkers did much hurt before I was apprised of it. At length, while we were thinking of quite another thing, we struck upon a method for which we have cause to bless God ever since.[8]

The ministry leader was John Wesley (1703-1791). The "method" Wesley employed was the small-group concept which Wesley called the "class meeting." Twenty years ago cutting-edge churches in America were realizing the value of small groups. Wesley instituted cell groups for all his churches 260 years ago!

As soon as people accepted Christ under his ministry, they were placed in a class meeting. The meetings met primarily in homes and consisted of groups of 10-12 people who met together for mutual ministry, prayer, and edification. Wesley organized other groups called "bands" for the purpose of developing Christian character and cultivating godly affections. He placed those with leadership potential in what were called "select bands." All the class meetings in a territory made up a "society" which met regularly for corporate worship services.

The Methodist churches Wesley founded derived their very name from the strict "method" that Wesley had for every aspect of the believer's life. There was a method for evangelism, a method for discipleship, and there were methods for raising funds and caring for the poor. Wesley's strict attention to detail and his organizational genius ensured that he was far more effective in almost any endeavor as compared to his ministry peers.

He produced over 400 publishable works, started over 6,000 cell groups, traveled over 225,000 miles on horseback preaching up to five sermons a day (the first beginning at 5:00 A.M.) in towns throughout England and America, and by the time of his death almost one in three people in England was a Methodist!

His primary gift mix of evangelism-administration was indeed powerful. Because his gift mix combined the winning of souls with devising the most efficient systems for containing the harvest, his ministry influence far superceded other prominent revival preachers of his day such as Jonathan Edwards and George Whitefield. His contemporaries transformed lives; Wesley transformed nations.

Not everyone with the gift of administration will change nations, but they will change your church or organization...and make it better. The word translated "administration" is the word *kybernesis* which means "guidance" or "leadership." It's related to the word *kybernetes*, which is a naval term meaning "helmsman" or "captain."

Some teachers only speak of one gift of leadership as found in Romans 12:8 while believing Paul's use of "administration" in 1 Corinthians 12:28 to be just another word for the same gift. I believe that view to be inaccurate. I believe Paul had two different abilities in mind and thus called them by different names to highlight two separate gifts.

Granted, they are related gifts in much the same way that helps and serving are related gifts. Leadership and administration both involve the concept of leadership; it's just a different kind of leadership. The leadership gift in Romans 12:8 is *prostemi* and evokes the image of one standing out in front of others or one providing a leadership covering for others. The gift of leadership involves vision casting, creating the strategy, and leading the people.

The administration gift involves creating a plan to implement the strategy and involves decision-making power over resources, but not necessarily people. It's true that the administrators are the captains of each ship, but the leaders are the admirals who give the orders to the ship's captains on where to go and what the mission is upon arrival of the destination.

Those with the gift of administration are known by three characteristics. First, they can bring order and efficiency out of chaos. These Christians are excellent stewards and they instinctively know how to use resources wisely, how to delegate effectively, and how to improve the existing state of things. They have a keen ability to evaluate a project and then set a course to ensure maximum effectiveness. They are able to make realistic projections for a set of goals and tell which ones can be accomplished now and which ones are to be implemented later on down the road.

Second, those with administrative gifts are usually organized people who have their own affairs in good order. Administrators lead ordered lives, love to compartmentalize, and are the kind of people who know how to motivate and assign the right tasks to others to ensure efficiency. Many have abilities in matching people with specific jobs, and thus have a good track record for making good fits.

Third, those with administrative gifts tend to notice what is wrong with things so they may sometimes feel bad and think that they are always focusing on the negative. This isn't true; actually it's just their spiritual gift operating. Their gift will always cause them to notice disorder, inefficiency, and personnel mismatches, because that's how God has wired them. They're supposed to notice such things so they can then get in there, roll up their sleeves, and fix things!

Those with this gift are a godsend to any church or ministry endeavor. These folks will ensure that there is a workable plan in place and that the work of the ministry is operating at a peak level of efficiency.

GIVING

The unique, God-given ability to give unselfishly of one's resources (time, money, affections, etc.) to ensure that the work of the church and the needs of others are taken care of. Romans 12:8, Matthew 27:57-60

Paul used the word *metadidous*, which means, "giving" to describe this gift. This is a perfect time to re-emphasize a point made in chapter three. Just because we do not have a certain spiritual gift we are not excused from performing roles associated with that gift if those roles are required of all Christians.

Giving is a great example. All Christians are commanded to give generously (2 Corinthians 8:1-7). This would imply, in my opinion, a minimal tithe of 10 percent of our income to our local church and extra giving from time to time as the Lord prompts us. That is a role that every Christian is to perform. Some Christians go way beyond that. For these saints, they don't give above and beyond because they have to, rather they give because they want to and are motivated by the Spirit to do so. That is to say, some Christians have a gift of giving, and what a blessing they are to the church.

Those with the gift of giving display two dominant traits. First of all, they get a profound sense of joy from being used by God to bless another person who is in need. This may involve providing some physical need for another person or family such as a piece of furniture or food or clothes. It oftentimes involves a direct gift of money to another individual or to some church or parachurch organization that needs the funds to continue their ministry work.

A second trait of those with this gift is that they are very sensitive to the needs of others. People with the gift of giving notice needs and they begin to pray about whether this is a situation God is moving them to do something about. Those with this gift are careful about where they give, and usually only give when the Spirit is prompting them. They are not softhearted "suckers" who can't say no to a hard case story. Since they rely on the Spirit to tell them when and where to give, you can't fool them nor manipulate them very easily. They give when God tells them to give.

The Lord uses these saints to meet the needs of others and to help the work of the church go forth. Oftentimes God will bless these folks with very good business sense and will greatly bless the work of their hands in their jobs and investments. This is because He uses these Christians to fund the works of the church. Because they are faithful with their money and know that it all belongs to God, He can trust these Christians with great wealth because they are willing to give it all away if the Lord instructs them to. In essence, saints with the gift of giving possess their money; their money does not possess them.

This was certainly the case with a pastor in Bristol, England. George Mueller (1805-1898) had a strong gift of giving and faith. He was a man who lived to give and minister to the needs of others. His heart was particularly touched by the thousands of orphans who roamed the streets in search of food, shelter, and love. Mueller began praying in faith for God to send him the funds to take these children in. His prayers were answered and after announcing his plans to build an orphanage to educate and raise society's unwanted children, God began to touch others' hearts to give to the ministry.

He eventually built five orphanages and took in over 2,000 orphans.[9] He never once publicly asked for money. The entire ministry expenses year in and year out came from donors who heard about the work from word of mouth. Gifts of thousands of pounds would come in and he would always put it into the work of the ministry.

Throughout his life, he spent his own modest personal salary and life savings on the work of various benevolence ministries. After his death, his personal financial books were audited and it was discovered that $180,000 to the work of the kingdom had been given from someone identified only as, "a servant of the Lord Jesus, who constrained by the love of Christ, seeks to lay up treasure in heaven."[10] The donor was of course, Mueller himself.

SIMPLICITY

The unique, God-given ability to voluntarily divulge oneself of most material comforts so as to simplify one's lifestyle for more effective ministry. 1 Corinthians 13:3, Acts 2:44-45

This gift is not explicitly listed in Scripture. But I believe the apostle Paul may have referenced it in 1 Corinthians 13:3 when he talks about how different gifts can be used and still be useless if they are not motivated by love. While commenting on the gifts of knowledge, prophecy, and martyrdom he also speaks of those who bestow all their goods to feed the poor. The word he uses is *psomizo*, which means "to give to eat or to distribute" (as in distributing alms). History, as well as modern experience, has shown that there are some Christians who feel a calling to live a very simplified lifestyle. These Christians have a heart for the disadvantaged and neglected in society.

That was certainly the case for a young Albanian woman named Agnes Bojaxhiu. Agnes grew up with a tender heart for the Lord and at age eighteen left her home to do missionary work in India where she taught school and studied nursing. One day as she was traveling by train, she heard the voice of God. She later recalled, "I was sure it was God's voice. I was certain that He was calling me. The message was clear: I must leave the convent to help the poor by living among them."[11]

Soon after that she started a new order, The Missionaries of Charity, and with the help of many others she began establishing homes for lepers, orphans, and other destitute people throughout India. Her heart of compassion never ceased and up until her death at age 87 she continued to bathe, feed, and minister to the sick and dying of the inner-city slums. She once commented, "they lived like animals, at least they die like human beings."

This great saint was known affectionately to the world as "Mother Teresa" (1910-1997). Her order eventually grew to over 1,000 nuns who operated over 200 centers of charity worldwide. She was loved and respected by leaders of every nation and religion and was aptly awarded the Nobel Peace Prize in 1979.

Mother Teresa had the gift mix of mercy-simplicity. Like Mother Teresa, those with the simplicity gift display two dominate characteristics. First, they are not materialistic. They do not derive their happiness from clothes, beautiful homes, or possessions of any kind.

They derive their happiness from serving other people in need. Because of the nature of their gifting they usually live very simplified lifestyles because they would rather spend their money on ministering to others. For example, in 1964 on a trip to India Pope Paul VI gave Mother Teresa his ceremonial limousine, which she immediately raffled away to further support her compassion ministries![12]

It is mistakenly believed that to possess this gift one has to be poor or that one voluntarily lives in poverty. Some teachers even call this gift "voluntary poverty," but I've never liked that designation. Many with this gift have plenty of money but you would never know it by how they live. Some choose to live at the poverty level and some live as the rest of us albeit with much less of the creature comforts that we are used to.

A second trait of those with this gift is that they have a noticeable heart of compassion directed toward the poor or hurting of society. It bothers them when they perceive someone in need has been overlooked by everyone else. Their heart of compassion always leads them to action. These are the people in the church who start the food kitchens for the poor and who organize the buying of Christmas gifts for the needy children in the community.

These believers are beautiful examples of Christian love in action. Blessed is the congregation that is fortunate to have a few of these Christians in their midst. While some talk about the love of God, those gifted in simplicity will go about showing it.

CRAFTSMANSHIP

The unique, God-given ability to work skillfully and creatively to design, build, or create things that are useful and inspirational in the work of the kingdom. Exodus 31:3-5, Exodus 35:30-35

At one point I hesitated in including craftsmanship in my inventory of spiritual gifts. I wondered if this ability was a one-time special anointing God distributed for the sole purpose of constructing and beautifying the Ark of the Covenant. That is, after all, the only mention of the gift. We read in Exodus 31:1-11 that the Holy Spirit filled Bezalel and Oholiab and gave them the ability to make beautiful artistic designs in gold and silver. The Hebrew word used in the passage is *melakah*, which means "to work" in terms of ministry. Bezalel and Oholiab were able to make elaborate furnishings and also had skill in designing the ceremonial garments worn by the High Priest.

The more I reflected on the matter, the more I realized that if those things were important to the Lord back then, surely they still are today. Therefore, it is my conviction that the Lord still gifts some in the body of Christ in the area of the creative arts. I think that's a good description of this gift but in keeping with other teachers who already refer to the gift as craftsmanship, I'll follow their lead. Let's take a look at this gift.

The gift of craftsmanship relates to the broad abilities to build, create, or design things of a physical nature that are needed in the work of the church. Those with this gift have an anointing to create beautiful works of art or design that help the church in its mission. These men and women are often the ones who create the colorful, eye-pleasing banners that adorn many sanctuaries today. Some with this gift use their creativity to make welcome baskets and other unique gifts to hand out to first time visitors in their churches. Some are gifted in creating more elaborate structures such as furnishings.

Those who have gifts in this area are especially helpful on short-term mission trips that require the construction or design of physical works. The common thread that runs through those gifted in craftsmanship is a strong desire to use their creativity and skills for the Lord. They seek ways to bless others with their works and they enjoy finding ways to reflect the love of God through the construction of physical works.

CHAPTER 8

The Ministry Gifts, Part II

DISCERNMENT

The unique, God-given ability to detect whether the actions and intentions of others are from a heavenly, a human, or a demonic influence. 1 Corinthians 12:10, Acts 16:16-18

There is a certain passage in Acts chapter 16 that used to really puzzle me. Perhaps it confused you too. I'm talking about the one where Paul cast a spirit out of a young woman who had been following him around for a while. Remember the passage? Paul and his entourage had recently arrived in the city of Philippi and Luke records that a young girl began following the apostle and exhorting the crowds he was preaching to with statements such as, "These men are servants of the Most High!" "These men are proclaiming to you the way of salvation!"

Now I don't know about you, but if I were a missionary in a strange city and a young girl joined us saying those things to the crowds I might be inclined to invite her to be a part of my prayer team or perhaps offer her a position on my staff. At the very least I would have thanked her and bought her an espresso! It makes sense, right? But that's not what Paul did. In fact, he turned to the girl and said, "I command you in the name of Jesus Christ to come out of her!" And the Bible records that an evil spirit left the girl at that very moment.

From the natural perspective, everything looked fine. The girl looked normal. She wasn't drooling green slime from the corner of her mouth and deep, male voices weren't heard coming out of her. She seemed eager to help Paul and his friends. She even said all the right things. She affirmed the divinity of Christ. She must be a Spirit-filled child of God, right?...Wrong.

Paul sensed that underneath that facade of normalcy something wasn't right with this girl. Paul knew that Satan oftentimes masquerades as an angel of light and his workers as workers of righteousness. Paul discerned that day that the girl was in fact under the influence of a demonic spirit and that she needed to be exposed and healed. At that moment Paul demonstrated the special gift known as the discerning of spirits.

All Christians have general discernment and according to Hebrews 5:14 it can be sharpened by studying the Word of God. But God grants to some a special measure of discernment. The reference for this gift is found in 1 Corinthians 12:10. The Greek phrase used is *diakriseis pneumaton*. In the Greek both words are in the plural so the literal translation is "distinguishings of spirits." The word comes from the verb *diakrino*, which means "to judge" or "to evaluate." The plural reference regarding this gift implies there are several levels of discernment and that there is more than one spirit that can be discerned with this gift. In fact, those with this gift can distinguish between demonic spirits, heavenly spirits, and human spirits.

If there was ever a gift needed in the body of Christ today it is the gift of discernment. I've seen many people get caught up in movements that looked spiritual and sounded spiritual, but were in fact not of God. I've seen false ministers of the gospel get on the airwaves and dupe God's people out of lots of money because these Christians lacked the discernment to know if these individuals were genuine or not. How many of us have invested time or energies into friendships or partnerships with others that we later realized was a mistake from the very beginning? Such observations ought to draw us to highly value those with this gift. God has granted this gift to the church to protect us and to help us make good decisions.

I think the best example of this gift in action is seen in the ministry of Jesus. Jesus was never fooled when He met anyone. He intuitively knew the condition of their heart. He knew their motivations. Often the Pharisees would approach Jesus with a question that seemed logical and innocent enough, but Scripture would record that "Jesus, *knowing their hearts* answered them saying...." Jesus knew when someone was genuinely asking a question or when one was trying to set a trap.

Jesus' discernment didn't only operate on a negative level. He could also just as easily discern the Spirit of God within someone as demonstrated when He approached Nathanael in John 1:47 saying, "Behold, an Israelite indeed, in whom is no guile!" Remember, in that narrative it was the first time Jesus had ever laid eyes on Nathanael, and yet He could make that character observation about him.

The primary characteristic of those with this gift is that they have an ability to see beyond the exterior of a person. They can make accurate observations about the motivations of others. They can sense if someone is operating from an anointing of God or from an influence of the evil one. Some with the gift can even discern if spirits are in the atmosphere such as in a home or even in a certain geographic location. Their level of discernment is, of course, dependent upon the level of anointing that they have from God.

As with all the spiritual gifts, we need to be creative and find ways to use our gifts for the work of the ministry. I have seen this gift operate beautifully so many times in a small group setting such as in cell groups. Oftentimes the Lord will reveal to someone with the gift that someone else in the group is struggling with something, perhaps with a spirit of heaviness or depression. When this is inquired about, often someone will disclose that need and then the group can intentionally minister to the person and see the Lord do a great work. It's so refreshing to see the body of Christ minister to one another because someone took a step of faith and moved out in the area of their gifting as they were prompted by the Spirit.

Before we close, I would be remiss if I didn't mention a caution associated with this gift. I've seen this gift abused sometimes. If they are not careful, some with discernment gifts can be judgmental about others because of the insight they get about the motivations of people. Some struggle with gossip. They can also be tempted to be prideful and show off the revelatory information that they have about someone. Those with discernment need to especially pray for the maturity to know when things that they sense are to be shared and when they are only meant to be privately taken to God in prayer.

SERVING

The unique, God-given ability to be aware of the physical and practical needs of others and to meet those needs in a way that blesses them. Romans 12:7, John 12:3

It's hard to imagine how the church could function without this gift. In every congregation God has gifted some men and women with the ability to take notice of the practical day-to-day duties that must be accomplished for any ministry endeavor to succeed. In the tenth chapter of Luke we see this gift in operation in Martha.

When Jesus enters her home she immediately begins to serve the needs of her guests. While she is unselfishly taking care of her guest's needs, she becomes a little perturbed when she notices her sister Mary sitting at the feet of Jesus instead of helping her serve. What happens next is a little surprising if one doesn't understand spiritual gifts.

When Martha asks Jesus, "Lord, doesn't it bother you that Mary isn't up serving the others like I am?" Jesus basically replies, "No, it doesn't bother me at all. As a matter of fact, Martha, I commend Mary for sitting at my feet and spending time with me which is where you both belong at this time." It's at that point in the story that I always felt sorry for ol' Martha. She tries to serve Jesus and ends up getting a mild rebuke for it!

We need to understand why she gets a correction. The Lord is not rebuking Martha for using her spiritual gift of serving. The Lord is rebuking her for projecting her gift on Mary and for misunderstanding the priority of the moment.

In His rebuke, Jesus was basically saying to her, "I didn't create Mary with a serving gift so I don't expect her to do all the same things that you do. Secondly, what was most important in this moment was that you both were in that living room with me so I could spend time with you and bring impartation into your lives." The very essence of what the Lord was saying was, "Martha, don't get so busy *working for Me* that you begin to equate that with *being with Me*." Wow, that's a lesson we all need to remember.

Although Martha was rebuked in that one instance, I am sure that throughout most of her life Martha used her serving gift in a wonderful way to bless many people. The Greek word used to describe this gift is *diakonia*, which literally means "serving" or "ministering." It's the same word often translated "deacon" elsewhere in the Bible. Since the primary role of deacons was to serve, it makes sense that many of them had a primary gift-mix that included the gift of serving.

The main characteristic of those with this gift is that they have a desire to meet the practical needs of others. Those gifted in service notice when the church needs painting. They notice when a neighbor has a physical or spiritual need that everyone else has overlooked. When they see a need they immediately go into action to meet that need.

Christians with this gift are usually very dependable, hands-on type of people. A second trait of those with this gift is their lack of desire to delegate tasks. Servers love to serve so you won't usually see them barking out orders for others to do something. They just roll their sleeves up and do it themselves. No matter whether the ministry endeavor is a large one or a small one, these Christians are a great asset to the team. And as a bonus you don't usually have to assign them a part to play; they will intuitively gravitate to wherever the greatest needs are anyway.

HELPS

The unique, God-given ability to partner and come alongside others for the purpose of greatly increasing the other person's ministry effectiveness. 1 Corinthians 12:28, Acts 13:4-5

Most of us in the evangelical church have a very high regard for the apostle Paul. One can tell that by the frequency with which we quote him. "Paul says this, Paul says that." We quote Paul almost as much as we do Jesus. Of course, it's well earned; I mean the man did write thirteen books of our New Testament, helped evangelize most of the known world of his day, and received special revelations from God that he was not even permitted to share with the rest of the church.

We often think of Paul and wonder, "How could one man accomplish so much?" Part of that answer was that Paul had a Holy

Spirit empowered special helper, a secret weapon of sorts that was responsible for helping his ministry to be so fruitful. Moses had Joshua. Batman had Robin. Paul had Luke.

Have you ever noticed as you are reading the book of Acts that it sometimes shifts to the first person where you run across several "we" sections? You know things like, "and when we finished the voyage from Tyre we arrived at Ptolemais," or "then we visited the churches in Ephesus." The "we" in those verses is the author of the book of Acts, which is none other than Luke. Luke accompanied Paul as he ministered in city after city in province after province.

He traveled thousands of miles with the apostle on horseback, on foot, and on the great ships of the sea. He assisted Paul in a variety of ways. Being a trained physician he probably looked after Paul's health. He served as a scribe and ministry record keeper making copious notes of all of Paul's journeys listing cities visited, churches planted, and the different jails the city officials invited Paul to stay in while he was in town! He provided Paul with the emotional support of a true friend when the apostle would get discouraged, and he no doubt ministered alongside his better-known friend throughout their journeys together.

The gift of helps is very similar to the gift of serving with one major difference. The gift of helps is a person-centered gift, while the gift of serving is a task-oriented gift. The gift of helps is given to help strengthen the ministries of others. It comes from the Greek word *antilempsis* that means "help" or "assistance."

There are three primary traits that those with this gift will display. First, they receive great fulfillment from helping another Christian with a ministry task. These men and women love to see others succeed, and they are instrumental in the success of others. The way they help another Christian is based on what they perceive is most needed at that time. Sometimes they assist in more intangible ways such as providing friendship and support during a needed season of someone's life. At other times their assistance is primarily hands-on as in various acts of manual service.

A second trait of those so gifted is that they have a passion to invest themselves in the lives of others. These Christians are not self-centered. When they meet you they instinctively ask themselves, "What can I do for this person?" rather than, "What can this person do for me?"

A third trait of those gifted in helps is that they are very loyal to those they help, especially for those God assigns them to work with on a long term basis. When this occurs, the Lord seems to knit their heart to the other person. We see a moving example of this in 2 Timothy 4:11 where Paul is lamenting the fact that so many of his so-called friends and ministry partners have deserted him during his trials. He then comments, "Only Luke is with me."

Oftentimes God will provide a pastor with one special person in the congregation who is gifted in helps and then assign that person to the pastor. This is nice seeing that oftentimes Satan will also assign one special person in a congregation to do nothing but make the pastor wish he had taken up engineering.

The pastors who are blessed to have such a person in their midst can see their ministry effectiveness increase exponentially. This is one of those spiritual gifts that can get overlooked because those that possess it are oftentimes behind-the-scenes kind of Christians. I personally believe however that it is exactly this type of gift, and thus these kinds of Christians, whom Paul says in 1 Corinthians 12:23 should receive more abundant honor. This is truly a beautiful gift the Lord has given the church, and we should never take these precious saints for granted.

INTERPRETATION OF DREAMS

The unique, God-given ability to decode the symbolism and explain the meaning of dreams and/or visions that others receive from God. Daniel. 1:17, Genesis 41:12

One of the most overlooked forms of communication that God is pleased to speak to us through is dreams. The Bible consistently reveals God as speaking to people through this universally experienced, yet mysterious phenomenon. The Lord uses dreams to warn global leaders of future events (Genesis 41:1-8), to provide revelation to His prophets (Numbers 12:6), to provide direction to His servants on what to do next in a difficult situation (Matthew 2:13-14), and for a host of other reasons as well. Scripture also points out that in these last days during the age of the church that dreams are to be expected as a normative means of communication between God and His people (Acts 2:17-18).

Even though the biblical evidence is clear, there are millions of Christians who would never entertain the idea that their dreams have meaning, let alone that God is actually trying to say something to them personally through their dreams.

Why is that? The main reason is they were never taught that God wants to speak to them that way. They probably never heard a sermon on the topic, key leaders in their lives never mentioned it to them, and thus they subconsciously skimmed over the many passages in Scripture about dreams with an attitude of..."Well, that's probably not for today."

Most of us develop our key theological beliefs based on what was taught and emphasized to us by influential spiritual figures during our formative years of spiritual development. While we gain much good from that, we also tend to inherit their prejudices and misunderstandings as well.

Of course everything I will say about dreams in the next few paragraphs applies to visions also. Visions occur when we are awake. Sometimes God will place us into a trancelike state and give us a vivid picture of some thing or event. However, I wish to focus mainly on dreams because all of us dream; but do keep in mind that God often speaks to people in visions as well.

The first question we need to ask is, "Are all dreams from God?" Every time we dream are we to wake up looking for some hidden spiritual message? The answer is simply, no. Dreaming is a natural physiological function that is common to every human being, and is necessary for maintaining adequate mental and emotional health. But God does often use this natural function in a supernatural way.

If I watch a good science fiction movie, I often dream about it that night. When I wake up the next morning I don't waste precious time trying to find God's hidden meaning in the scene where I shot an alien Death Star droid into bits with my laser rifle. I know I dreamed of aliens and starships because my subconscious mind was still processing the images from the night before.

While many dreams are just the result of natural human functioning, every Christian needs to be aware of the fact that some could be from God. I remember as a child I often had a recurring dream that I was preaching. I would see myself in the dream as a very young boy passionately exhorting a group of children to live for God. The group seemed to listen intently and was being changed inwardly by the message I delivered.

I had this dream repeatedly from about age five until about age nine or ten. I always wondered why I would dream such a thing. The last thing I wanted to be was a preacher! Like most boys, to the extent that I ever even thought of a life vocation, it certainly didn't revolve around ministry, but rather around astronauts, army men, and ninjas. Years later, at age sixteen, God called me to preach the gospel. I now know that He was prophetically revealing to me as a child part of that which was to be my destiny.

Not realizing that God spoke to us by dreams, I never paid attention to my dreams in my early years of the faith. It was not until many years later that I began to notice a correlation between my dreams and actual events that occurred in my everyday life. I would have a very vivid dream about a person or a family and then a little later some dramatic event (sometimes good and sometimes bad) would occur within that family.

I also noticed that many of my dreams contained recurring themes and symbols. I also realized that I instinctively knew what these symbols meant and could usually decode the meaning of my dreams rather quickly. For example, I have always loved tropical fish and have maintained aquariums for most of my life. I know all about them and can tell you their scientific name, their sex, their health, and identify certain diseases that these types of fish can acquire.

Interestingly, I noticed that in seasons of my life when I was not close to the Lord I would often dream of sickly, lethargic aquarium fish. This dream was God communicating to me that spiritually I was sickly and weak and that I needed to repent and move closer to Him.

In my dreams, churches or denominations often take the form of vehicles or large buses. New Christians are usually represented as infants in diapers. And we all tend to have very unique symbols for the demonic realm. In my mother-in-law's dreams they're represented by alligators, in most Christian's dreams, they take the form of snakes, but in my dreams, demons are often represented by big, bearded, tattooed men on motorcycles (long story - don't ask!).

In talking with others who receive spiritual dreams frequently I learned that it is quite common for persons to have their own recurring symbols. Each of us must learn our own "dream vocabulary" and ask God to give us the meaning of the more common symbols that often accompany our dreams.

Gradually as I grew in my understanding of dreams, and from studying what Scripture had to say about them, I realized how valuable they are for us. I am now fairly confident in discerning for my own life which dreams are from God and which are just natural dreams. When we do receive dreams from the Lord, they are usually one of three different types:

1. *Warning Dream* – This type of dream is meant to warn us about some future attack from the enemy or some difficult time ahead. This could be a warning about a friend, spouse, or your children. The Lord gives us this dream so that we will begin to pray and intercede for ourselves or other individuals. He also gives it so that we will be prepared for that which is coming. Sometimes God has not decreed that it *must* come to pass; thus **through** prayer the hardship could be avoided. Example from Scripture: Abimelech warned not to sleep with Abraham's **wife** (Genesis 20:3-7).

2. *Confirmation Dream* – **This dream** simply confirms that what you believe to be the **case about** a person or a situation is in fact true. This type of **dream** can also be used to give you the emotional impetus **to act** on what you already know but have thus far been **unresponsive** toward. My dreams of sick, lethargic fish **were confirmation** of what I already inwardly knew to be true **at** the time, and were thus confirmation dreams. Example from Scripture: Pilate's wife's dream confirming that her husband should release Jesus from custody (Matthew 27:17-19).

3. *Prophetic Dream* – This type of dream reveals the secrets of the future as only God knows them. This type of dream may also shed new light into some aspect of God's dealings with mankind or some issue that is vague in Scripture. The

book of Revelation is a recorded prophetic vision that was given to the apostle John. It both reveals the future as well as explains the past and present. Example from Scripture: As a 17 year old, Joseph dreamt about his future place of honor and high governmental service (Genesis 37:5-8).

Sometimes our spiritual dreams may be a combination of two types. Like all of us, I will never forget the terrible morning of September 11th, 2001. At the time I was working for Regent University and was participating in a weekly Tuesday morning prayer meeting with some co-workers when we all received news that several jetliners had smashed into the World Trade Center towers and into the Pentagon.

I'll never forget the look of horror that overcame one co-worker of mine as she burst into tears and wept uncontrollably. She told me that she had been having several disturbing dreams recently about airplanes crashing into things, and mentioned one in which she saw a plane tear into a building. I also remembered that roughly one week before the attacks the chancellor of our university, Dr. Pat Robertson, had told the entire CBN and Regent University staff that the Lord had showed him that major terrorist attacks were soon coming to the United States.

This warning was even recorded and made public on the 700 Club telecast that week. There is no telling how many other Christians had similar dreams such as these in the weeks and months before September 11th but I suspect that many did. In this case, the dreams were a combination of prophetic/warning dreams that God was giving to the church.

Over time one can begin to differentiate between a natural dream and a dream from the Lord. But sometimes it is not so clear and only prayer can tell. I believe that if we pray for the interpretation of our dreams that God will reveal them to us. However, we can also rest assured that God has gifted some individuals within the church with a special ability to do so. They can be very helpful in bringing out the meaning of difficult dreams. Those with this gift are identified as such because they have an ability to decode the strange symbols that usually accompany spiritual dreams. Perhaps the person best known for this particular gift in Scripture was Joseph. The Hebrew word used in Genesis 41:12 is *patar*, which means "to interpret."

The Lord used Joseph to interpret many dreams. God gave Joseph as a young boy a series of both confirmation and prophetic dreams that foretold the high place of honor and authority that would one day be his. There is no doubt that those dreams from his youth kept him going in the years of difficulty that lay ahead of him.

In Genesis chapter 40 he interprets two prophetic dreams from Pharaoh's cupbearer and chief baker. One chapter later he gives an interpretation to a prophetic dream of Pharaoh's which has worldwide ramifications and ends up saving an entire nation from starvation. God is giving the same kinds of dreams today. He gives us dreams to warn us, to shake us from our apathy, or to confirm our deepest desires or greatest questions.

INTERPRETATION OF TONGUES

The unique, God-given ability to interpret and translate a message in tongues into an understandable language that others can receive and benefit from. 1 Corinthians 12:10, 1 Corinthians 14:26

The Greek phrase used to describe this gift is *hermeneia glosson*, which means "interpretation of tongues." The sole purpose of this gift is to translate a message in tongues into the native language of the hearers. Only one time in Scripture did God not use an individual to do this. That of course was Acts chapter 2 when the 120 were filled with the Spirit. Acts 2:7-8 records, "And they were amazed and marveled, saying, Why, are not all these who are speaking Galileans? And how is it that we each hear them in our own language to which we were born?"

This passage doesn't definitively tell us if the 120 were speaking in ecstatic utterances (*glossolalia*) or if they were supernaturally given the ability to speak in languages they had never learned (*xenoglossolalia*). Another possibility is that the 120 were speaking in their native language and that the real miracle was in the hearing by the others who heard the disciples in their own native languages (*heteroglossolalia*). The text specifically mentions tongues of fire sitting upon the 120 so the miracle strongly seems to be within the 120, not within the hearers.

This is a unique occurrence in Acts 2 because Paul's mention of the gift of interpretation in 1 Corinthians 12 implies that tongues are usually interpreted by a single individual with this specific gift. Those with the gift of interpretation are able to help everyone in the congregation receive the blessing of a message in tongues.

These Christians are very important indeed as Scripture forbids public proclamation of tongues unless Christians with this gift are present. I am not aware of a prominent Christian in church history who had this gift, but I have been present many times in a corporate worship service when someone with this gift used it. Their contribution to the service was a great blessing appreciated by all as we heard before us a translation of a message the Lord had specifically for us that day.

MISSIONARY

The unique, God-given ability to effectively minister in a foreign culture for the purposes of establishing and/or strengthening the church within that cultural group. Acts 13:1-5, Acts 22:21

The missionary gift is not specifically labeled as a *charisma* in Scripture, but I believe it to be one. Most church leaders have come to recognize that there is indeed a particular calling some have to minister to a different cultural group than their own. Commensurate with this calling is the ability to be successful at it and to have the perseverance to endure the hardships that come with this. Seeing that these two criteria exist, that is, a special calling and a special ability for the task, it is proper that we view the ministry of a missionary as a separate spiritual gift.

Those who possess the missionary gift can be identified by three dominant traits. First, they have a strong emotional attraction to foreign cultures. Missionaries love other people groups. They have an interest in other cultures' unique heritages, customs, and idiosyncrasies. They usually begin learning foreign languages without any prompting from anyone else. They do this because of their strong desire to connect with others and to become assimilated into their world.

These Christians many times have huge world maps hanging in their offices or at home. When they are not in the field they at least want to be reminded of the big picture of God's redemptive plan for this world. Just seeing a map of the world each day stirs their spirit for missions.

Second, those with the missionary gift have a deep burden to see the gospel penetrate foreign fields. It burdens them to think of people groups with no indigenous churches present. It vexes their spirit to learn of a tribe that still has not had the Bible translated into its native tongue.

The third characteristic associated with this gift is that these folk assimilate more easily into new cultures than do others. Those with this gift are accepted more quickly by the other culture as well. God has given them an anointing that causes other people to sense the genuineness of their heart, and they are honored and appreciated by those they minister to.

One of the great missionaries the Lord gave the church was Mary Slessor (1848-1915). Mary knew she was called as a missionary to Africa from the time she was a young child. As a little girl she would often pretend to be teaching and ministering to little African children.[1] Her home life was very difficult. Her father was an alcoholic who spent all the family's money on liquor, leaving the family to subsist at the poverty level. Because of this, at a young age Mary began working fourteen hours a day in factories to help support the family. Having to confront harsh, godless men at the factories all day and a terrorizing father at night, toughened Mary and made her one who could hold her own against anyone.

At the age of 28, with a blessing from her mother, she took leave of Scotland, and with a charge from the United Presbyterian Church, headed to Nigeria, "the white man's grave." Calabar, Nigeria in 1876 was a former slave-trading port and was inhabited by a completely pagan people. The locals in Calabar practiced witchcraft, human sacrifices, mass tribal slaughters of their rivals, and a particularly cruel idea about twin babies. These children were thought to be an omen of the devil and women who had twins were put out in the woods with their babies to die by the elements or the animals, whichever got them first. If that wasn't enough, the area's swamps and rivers were infested with disease so most people never lived to see old age.

Upon her arrival, Mary immediately began rescuing the abandoned twin babies and raised them in her home as her own. In no time she mastered the local language and began preaching the gospel traveling by foot from village to village, and along the way built schools and churches. She taught the local women advanced trade skills and medical work so that they could better trade with the Europeans who would visit the coast. These skills began to raise the standard of living for the whole village.

When people were sick, she would nurse them back to health. After a time she gained the respect of the local chiefs who invited her to move into the interior of their villages. She saved many from death by walking up to rival chiefs and demanding a stop to the raids and killings of rival villages. Instead of killing her where she stood, they obeyed and returned to their own regions.

Recognizing the enormous sway she held with the natives, the British government in 1892 appointed her as a vice consul of the area where she had the authority to judge disputes and issue rulings. She was the first woman ever named to such a post. She would later write, "No tribe was formerly so feared because of their utter disregard of human life, but human life is now safe in Okoyong. No chief ever died without the sacrifice of many human lives, but this custom has now ceased."[2] For thirty-nine years she preached the gospel and served the people of Nigeria. Through sickness, poverty, exhaustion, and threats against her life she never lost sight of what she was there for, to show the people of Africa that God loved them.

All of us need to remember our Lord's command in Acts 1:8 regarding world evangelism. We are to be witnesses in Jerusalem (our own city), Judea (our surrounding region), Samaria (surrounding nations), and to the uttermost parts of the earth. The task for world evangelization requires the mobilization of the entire church.

For those of us not called to be missionaries, our support should be in two areas, intercessory prayer and financial support. It would be a wonderful thing if every Christian would consider adopting a missionary and then praying for them and corresponding with them regularly. These men and women are on the front lines in a war for the souls of others. They deserve a place of special honor among the household of faith. We also need to be financially supporting missionaries and/or missions organizations every year.

Still today, in the early twenty-first century, there are hundreds of groups that have yet to have one indigenous church planted in their tribe or people group! There are still over 1,000 languages that have yet to have the Bible translated into them! These statistics are hard to believe in light of 2,000 years of Christianity on the earth, but missiologists confirm that they are indeed true.

We in the universal body of Christ cannot continue to spend almost the entirety of our church budgets on trying to reach only those in our own city and nation. We must allot some of those funds to the work of foreign missions. No one should be allowed to hear the gospel twice until everyone has heard it once.

MERCY

The unique, God-given ability to comfort and restore others who are experiencing a physical, spiritual, or emotional hardship. Romans 12:8, Luke 10:33-35

Since all of humankind is infected with the disease of sin, it is no surprise that our world is one where much cruelty, injustice, and suffering occurs. Therefore, since one of the five primary purposes of the church is "service" (or ministry), it is no surprise that God supernaturally gifts some Christians with an ability to minister to and restore those who are suffering. He does this primarily through Christians with the gift of mercy. The Greek word used in Romans 12:8 to describe this gift is, *eleon* which means "mercy" or "pity." It comes from the verb *eleeo*, which means "to show mercy; to have compassion." Those with this gift are supernaturally endowed to do just that.

Those with the gift of mercy usually manifest four dominant characteristics. First of all, they are very drawn to people in distress. These Christians will notice when someone is hurting or being mistreated, and compassion wells up in their heart to do something about it. Second, these Christians have a supernatural ability to love and care for others, even total strangers. Saints gifted in mercy have the love of God flowing through them in a huge way. They have a strong desire to meet the needs of others and to share the love of Christ with them.

Third, these Christians will be drawn to ministries or other acts of service that seek to restore the hurting. Perhaps the main difference from the compassion that all Christians feel for the hurting as opposed to those gifted in mercy is that others are content with making a financial contribution to help someone, but those gifted in mercy feel the need to physically serve others as well. Their gift drives them to get personally involved in the lives of others and to form a relationship with those to whom they are ministering.

And last, those with the gift of mercy have a hatred of that which causes injustice and suffering upon others. They will often be drawn to publicly speak out against that in society which causes others to suffer. In this one regard those with mercy gifts are similar to prophets who also have a special imprint from the Spirit to hate sin, evil, and injustice.

One particular Christian who had a very obvious gift of mercy was Pandita Ramabai (1858-1922). Sarasvti Ramabai was born in the Gangamula Forest of India to a strict Hindu family. She was somewhat of a child prodigy. Even though it was unheard of to educate a woman in Indian culture at the time, her mother and father taught her from her youth.

She was fluent in at least five languages. By the time she was twelve she had memorized 18,000 Sanskrit verses. Later, Hindu scholars gave her the title "Pandita" (Learned) and some thought she was the very incarnation of Saraswati, the Hindu goddess of learning. She had a very difficult life as her entire family eventually died of starvation and she was on the edge of death herself. Later she married, but her husband died of cholera less than two years later.

Although a strict Hindu, she was extremely bothered by the treatment of women in Indian culture. Girls there were routinely condemned to serve as temple prostitutes, women could not be educated, own property, and were expected to burn themselves alive on funeral pyres when their husbands died, since a woman had no worth without a husband.

On a trip to England in 1883 she met some Christians and was extremely impressed by their love and ministry to all people, including women. After being there some time she was pricked to the heart after a missionary read her the story of the Samaritan woman at the well in the fourth chapter of the book of John. Pandita later recalled of that episode:

> She read me the story of Christ meeting the Samaritan woman, and His wonderful discourse on the nature of true worship, and explained it to me. She spoke of the infinite love of Christ for sinners. He did not despise them, but came to save them. I realized, after reading the fourth chapter of St. John's Gospel, that Christ was truly the Divine Saviour He claimed to be, and no one but He could transform and uplift the downtrodden womanhood of India and of every land. Thus my heart was drawn to the religion of Christ. I was intellectually convinced of its truth...I knew full well that it would displease my friends and my countrymen very much; but I have never regretted having taken that step. I was hungry for something better than what the Hindu Sastras gave. I found it in the Christian Bible and was satisfied.[3]

After her conversion, Pandita returned to India and began several ministries to help the plight of women in India. She opened the

Mukti Mission at Kedgaon that took in widows, orphans, and other girls of lower caste, saving them from a life of begging or death.

She later became a political activist and lobbied for women's rights. She wrote a very influential book entitled, *The High Caste Hindu Woman*, which exposed the treatment of Indian women to the West, and is credited as one of the primary influences for the reforms that later came to India.

Pandita used her brilliant intellect to also do the work of a missionary evangelist. After mastering Greek and Hebrew, in her final fifteen years she single-handedly began to translate the Bible into Marathi. During the final stages of the translation she fell very ill and was on the verge of certain death. She cried out to God to give her ten more days before calling her home so she could finish proofing the translation. She finished the final proofs ten days later and then died. Her gift of mercy saved the lives of thousands of women and helped change social policy for an entire nation, for the glory of God.

KNOWLEDGE

The unique, God-given ability to perceive the truths of God and the mysteries of the faith and to share these insights for the edification of the church. 1 Corinthians 12:8, Acts 18:24-26

There is disagreement in the church today regarding the exact nature of this gift so we will take a closer look at it. It began to be popularized years ago in some charismatic circles that a "word of knowledge" was a spontaneous revelation by the Spirit. These spontaneous revelations usually revolve around some future event or some piece of information about a person that could not have been known by natural means.

For instance one might declare, "The Lord has given me a word of knowledge that there is a person in the congregation this morning who just lost their grandmother. Please come forward so that we may pray for you and your family."

The most common view of the gift of knowledge that is held by most non-charismatics is that it has to do with a special knowledge of God's truth or of God's ideal operations in His dealings with people today. After much biblical study and research I have come to the conclusion that our non-charismatic brothers and sisters have it right on this gift and that we in charismatic circles have had it wrong.

Biblical exegesis does not strongly support the revelatory view of the gift of knowledge. Before we look at what Paul probably meant by this gift, let me give you my reasons for holding to the view that the gift of knowledge has to do with deeper insights into God and His Word.

First, since Paul never defines the gift, the burden of proof lies on those who would say *gnosis* (knowledge) refers to spontaneous revelations. The word is simply not used that way throughout the rest of the New Testament. It occurs numerous times and refers to knowledge in the same sense as we use the word today, not in the sense of spontaneous revelations that suddenly come upon us.

Second, the context of 1 Corinthians 12-14 supports a non-miraculous view of knowledge. The Corinthian church is rebuked by Paul in chapter 12 because of the very fact that they were overly enamored with the more miraculous gifts like healing, miracles, and tongues. It makes sense then in 1 Corinthians 12:8-10;28 when Paul speaks of spiritual gifts to include other items deemed not so impressive (like knowledge, wisdom, helps, administration, etc.) to show the Corinthians that Christians with these kinds of gifts are also "Spirit filled" just as much as those who operate in the miraculous gifts.

Moments later Paul specifically starts a series of rhetorical questions such as "Do *all* speak in tongues, do *all* work miracles?" in an effort to further prove his point that the reception of miraculous gifts such as tongues do not equate to some new higher level of spirituality, but rather are sovereignly given by the Spirit regardless of the spiritual level of the recipient!

In other words Paul is purposely mixing so called "miraculous" gifts (tongues, miracles, healings) with so called "non-miraculous" gifts (helps, knowledge, wisdom) in an effort to show they are all from the Spirit and that there doesn't need to be any pride associated with receiving any of them.

Finally, the ability to receive supernatural revelations is indeed a valid New Testament gift, but when these occurrences appear in Scripture they are always referred to as "prophecy" not as "words of knowledge." In essence, there is already a biblical label for this phenomenon of spontaneous revelation, so good interpretation rules would require us to take Paul's use of the word "knowledge" at face value and infer that this refers to a special anointing of knowledge concerning the things of God that some receive.

I must say when I came to my own conclusions about this gift I was very pleased to find that several prominent Pentecostal and charismatic scholars such as Donald Gee, C. Peter Wagner, and most significantly, J. Rodman Williams, held similar views on the gift of knowledge.[4]

So we now arrive at the question, "What is the gift of knowledge?" Well, it's essentially an anointing from God to understand His Word, His ways, and His divine order for things. The gift of knowledge is usually shared with others in the context of a teaching although it can be equally used in a one on one basis. Some Christians seem to be able to understand God's ideal plans for the church, evangelism, relations with Islamic fundamentalism, or anything else for that matter. These Christians receive a deeper insight into these things than do the rest of us who wrestle with such things.

The primary characteristic of those with this gift is that the Lord regularly gives them special insight into His Word and His ways. Other Christians recognize that the insights and instructions from these believers are specifically given to them by the Holy Spirit.

I believe pastor Rick Warren's book, *The Purpose Driven Church*, was born out of a gift of knowledge regarding the five purposes of the church as revealed in Acts 2:42-47. That book has caused an ecclesiastical revolution of sorts within the modern church as a generation of pastors learned a better way to "do church." However, if I had to think of a Christian today that best illustrates this gift I would choose Dr. C. Peter Wagner.

Peter Wagner served as Professor of Church Growth at Fuller Theological Seminary for over thirty years. He has authored numerous books and conducted countless seminars throughout the world. God has revealed many truths to him regarding how the body of Christ can be more successful and productive in its ministry to this world.

He has been a real pioneer and has helped the church greatly in our understanding of evangelism, church growth, spiritual warfare, spiritual gifts, and on and on. His many books are basically words of knowledge that he has preserved in book form. He demonstrates greatly one who has a powerful gift mix of teacher and knowledge. When reading his books, one can easily see the teaching and knowledge gifts flowing forth from the pages. And after you finish his books, you generally understand what all was communicated and are blessed by it.

WISDOM

The unique, God-given ability to discover principles and precepts in the Word of God and to accurately apply them to everyday living so that oneself and others live skillfully and are blessed by God. 1 Corinthians 12:8, Acts 15:13-20

Sometimes the natural concepts of wisdom and knowledge get confused. Knowledge relates to knowing facts or having understanding about an issue. It is gained through study, insight, and educational experiences. Wisdom, however, relates to a mastery of the intangibles of life such as relationship dynamics, making smart decisions, and discerning the proper timing for things.

Wisdom is not dependent on one's educational level, but rather is given by God as one diligently studies the Scriptures. Every Christian who makes the serious study of the Word of God a lifetime pursuit will grow in wisdom, but some Christians receive an extra endowment of wisdom in the form of this unique spiritual gift.

Some situations in life can only be dealt with successfully by choosing the wisest course of action. For example, only wisdom can enable one to know when to apply Proverbs 26:4 vs. Proverbs 26:5. These verses read:

> Proverbs 26:4 - Do not answer a fool according to his folly, lest you also be like him.
> Proverbs 26:5 - Answer a fool as his folly deserves, lest he be wise in his own eyes.

A first reading of these two verses would appear that Solomon is offering totally contradictory advice. Well, in a sense he is. What he is saying is that there are times when you ignore foolish people because speaking to them at that time will get you nowhere. At that particular point in their lives they are not open to any correction, so don't waste your breath. However, there are other times when a rebuke given at just the right time and in just the right way will actually save a fool from the stupid decision he is about to make. How do you know when to answer a fool and when to just keep quiet? Only the wise can discern the timing.

The Lord gave Solomon the gift of wisdom in 1 Kings 3:11-12 and the Lord Himself stated that there would never be another with a stronger endowment of wisdom than Solomon. But thankfully, according to 1 Corinthians 12:8 the Lord is still distributing "words of wisdom" to His people in the form of a special gift.

The Greek word used here is *sophia*, which simply means "wisdom." First Kings 3:28 states that Israel realized God gave Solomon this ability so that he could properly administer justice. I think Paul had this in mind as well in 1 Corinthians 6:4-6 when he rebuked the Corinthians for taking each other to civil court over their disagreements rather than finding the men or women in the church gifted in wisdom who could have settled their disputes.

The Lord gives the church this gift to help her members make wise life decisions and to settle disputes so that they need not ever get beyond the walls of the church where bickering parties can bring dishonor upon God's people. It would be nice if our churches could begin to actually practice this with those in their congregations who are recognized to have this gift.

Those with the gift of wisdom have two dominant characteristics. First of all, they have their own affairs in good order. Those with the gift of wisdom, over time, show their wisdom in the life decisions they make. They make the right decisions in their personal lives, in their finances, in their dealings with those in authority over them, in their dealings with peers, and in their dealings with those subordinate to them. After a while, it becomes pretty obvious when speaking with them that they are gifted in wisdom.

A second characteristic of those with the gift of wisdom is that they can make tough decisions quickly and instinctively, and they usually don't mind confronting people with tough love and tough advice for those who seek their opinion. There is a confidence that comes from knowing that one's advice is birthed from the will of God, so there is no need to dance around issues or be uncertain when dispensing godly counsel.

A contemporary Christian of today who I believe has the gift of wisdom is Joyce Meyer. I love listening to her teaching because often somewhere in the teaching is a gem of wisdom about how to get better results when dealing with one's boss, or getting ahead in life, or dealing with a friend who is trapped in sin, or some other issue.

After I analyze the simple point she made, I can often find a proverb or other biblical verse that encapsulates the essence of what she just brilliantly stated in a unique way. By listening to her teachings, I have been able to live my life a little more skillfully by her ministering to me through one of the spiritual gifts she possesses. She happens to incorporate her gift of wisdom through one of her other primary spiritual gifts, the gift of teaching.

WORSHIP

The unique, God-given ability to usher in the presence of God during a time of worship for the purpose of drawing others into an intimate encounter with God. 1 Corinthians 14:15, 1 Samuel 16:23

In the sixteenth chapter of the book of First Samuel we read that a troubling spirit would often come upon King Saul causing him great depression. It was later discovered that if the young shepherd boy David played his harp in the presence of Saul, the troubling spirit would leave. In all of Scripture this one verse best illustrates the power of anointed worship and what it can accomplish.

Music and song have a profound impact upon the emotional and spiritual state of people. We've all felt its power. We were divinely designed to enjoy both giving and receiving music. God Himself is a lover of music and worship. It existed in heaven before the creation of humankind in the angel Lucifer who may have had musical instruments built into his very body by God (Ezekiel 28:13-14).

It's clear from Scripture that God specifically gifts some people with abilities related to worship. The Hebrew word used to describe this gift in 1 Chronicles 23:5 is *halal*, which means "to praise." There are two primary characteristics of those with this gift. The first is that they are gifted musically. These Christians are extremely talented musicians, songwriters, singers, and in some cases all three.

The second characteristic is an intangible anointing they have that has the effect of being able to draw others into a state of reverence and worship of God. I've met many Christians who have beautiful voices or who are accomplished at instruments and yet do not possess the gift of worship.

With enough determination, most people can learn to strum a guitar or play the piano, but one cannot simply acquire a spiritual gift through force of will. The anointing to lead others into worship isn't learned; it's given by God. True worshipers affect others at a spiritual level. They can transport us from where we are into the very throne room of God.

David could do that. His worship drove out evil spirits, his worship invited in the very Prince of Peace into any room he was playing in. People in the room where he was leading worship were changed. David was also an accomplished songwriter. He penned almost half of the book of Psalms by himself, contributing seventy-three out of the 150 total. Many of the psalms were put to music and became the popular hymnbook of the early Hebrews.

One of the many characteristics of our Lord is His omnificence, which He also seems to deposit especially in those with the gift of worship. These Christians seem to be able to produce new and original works throughout their lifetime that continue to bless the church.

That is certainly the case with Fanny Crosby (1820-1915) who I believe to be the most gifted worshiper of the 19th century. She composed over 5,000 hymns during her lifetime, many of which were translated into dozens of languages. Some of her greatest works came later in life while in her 70s and beyond. It has been said that her hymn, "Pass Me Not O Gentle Savior" has led more people to Christ than any other hymn. Even Ira Sankey, the song leader for the great evangelist D.L. Moody, commented that the success of their evangelistic crusades was due in large part to the anointed hymns that Crosby wrote, hymns that literally drew people to Christ.[5]

As I sit here writing, I am listening to a worship CD by Darlene Zschech, God's gift to my generation. Darlene is the worship leader of Hill Song Church in Sydney, Australia. I believe Darlene may be one of the most gifted worship leaders of the 21st century church. There is a very recognized anointing upon her music. I've done my own little experiments to test this out.

Oftentimes when I visit other churches, I observe people during worship. When a Darlene Zschech song is played, hands begin to come up all across the congregation and one can sense a change in the level of receptivity in the room. There is a noticeable effect her music has on people that can't be said to be equally true for all Christian music. I first became aware of the fact that she was not just another song leader, but a gifted worshiper when I first became aware that her songs had this effect on me.

Perhaps you've also seen the intimacy in worship go to another level when the congregation breaks into "Shout to the Lord," "I Will Run to You," "The Potter's Hand," or "I Will Bless You Lord." Those with the gift of worship have a unique gift in that it is used as a healing balm upon the hearts of the people and used to minister directly to the Lord Jesus Christ Himself.

CHAPTER 9

The Sign Gifts

MIRACLES

The unique, God-given ability to perform supernatural acts which supersede natural law for the purpose of causing others to recognize the power and glory of God. 1 Corinthians 12:10, Acts 19:11-12

Jesus told us in John 14:12, "Truly, truly, I say to you, he who believes in Me, the works that I do shall he do also; and greater works than these shall he do because I go to the Father." Verses such as this are powerfully realized in those who are endowed with the gift of miracles. The Greek phrase used for this gift in 1 Corinthians 12:10 is *energemata dunameon*, which is plural and is translated "workings of power." *Dunameon* is another form of the word *dunamis* which is usually translated "power" or "miracle" and is used in Scripture to describe a variety of supernatural feats performed by Jesus and the apostles.

One of the most amazing examples of this gift can be seen in the life of Gregory Thaumaturgus (c.210 -c.270). Born in Neocaesarea (modern-day Turkey), Gregory gave his life to Christ as a young teenager. He was taught at the feet of the great church father Origen, under which he proved to be a brilliant student who excelled in the study of philosophy and theology.

Gregory was a man of rare character and holiness who was respected by all his contemporaries. The ancient church historian Eusebius even mentions him in his writings referring to him as, "that illustrious bishop of my own day."[1] He later became bishop of Neocaesarea and it was said that his ministry and influence was so profound there that in the beginning there were only seventeen Christians in the entire city but at the time of his death there were only seventeen pagans.

Although Gregory contributed greatly to the faith through his theological writings and his pastoral care for his flock, he is most known for the miraculous deeds that were a constant throughout his ministry. The Christians of his day eventually gave him the surname "Thaumaturgus," which is Greek for "wonderworker."

We'll take a look at just a few of the miraculous feats that were performed through Gregory's ministry. One well-known deed of his involved a feud between two siblings. It seems that two young brothers were dividing their inheritance and could not agree on who was the rightful heir to a small lake on their property. Neither would compromise or agree to share the lake.

They brought the dispute to Gregory each hoping to find a ruling in his favor. Gregory would not commend the lake to either brother, but instead urged them to reconcile in Christlike love and to put peace ahead of material gain. The brothers refused and became so embittered over the property dispute that each side armed their servants and prepared to meet on a set day to literally war over possession of the lake.

Word of this got out to Gregory who went to the lake the evening before the battle was to begin and spent the whole night there in prayer. By morning the entire lake had completely dried up and the battle was called off because there was no longer a lake to fight over.[2]

Another instance involved a certain region that had a terrible stream that ran near it. This stream was given to frequent flash floods from some mountainous runoffs that also fed into it. The torrent of water from the stream's floods had many times destroyed the cattle, crops, and sometimes even homes of the locals. The town had tried to erect dikes and other measures, but nothing seemed to work.

The Christians in the town begged Gregory to come look at their situation in person and he assented. Upon looking over the banks of the stream he told the townspeople that it did not belong to man to mark the boundaries of the waters and that only God could command the limits of the stream. After his remarks he shouted loudly for the Lord to give assistance. He then placed his staff at one point at the edge of the bank and it slowly sank below. Soon thereafter a very large tree grew up where his staff had sunk. The tree created a natural barrier that prevented the stream from flooding that area ever again, much to the joy of the locals.[3]

Another incident involved Gregory traveling through a certain town full of pagan idolatry. He could find no church to enter in and pray, so he walked into a local temple and immediately felt the presence of the demons that inhabited it. He invoked the name of Jesus and ordered all demonic spirits to leave. They immediately obeyed and he stayed there all night in prayer in the consecrated "church" he had created by expelling the old tenants.

The next morning as Gregory was walking out of the city the pagan priest went into the temple and noticed that the demons were gone. No matter what invocations he tried he could not compel them to come back into the temple. When he learned what had happened the night before he was furious and caught up with Gregory and began threatening him with violence and arrest by the local authorities. Gregory rather calmly replied that his faith and

202 · Spiritual Gifts: Their Purpose & Power

power were derived from God and that he had the right to expel the demons and to send them wherever he wanted.

The priest challenged him to send the demons back in his temple to prove to him with his own eyes that Gregory had the power he boasted of. Gregory decided to assent to the man's wishes so he asked for a piece of paper. He was given it and after scribbling a message he handed it to the pagan priest. The pagan custodian took the paper and placed it on the altar and called the demons back into the temple. This time they entered again. On the paper was written, "Gregory to Satan: Enter." The demons did indeed return, having seen that the man of God had given them written permission to do so.

The priest was utterly shocked at this marvel and returned to Gregory and asked him for one more demonstration of power. He asked Gregory to move a huge rock that lay ahead that no man could possibly lift. Gregory immediately gave a command to the massive rock to move to a certain place and the rock obeyed by moving itself to that exact spot. The pagan priest was so convinced of the power of Gregory's God that he immediately left his pagan priesthood, his town, and all his possessions to follow Christ and to travel with Gregory.[4]

These are just a small sample of the miraculous events that occurred in Gregory's ministry. When it drew near to the time of his death he ordered his burial spot to remain secret so that people would not be tempted to venerate his body and thus rob God of his glory.[5]

We can see from the examples in Gregory's life just how useful and powerful the gift of miracles can be. The gift is used first of all to bless and help people that are in need. God in His wisdom sometimes allows His people to go through hardships. Sometimes the trials we go through in life are good for us because we learn to better trust Him and it causes us to mature in some aspect of our character. At other times God provides a supernatural deliverance in response to the cries of His children. Many times He chooses to use a human intermediary to bring about that deliverance.

Another purpose for the gift of miracles is to serve as a sign to the world. This gift reminds those who experience it that there is indeed an almighty, all-powerful God who commands the seas, the lands, and every living creature on the earth. Christians gifted in miracles cannot perform the miracles at their will. They must be sensitive to the voice of the Holy Spirit and act only when prompted by Him. But when so prompted and released by God to act, these servants of God can create in the Christian community a great sense of thankfulness, awe, and fear of God.

HEALING

The unique, God-given ability to cure and restore those who suffer from physical and/or emotional ailments. 1 Corinthians 12:9, Acts 3:1-8

This is a gift for which we should all be especially thankful. How good and merciful is our Father that He should grant this ability to some in the body of Christ. The whole issue of divine healing is one in which there is much confusion in the church. Two extremes exist today.

Many churches and denominations with cessationist leanings downplay this gift and don't encourage their members to seek it nor expect its operation in their midst. Sadly, this creates an institutionalized weakening of faith for millions of Christians subjected to years of such teaching. On the other side some churches teach an unbalanced view of sickness and healing in which the culprit for all sickness is said to be sin or satanic attack. This theology holds that God will always heal anyone if they only have enough faith.

As the case often is, balance is the key and the truth is somewhere in the middle. We must remember that the kingdom of God has not yet been fully established upon the earth. Jesus' earthly ministry and our current New Testament age are but first fruit tastes of that which will fully come when God fully ushers in His new kingdom (Revelation 21:1-4). Until that final consummation, the reality is that we live in a fallen world where evil exists, where we still struggle with sin, and where our bodies wear out and eventually die.

Many of society's ailments are brought on by people's foolish lifestyle choices such as excessive drinking which leads to alcoholism or the various sexually transmitted diseases due to promiscuity. How many more millions contract diabetes and other diseases each year due to gluttony or a refusal to heed to a responsible diet?

Nonetheless, in addition to these causes Scripture also points out that some illnesses are brought on by direct demonic attack (Luke 13:10-11). And though this is not popular, I would be remiss if I failed to mention divine sickness. Yes, the Bible does reveal to us that some sickness and disease is a result of the judgment of God.

Numbers 12:1-14 is a powerful reminder of this reality. Due to her rebellion and pride, Moses' own sister, Miriam, was once struck with leprosy from which God refused to heal her immediately. He allowed the disease to linger on for seven days as a warning to her. And lest we New Testament era saints feel immune from God's judgment we would all do well to read 1 Corinthians 11:27-30 and to see what the apostle Paul taught about this subject.

As we can see, there are many causes for sickness, but thankfully our God is also a God of mercy and is eager to heal His people who cry out to Him in faith. The New Testament provides us with many reasons why God healed people in biblical times and why He heals today. Let's take a look at a few of these:

REASONS GOD HEALS TODAY

Due to His compassion...	beheld the need of the crowds	Matthew 14:13-14
In response to faith...	the Canaanite woman	Matthew 15:28
For forgiveness of sin...	congregational prayer for the sick	James 5:14-15
For His own glory & honor...	an unnamed blind man	John 9:1-3
As a catalyst for evangelism...	many saved after lame man's healing	Acts 3:2 - 4:4

The Bible teaches that local churches should regularly practice prayer for the sick as part of their healing ministries (James 5:14-15), but Paul mentions in 1 Corinthians 12:9 that some Christians are specifically gifted in this area. The Greek phrase used to describe this gift is *charismata iamaton*, literally "gifts of healings." This word is related to *iaomai* which means, "to heal, to make well."

This plural reference probably refers to the fact that God distributes several varieties of the healing gift. Some may be anointed to heal the body while others have an anointing to provide deep inner healing for those with emotional and/or psychological hurts. These healers would be Spirit-anointed counselors who know how to get to the root issues of a problem and help bring the person to a place of wholeness again.

I believe the best way churches can identify those with healing gifts is to organize formal healing ministries in their churches or actively encourage prayer for the sick at special services or at the altar on Sunday mornings. Over time there will be some Christians who will rise above the others in terms of their effectiveness in praying for the sick. Once found and identified, these Christians can then be a great blessing to the church. In essence, the primary characteristic of this gift is that those who have it see people greatly improved or outright healed when they lay hands on the sick and infirm.

One misconception we need to clear up is that those with the healing gift can heal at will. On the contrary, they have to be sensitive to the Spirit and can only have effective ministry with those to whom the Spirit of God directs them. The role of discernment is especially crucial in those with healing gifts. Oftentimes before a healing can occur the root cause of the sickness must be discovered. Is the person's illness due to a satanic attack? Is there a psychosomatic root issue that needs attention first? Is the illness spiritually related, which will require repentance and confession?

Successful healings don't occur because we speak the right word/prayer formulas and manipulate God to perform a miracle. Those highly gifted in healing have learned to rely on the Spirit of God and much discernment while they minister to those the Lord brings across their path.

That being said, this is a very powerful gift of the Holy Spirit that can bring tremendous blessing to the churches that ask God for this gift and who are willing to cultivate it in those so gifted. A powerful example of this gift in operation occurred in the ministry of British evangelist Stephen Jeffreys (1876-1943). Jeffreys came out of the great Welsh revival of 1904-1905.

Accustomed to the hard labor of the coal mines at which he worked for over twenty years, he was asked to preach in 1912. He did and the results were dramatic. Always an avid soul winner since his conversion in 1904, his public preaching soon led to hundreds of conversions and invitations to preach in other towns and cities across England. However, it was soon discovered that brother Jeffreys had another gift as well. Scores of people from meetings all across England were reporting healings from every kind of sickness and affliction imaginable. Life-long bed-ridden cripples were brought to the services and left later walking out on their own. Debilitating rheumatoid arthritis was cured, along with gallstones, heart disease, and other disabilities.

One of the most notable miracles occurred one night when a little girl was brought to pastor Jeffreys by her mother. The girl had only one eye. The other was described as an empty socket covered with blank skin that resembled a thumbnail. Pastor Jeffreys laid his hands upon her and entreated the Lord for her healing. When he removed his hands from her eyes, to the absolute astonishment of the crowd, was a brand new perfectly proportioned blue eye that matched the other! They blindfolded her old eye and she reported that she could see fine with the new eye the Lord had just given her.

A skeptical pastor from another town who was in attendance that night at the urging of a friend, stuck around and later declared, "At these healing services I was privileged to witness a hundred miracles in that one week. It is the Lord's doing, and like living in the Acts of the Apostles."[6]

PROPHECY

The unique, God-given ability to receive an inspired message from God that is then shared with others to bring encouragement, edification, or correction. 1 Corinthians 12:10, Luke 2:25-35

The Greek word used to describe this gift is *propheteia* from which we get our word "prophecy." It comes from the verb *prophemi*, which means, "to speak forth." Another related verb used commonly in the New Testament would be *propheteuo* which means, "to proclaim; to make known." In my opinion, many teachers incorrectly define the gift of prophecy as the ability to speak well and thus associate it with the ability to preach good sermons. Scripture does not define prophecy as great oratory skill.

Both Moses and the apostle Paul had recognized prophetic gifts, and yet the Bible portrays both as unimpressive public speakers (Exodus 4:10, 2 Corinthians 11:6). The essence of the gift of prophecy is the ability to receive an immediate revelation from God about something and to then proclaim or "make known" that revelation for another person's well being.

There can definitely be a revelatory, predictive element to prophecy, but a message from God does not always have to be about some future event. As we observed earlier, prophecy in the Bible is portrayed as both forth telling and foretelling. The key ingredient that makes something a "prophecy" is that the message is divinely given by God for that specific occasion. It doesn't come from our observation of others, our own wisdom, or what we think would be "helpful" to share with another person.

Therefore, sometimes a prophecy could be something as simple as one declaring in a congregation, "I feel the Lord is saying the time for weeping is over, your sin is forgiven, behold the Lord says to you my daughter, 'Behold I make all things new, I have separated your sin as far as the east is from the west, I remember them no longer.'"

Now suppose a young woman in the congregation has been unable to forgive herself for a recent transgression and has spent the last eight nights literally crying herself to sleep. In the midst of a worship service, the Lord places those very words on the heart of someone to share publicly. The one gifted in prophecy shares it and the Holy Spirit uses those words to cut to the heart and release her from her condemnation. She leaves able to forgive herself and feels as if a ninety-pound weight has been removed from her shoulders.

That is "prophecy" just as much as if one also called out the girl by name and gave other details which couldn't possibly have come to the person by natural means. Prophetic messages are sometimes about the future and sometimes about the divine timing to say something just the right way, at just the right moment, to just the right person, so as to cause a spiritual change in the heart of the recipient. How is this done? It's done because the Holy Spirit tells the person the essence of what to say. When the Holy Spirit tells you what to say, it's always the right thing for the right occasion! This is what Paul had in mind when speaking of the gift of prophecy in 1 Corinthians 14:3.

Prophetic statements usually come in the midst of an assembly of believers or in our one-on-one ministry to others. However, sometimes the Lord will use them in the middle of a sermon or teaching in which one particular point will leap out and minister to the heart of the hearers.

I sometimes wonder if this is the case with one of my favorite preachers, Dr. Tony Evans, of Oak Cliff Bible Fellowship in Dallas, Texas. Often in the middle of one of his sermons there seems to be an especially anointed part of the sermon where my spirit receives deep ministry from what he is saying. I get the sense that the Holy Spirit perhaps even directed the way in which he delivered the point.

An example of one who I believe had a prophetic gifting was the great 19th century Baptist pastor, Charles Spurgeon (1834-1892). The Lord used the prophetic gift quite often through Spurgeon's preaching, which was recognized by everyone in his day as being especially anointed by the Spirit. Spurgeon himself knew where the real credit lay in his phenomenally effective preaching ministry:

> Now I believe the Holy Spirit led me to read that hymn. And many persons have been converted by some striking saying of the preacher. But why was it the preacher uttered that saying? Simply because he was led thereunto by the Holy Spirit...Rest assured, beloved, that when any part of the sermon is blessed to

your heart, the minister said it because he was ordered to say it by his Master...

Until our churches honor the Holy Spirit, we shall never see him abundantly manifested in our midst. Let the preacher always confess before he preaches that he relies upon the Holy Spirit. Let him burn his manuscript and depend upon the Holy Spirit...And best of all, if you all would have the Holy Spirit, let us meet together earnestly to pray for him. Remember, the Holy Spirit will not come to us a church, unless we seek Him.[7]

Spurgeon's prophetic gift would cause him to sometimes stop in the middle of his sermon and speak out a revelation that God had just given him. Some of these revelations would shock the congregation or the guests who were visiting, and many of them led to the person's salvation after the power of God was demonstrated before their very eyes.

One notable case involved a man who was converted under Spurgeon's preaching. The man's wife refused to attend with him. However, hearing of Spurgeon's powerful preaching and his notoriety in the city, she plotted to attend one of his services out of curiosity.

Disguising herself with a thick veil and shawl, she entered the hall after the service had already begun. Upon ascending the stairwell to the upper gallery, Spurgeon turned, pointed directly at her, and quoting 1 Kings 14:6 declared, "Come in, thou wife of Jeroboam; why feignest thou thyself to be another? For I am sent to thee with heavy tidings."[8]

Another occasion occurred while preaching in Exeter Hall. Spurgeon stopped mid-sentence, and pointing to one in the congregation said, "Young man, those gloves you are wearing have not been paid for. You have stolen them from your employer." After the service the young man, shocked and startled, tearfully confessed to Spurgeon, "It's the first time I have robbed my master, and I will never do it again. You won't expose me sir, will you? It would kill my mother if she heard that I had become a thief."[9]

In his autobiography, Spurgeon remarked that:

I could tell as many as a dozen similar cases in which I pointed at somebody in the hall without having the slightest knowledge of the person, or any idea that what I said was right, except that I believed I was moved by the Spirit to say it; and so striking has been my description, that the persons have gone away, and said to their friends, "Come, see a man that told me all things I ever did; beyond a doubt, he must have been sent of God to my soul, or else he could not have described me so exactly." And not only so, but I have known many instances in which the thoughts of men have been revealed from the pulpit. I have sometimes seen persons nudge their neighbors with their elbow, because they had got a smart hit, and they have been heard to say when they were going out, "The preacher told us just what we said to one another when we went in the door."[10]

Those with the gift of prophecy will regularly receive revelations from the Lord. This is the primary distinguishing characteristic of those with this gift. These revelations are generally given to minister to others in a more effective way. They are usually words of encouragement, confirmation, or consolation. Although sometimes the Lord will reveal dangers, traps by the enemy, or even the sins of others that He wants them to deal with. These revelations usually come in the form of deep inner impressions. Sometimes prophetic revelations can come through dreams, visions, or while reading a passage of Scripture.

The only way to confirm if one has this gift is to step out in faith in the promptings God gives and see what effect it has on others. Are their predictive messages later proved to be accurate? Are their messages of comfort or confrontation effective; do they cause a change in the hearts of others? True prophetic gifts are eventually recognized by the larger body of Christ and are therefore confirmed over time.

Those possessing this gift must learn how to share a word in such a way as to cause it to be received by the one it's directed to. As much as I admire Spurgeon, I do not agree with the practice of calling out the sins of others in a public worship service!

If the Holy Spirit strongly indicates that the revelation is not just to be prayed about, but is also to be shared, then it can be done quite sufficiently in private where it does not cause embarrassment or humiliation to the recipient. If he were alive today and Spurgeon's ability was recognized in the churches I've attended in the past, the leadership would have spent some time teaching him prophetic etiquette and protocol so that his gift could be more properly integrated into the ministry of the church. By all means share positive encouraging words publicly when appropriate, as they are a great testimony to the power of Almighty God and are a wonderful demonstration to unbelievers who may be visiting the service that day.

DELIVERANCE

The unique, God-given ability to perceive and confront demonic forces and to bring freedom to those trapped in demonic bondage. Mark 16:17, Luke 10:17

Mark 16:17 speaks of some Christians who will cast out demons. The Greek word used there is *ekballosien*, taken from the verb *ekballo*, which means "to throw out, to drive out."

Many Christians who have come to believe in the reality of spiritual warfare have become unbalanced in this area so some cautionary directives are in order. First of all we need to realize that the Bible does teach that there is a real devil and that there are literal real demons under his control. Those who don't believe this or who don't teach that we should bother ourselves with demons are actually under a demonic deception themselves and are playing right into the strategy of the enemy.

As far as I know there was no "Demoniac Treaty of A.D. 95" in which the demons and apostles made a deal saying to each other, "We apostles agree to all die off if you demons all agree to go underground and not harass God's people any longer." It would have been nice, but that's just not the case. That being said, there are demonic legions at work in the world today operating under the Lord's sovereign parameters.

However, we must not make the opposite error, which is to see a demon under every bush. I've met Christians who attribute almost every sin or hardship in life to the devil and who go around rebuking Satan at the drop of a hat. The only remedy for such imbalance is the same remedy that solves much of everything else—spiritual maturity. We have to realize that demons are real and that we should not go seeking to confront them, but when they do rear their ugly head in our lives or in the lives of those we are ministering to, we should deal with them with the power and the blood of Jesus.

The New Testament is full of examples of demonic activity, and we can learn much from studying the passages that speak of them. Scripture portrays both Christians and non-Christians as being demonically harassed at various times and in varying degrees throughout their lives (see 1 Chronicles 21:1, Luke 9:51-56, Acts 5:1-3). However, there is a great deal of disagreement as to whether a Christian can fully be demon possessed.

Incidentally, the very designation "demon possession" is misleading because it forces us to think of demonic activity in terms of two extremes, those "possessed" and those "not possessed." Actually this rigid distinction is foreign to the New Testament. The Bible actually uses the Greek term *daimonizomai*, which means to be "afflicted by" or "oppressed by" a demon. This word is sometimes more accurately translated in our English Bibles as "to have a spirit," but it is sometimes translated as "possessed by a spirit" which is a much harsher translation than the original Greek meaning of the word.

Therefore when we speak about a person who is "possessed" by a demonic spirit, the Bible would simply say that the individual is being oppressed by or troubled by a spirit. This vexation, however, may range from mild to severe. I prefer the term "demonized" rather than "demon possessed."

One could classify the severity of demonic influence by looking at the extent to which the demon has control of an individual's will. In light of this, it may be helpful to look at demonization in terms of three stages of severity. These three stages are: demon suggestion, demon oppression, and demon possession (or severe demonization).

Demonic harassment could be mild, as was the case of the apostle Peter in Matthew 16:23 when Jesus recognizes the influence behind Peter's confession. This mild influence of demons working in the thinking of God's people is quite common and ought to drive Christians to be in a constant state of repentance and watchfulness.

Others may be more demonized to the extent that they are oppressed by a constant demonic presence that affects their thinking, personality, and lifestyle. Habitual patterns of unhealthy behavior and sin are a possible indication that an individual is demon oppressed. This could manifest itself as habitual negativity, continued sexual promiscuity, or a compulsive addiction that one cannot seem to shake. People in this stage of demonization are many times aware of a driving force that seems to control various aspects of their will. At this stage individuals may find it hard to rid themselves of the spirit and may require the assistance of other Christians in prayer and accountability to do so.

The most severe form of demonization is what most call "demon possession." At this stage the individual cannot break free from the demonic bondage without assistance from others. In this stage the demons have almost complete control of the victim's mind, will, and emotions, and the victims are easily manipulated and controlled by the demon or demons. At this point the demons can actually speak through the people they have invaded and can control their motor actions as well, as was the case with the Gadarene demoniac in Mark 5:1-20. It is this state of severe demonization that requires deliverance or the person has no hope of getting any better.

Thankfully the Lord has provided in the body of Christ certain Christians who seem to have an anointing for deliverance. Most of those gifted in deliverance also have the gift of discernment that is a natural complement to this gift. One of the most gifted Christians that I know of today who sometimes ministers in this area is a Southern Baptist evangelist, Dr. Sam Cathey. He is a very well-respected minister and has preached hundreds of revival services in Baptist churches across the country. He's also given numerous addresses at the annual convention and many of the state conventions as well.

Brother Sam disagrees with me on this topic in that he doesn't consider deliverance as a specific spiritual gift, but rather as a function of the church that every Christian can perform. However, I'm the world's foremost authority on my own opinion and I say he has the gift! In his years of ministry he has been used by the Lord to help bring deliverance to hundreds of people.

What I so appreciate about him is that he keeps the Lord Jesus as the focus of his ministry. He doesn't glorify the supernatural deliverance ministry, but he is certainly prepared to do warfare in his dealings with people who come to him for help. One dramatic deliverance session he once told me about occurred during a week of revival services in a certain church in which a young woman came to him wanting to be free from several compulsive sins that plagued her. She was involved in immorality, continually used drugs, and often stole from her parents to support her sinful lifestyle. She wanted desperately to stop but couldn't.

As brother Sam was counseling her and leading her in a confessional prayer of repentance, the young woman began violently shaking and spitting. An evil voice came shrieking out of her cursing and taunting brother Sam and his wife and the local pastor and his wife who were in the room. At the same time, the woman and the chair she was sitting in began to rise three or four feet into the air and began floating! The powerful name of Jesus was invoked and deliverance was wrought that evening in the life of that young woman and she was never the same.[11] To the best of his knowledge, she is still free to this day.

Some sins and addictions are not just the flesh; they are demonic in origin, and unless spiritual weapons are used there can be no victory. One doesn't counsel demons out. They have to be cast out. Brother Sam pastored Graceway Baptist Church in Oklahoma City, Oklahoma in the early 1990s where the church developed a "warfare council" of trained Christians who were able to minister and see others set free. I wish that all of God's churches recognized the need for this type of ministry today.

It is indeed sad as I look at the body of Christ today and see so many Christians living defeated lives and not realizing that in many cases they cannot have the victory because of demonic strongholds that have never been diagnosed, let alone broken in their lives. How true is the Word of God when it tells us, "My people are destroyed for lack of knowledge…" (Hosea 4:6).

TONGUES

The unique, God-given ability to communicate with God in a special, heavenly language for the purpose of praise, intercession, and spiritual edification. 1 Corinthians 12:10, Acts 19:6

A careful read of Scripture will reveal that the New Testament speaks of two distinct types of speaking in tongues. The first type involves tongues that are known, understandable languages, and the second type are unknown tongues which are not representative of any known language on the earth. We see an example of this first type in Acts chapter 2.

At the Day of Pentecost the believers were all filled with the Spirit and began to speak in foreign languages they had never learned. Luke records for us in verses 7-8 that the unbelievers gathered around and said to one another, "…Why, are not all these who are speaking Galileans? And how is it that we each hear them in our own language to which we were born?" There are reports from time to time of the Lord using this type of tongues still today. I have heard a few missionary stories about the Lord using a brother or sister on the field to reach a tribe by enabling the missionary in a special circumstance to speak the natives' language they have never studied.

When we get to the book of 1 Corinthians we hear the apostle Paul speaking about another type of tongues which he refers to as "tongues of angels" in 1 Corinthians 13:1. He also states in 1 Corinthians 14:14, "For if I pray in a tongue, my spirit prays, but my mind is unfruitful." This of course refers to the fact that when praying in tongues even the ones praying have no idea what they are saying. It is in the context of this second type of tongues about which Paul speaks of its distribution across the body of Christ in the form of a distinct spiritual gift. Paul emphasizes in

1 Corinthians 12:30 that this gift is not given to everyone, but for those who do have it, they enjoy a powerful and intimate gift from the Holy Spirit.

The charismatic movement has greatly emphasized the blessings of this particular gift and the result has been that many people have sought the Lord to bestow this gift upon them. Paul teaches in 1 Corinthians 14:1 that we can earnestly desire and pray for certain gifts. For many who have desired this gift their prayers have been answered. The word used to describe this gift is *glosson*, which means, "tongues." Exactly as in English, the primary Greek meaning of the word is the physical organ of speech; the secondary meaning of the word is language. This is a gift of language, a spiritual language.

Tongues are used as a special language of prayer in which the spirit more than the mind does the praying. Those who pray in tongues do not know what they are praying. The Christian may be praying for foreign missionaries, praising God with majestic adulations, or he or she may be praying that their faith be matured through a season of trials, which is something that we would not normally pray for when our mind does the praying!

Praying in tongues is a beautiful sign of intimacy with God in which the spirit communicates directly to the Lord. Some espouse that praying in tongues has added benefits in spiritual warfare as the enemy cannot understand what is being said when Christians pray this way. I would lean that they may be right, but to be honest the Bible simply does not tell us this, so at best it is just an opinion.

A secondary function of the gift, besides the private devotional use, is when the Lord will impress on someone with this gift to give a public proclamation in tongues. When this occurs the Lord will often grant someone the gift of interpretation so that the message delivered in tongues can be translated into an understandable message that can exhort or bless the entire congregation. In this use, the gift of tongues becomes very similar to the gift of prophecy in which the tongues are used to send an edifying message to God's people.

If no interpreter is present, then the one speaking in tongues should not continue to speak in a loud, public way, as without interpretation the gift cannot edify anyone and it could cause confusion for those who don't understand this unique phenomenon (1 Corinthians 14:23-28).

Perhaps one of the greatest examples of one with this gift would be William Seymour (1870-1922). Seymour, born in Centerville, Louisiana, was the son of former slaves. He was an old-fashioned holiness preacher who had later come to believe in the gifts of the Spirit and the validity of speaking in tongues. In the early 1900s the small Pentecostal movement was not yet respected or accepted by mainstream Christianity, but that was about to change. In 1906 Seymour accepted the call to pastor a holiness church in Los Angeles, California.

The church was located at 312 Azusa Street. Soon after his arrival, a revival broke out that lasted three years.[12] During those three years the gifts of the Spirit were poured out in an unprecedented way. Seymour also spoke in tongues, and from his little church the revival spread all over California, America, and across the world as people were drawn to the church to witness the power of God. It was later known as the Azusa Street Revival. It was the birthplace of the modern Pentecostal/charismatic movement.

How typical it is of God to use vessels man would never consider. Who in the early 1900s in that day of racial strife and discrimination would have ever guessed that God would use an uneducated black holiness preacher from the deep South to be His choice of who would inaugurate the most powerful worldwide revival the church had ever experienced. Let us always remember that "…God sees not as man sees, for man looks at the outward appearance, but the Lord looks at the heart" (1 Samuel 16:7).

MARTYRDOM

The unique, God-given ability to endure suffering and persecution for the cause of Christ and yet maintain a spirit of joy and thankfulness for the purposes of witnessing to the oppressors and inspiring the church at large. John 21:18-19, Acts 21:13

One October morning in 2001, Pakistani pastor Emmanuel Atta preached from Ephesians 3:13-16. He was exhorting his congregation to stay faithful to God in prayer and to not lose heart in their tribulations. Life can be very difficult for Christians in Pakistan, who number less than 5 percent of the population.

As he was concluding his message three Muslim fundamentalists stormed into the worship service and pointing automatic weapons at pastor Atta, demanded he throw his Bible onto the ground. Pastor Atta refused, but instead he tightly embraced his Bible and moved it toward his heart. Angered by his refusal to disrespectfully throw God's Word onto the floor the three men opened fire on the entire congregation and fled away. Moments later Pastor Atta lay dead in his pulpit along with fifteen members of his congregation.[13] He left behind a wife and six children.

As tragic as this is, what's more tragic is that this threat is the norm for millions of Christians every day in other parts of the world. When most of us think of Christian martyrs, we think back to biblical times when evil Roman emperors like Nero or Diocletian made sport of killing Christians in the coliseums. But the truth is that more Christians were killed for their faith in the twentieth century than in all previous centuries combined.

It is as if the spirit of anti-Christ and the forces of darkness grow more desperately wicked as they sense the coming of the Lord drawing ever closer. Satan's last-days strategy has been to stir up in groups and nations a hatred of Christ and His people on a scale that is almost unimaginable. World Christian scholar David Barrett states that seventy million Christians have been killed for their faith in the last two thousand years and that forty-five million of those deaths occurred in the twentieth century alone.[14] Said another way, of all the Christians ever killed for their faith, 64 percent occurred in the century we were born and grew up in!

Until the return of the Lord, we must all realize that we are active combatants in a cosmic war between God Almighty and Satan and his forces. As in every war, there are causalities on both sides. Satan attempts to undermine the work of the gospel by attacking God's people in many ways.

One of the ways he seeks to do this is by influencing various groups and nations to actively oppose and persecute God's people. The early church had to endure the pagan Roman Empire, and saints in the Middle Ages had to worry with despot monarchs and the Inquisition.

Christians in the twentieth and twenty-first centuries have to contend with communism and radical Islamic fundamentalism. In the past few decades millions of believers in the former Soviet Union, China, and North Korea have been brutally murdered or sent to harsh work camps where they died of starvation or exhaustion. Millions of others have died in places like Sudan where Islamic Sharia law was instituted in 1983. Due to a policy of forced Islamization, Christians there routinely have their homes burnt to the ground, are harassed, and oftentimes killed by their radical Muslim rulers.

In Matthew 10:17-18 Jesus states that some of His people will be brought before kings and rulers to serve as witnesses for Him. Their abuse, and sometimes death, serve as tangible proof or "signs" of the wickedness of humankind and their refusal to heed the gospel. In this sovereign role of suffering and ultimate sacrifice laid before them, the Holy Spirit supernaturally endows some brave men and women with the ability to undergo the persecution and maintain the perspective and love of Christ while going through it. While martyrdom is not specifically called a spiritual gift in Scripture, Paul does seem to allude to it as such in 1 Corinthians 13:3.

Those with this gift and calling are very similar to the brave soldier who in the midst of battle sees his country's flag lying on the ground in an open field. In an act of bravery and respect for what he's fighting for, he wades out amidst the continued gunfire and picks up the banner and waves the flag rallying the pride, courage, and determination of his comrades. His selfless act rallies the troops to fight on for their cause, but while standing and waving the flag he is hailed down in a sea of gunfire.

All the soldiers in the trenches saw the battered flag being mocked as it lay in the mud, but none dared move. How is it that some seem to have a courage to rise up in holy anger and hoist the flag up knowing it may cost them their very life? Only God knows. In some parts of the world the wicked rulers say, "There is no God," "The party is your God," "Throw your Bibles down and let none speak the name of Jesus in this place!"

While many Christians feel compelled to go underground and pray for a change of circumstances, ministering in whatever ways they can under the terrible circumstances they find themselves in, others feel another call. Knowing that defiance will mean certain death, they feel the Spirit's call speaking gently to their heart saying, "take no thought for what you shall say, I will give you the very words in this hour." These Christians stand in the midst of their comrades and to the rulers say, "I will not throw down my Bible and I will not cease to proclaim the name of the one true God, the Lord Jesus Christ." And down they go. Precious in the sight of the Lord is the death of His saints. (Psalms 116:15).

DISCOVERING AND GROWING IN THE GIFTS

CHAPTER 10

Discovering Your Spiritual Gifts

TAKE NOTE OF YOUR MINISTRY PASSIONS

I hope that while reading over the thirty different gift vignettes your heart was particularly stirred by some of them. As a Christian you have a guarantee from God Himself that you too possess some of those amazing gifts that you were just reading about!

The first step in discovering your spiritual gifts is to take a careful introspective look at yourself in regards to spiritual matters. What aspect of serving God do you most enjoy? What ministry activities bring you the most fulfillment?

When we are serving in the areas that utilize our giftings, we will be content and enjoy our service to God. When we try to operate in areas outside of our giftings, we will be frustrated, bored, overwhelmed, and generally not very happy. The reason for this is that we are "out of our element" so to speak. We are attempting to produce spiritual results in an area where we are not especially gifted to function. Therefore, the first key to discovering your unique giftedness is to spend some time thinking about what you enjoy doing in your service to God.

Do you love seeing people grow by sharing what the Word has to say about a particular issue? Is studying the Bible something the preacher has to keep telling you to do, or do you do it naturally because you love to discover its teachings? If this sounds like you, you may have the gift of teaching.

Are you always the one who notices the little things that others overlook? Are you the one who doesn't seem to worry about the limelight, you just want to help people in practical ways? Does it give you a profound sense of joy to clean someone's house, to bring over a meal when a neighbor is sick, or to spend time serving someone who you sense really needs it? If this is you, you probably have a gift of serving.

What are your ministry passions? What do you dream to do, hope that you get asked to do, and love to do for God? Individual Christians will naturally drift toward and be attracted to ministries that utilize their gifts. Therefore, "gift drift" is a phenomenon that needs to be carefully observed by individuals themselves and by the leaders of a church as a means to identify a person's gift. Spend some time examining your feelings and ministry passions. Your conclusions to these thoughts will point you toward your gifts.

PRAYER

A second and equally important step is to begin spending serious prayer time with the Lord, asking Him about your giftings. We are told in 1 John 5:14 that if we ask anything according to His will He will hear us. We know from 1 Corinthians 12:1 that the Lord specifically does not want us to be ignorant about our spiritual gifts. Now I'm not a gambling man, but there are two things I'll bet the Carraway farm on: 1) The District of Columbia will go for the Democratic presidential candidate in the next election, and 2) If Christians ask God to reveal to them their spiritual gifts, He will.

The Lord desires for His children to know their gifts, and if we earnestly seek Him about them, He will reveal them to us. As you have no doubt learned by now spiritual discovery is a process and it takes time. Be patient; trust God. As you continue to grow in your faith, live for Him each day, and what your hand finds to do, do it well as unto the Lord.

Tell Him of your desire to not want to waste your talents. Tell Him that you want to put the majority of your time and energies into the ministries that He has best suited you for. Thank Him for His kindness in gifting you and let Him know that you are thankful that He is going to steadily reveal His will to you and that the gifts of the Spirit He's placed within you will become more and more obvious as time passes. If you already believe you know your giftings, you can ask the Lord to confirm them. Remember, Jesus promised us in Matthew 7:7-8, "Ask and it shall be given to you; seek, and you shall find; knock, and it shall be opened to you. For everyone who asks receives, and he who seeks finds, and to him who knocks it shall be opened."

ANALYZING YOUR EFFECTIVENESS IN MINISTRY

Another aspect we need to consider is our past and present ministry effectiveness, for it will be another key that will point us towards our gift. Because of our gifting we should naturally be more successful in certain ministries than others in our church. What do you seem to be better able to do than most of the Christians you know? What commands of Jesus do you perform more consistently than do other Christians you know? Which activities around the church do you usually get involved with because you know you can do them and do them well?

These are important questions you need to consider. If you are gifted in evangelism, you'll be winning souls much more regularly than the average Christian. If you are gifted in intercession, you will pray harder, longer, and more often than those around you. In essence, what you are now doing, and doing well, will also shed much light on your giftings.

You may be saying to yourself, "I don't know where I'm effective in ministry." It may be that you have never stepped out in faith and begun to serve the Lord in a certain ministry area. That's OK, because after you finish reading this book that is going to change. You are going to begin getting involved in the ministries of your church because you know that God has given you a gift and you're not going to waste it a day longer!

You need to begin trying your hand at the different ministries your church offers. Over the next year or two you'll begin to see which ministries you *enjoy*, and you'll also see which ministries you're *good at*. These two criteria alone will take you far down the path of spiritual gifts discovery.

A word of advice needs to be said here. When you begin analyzing your effectiveness in ministry, you need to be honest with yourself. When you attempt to teach a lesson and everyone (including your dear old mama who is so proud of you) falls asleep, you're probably not gifted with teaching. If you have a habit of giving "prophetic words" to people and they habitually don't come to pass, nor do they seem to inspire the body of Christ around you, you're probably not the prophet you think you are.

Most of us have at one time desired to have the really miraculous glamour gifts like miracles and healing. It's much more prestigious to be introduced as…"This is Martha Shlumpberger, one of the most powerful deliverance ministers in our church!" rather than, "This is Martha Shlumpberger, one of the best helpers in our church!" We need to put the flesh aside and not try to convince people that we operate in gifts we don't have. We need to be thankful to God for the gifts we do have and use them for His glory and for the advancement of His kingdom. To do anything less than that only leads to wasting precious time and eventually ruining our credibility.

Take a Spiritual Gifts Test

I've heard people bash spiritual gift tests saying, "You can't determine someone's God-given gift by using a man-made questionnaire." I strongly disagree. We know a lot about spiritual gifts in the twenty-first-century church and we've had our theories confirmed through time and observation. People with certain gifts exhibit specific behavioral traits and specific abilities. We can do a fairly good job of describing these abilities and traits, create an objective set of questions that test for the presence or absence of these traits, and then ascribe a numerical value or "score" that an individual has in relation to a particular gift.

While spiritual gifts tests are not the final say, they can be a valuable tool in confirming your gifts, and I highly recommend them. I believe the primary way we discover our gifts is through examining our passions and by evaluating our level of effectiveness in various ministries that we try. Therefore, I advise the use of spiritual gifts tests as a confirming tool, not as the primary way to discover our gifts. The key factor in the effectiveness of the various spiritual gifts tests available today is that they be well written and that people answer the questions honestly.

The Carraway Spiritual Gifts Inventory is a statistically validated instrument in which the questions are designed to test both inward motivations and outcome-based abilities. Since this is a self-assessment instrument, the true key to the accuracy of the test is that you answer the questions honestly.

Most people who take the test score in the high 15-20 range in perhaps two to five gifts. There will be some variation of this as we are all gifted differently, but if you find yourself scoring in the

15-20 range for ten or fifteen different gifts, then there is a very good chance you are answering inaccurately as most people don't have that many spiritual gifts!

Only the Lord Jesus expressed all the gifts perfectly, so it will be extremely rare to find one Christian who prays constantly (intercessor), *and* regularly leads people to Christ (evangelist), *and* gives liberally and above at all times (giver), *and* regularly gives accurate prophetic words (prophet), *and* is a constant source of encouragement (exhortation) and on and on. When taking the test, only score yourself as a "4" if you really engage in that activity all the time. It is in your best interest to be accurate in your answers so you can narrow down your list of true spiritual gifts. That way you'll only be spending time developing in the areas where you truly are divinely created to succeed.

GET CONFIRMATION FROM OTHER CHRISTIANS

Lastly, when trying to determine our gifts, we need to be open to the observations of others. God often uses other people to speak into our lives. The Lord will often send someone our way who will encourage us and prove to be instrumental in our further ministry development. These individuals will have insight that we don't have, and they may be able to see potential gifts within us that we ourselves never realized were there.

If you feel you know what your primary spiritual gifts are and you've had them confirmed with a gift inventory also, then the next step is that you need to speak with those closest to you and get their feedback as well. Do they not agree with your own assessment of your spiritual gifts? If not, rather than getting upset with them, perhaps you need to spend more time in prayer and reflection to see if you've missed something. Could it be that your flesh wanted those gifts but God has in fact gifted you in another way?

I firmly believe that the body of Christ confirms the giftings of other members in the body. If those closest to you agree with your own assessment of your gifts then you can begin to get more and more confident that you do indeed possess those specific gifts. Pay attention to the comments, compliments, and even the constructive criticism that other Christians offer you. Within those comments could be revelation that you need to receive.

CHAPTER 11

Maturing in Your Spiritual Gifts

CULTIVATE YOUR RELATIONSHIP WITH JESUS

Without a doubt the single most important factor in determining the growth of our spiritual gifts is the quality of our relationship with Jesus. Our growth will be proportionally related to our personal daily walk with Him. In John 15:1-11 Jesus tells us that we can do nothing apart from Him. Only those "in the vine," those intimately connected to Him, can ever truly do a significant work for God.

As Christians we must understand that true spiritual maturity is an awareness of an ever-increasing dependency upon God. As the apostle Paul so aptly said in Acts 17:28, "In Him we live and move and have our being (KJV)." As we grow closer to Jesus day-by-day and year-by-year, we begin to experience growth in every area in our lives. We become more patient. We become more sensitive to the sin in our lives. We tend to lose the desire for notoriety, and simply want to be servants in the kingdom of God. The still small voice of the Spirit, which was once so difficult to hear, gradually becomes clear.

And as we grow closer to our Lord, the endowments given to us by the Holy Spirit grow stronger as well. If our gift is discernment, our discerning abilities grow stronger. If we are gifted in evangelism, our passion for souls increases throughout our lives. The gifts grow in us as we grow in Him.

To see our spiritual gifts developed to their fullest extent, we must make our relationship with Jesus our number one priority. The Lord Jesus and His supremacy in our life can never be compromised. Our desires, our schedules, our affections, all belong to Him. If we will keep Jesus in His proper place as Lord of our lives, our Christian lives will indeed be a success. As we maintain that close intimate walk with Him, the gifts of the Spirit flow out of us as we minister in His name.

How do we cultivate our relationship with Jesus? The same way we keep our other relationships strong. We spend time with the Lord and do those things that are pleasing in His sight. Our relationship with God is a personal one, and there is no formula for getting closer to God. There are, however, certain things that must be done to keep that relationship strong.

In my life I have five spiritual disciplines that I live by. These are like five core values that I observe in order to keep my heart tender towards God. They are: meditation on the Word, prayer, separation from the world, fellowship with the church, and obedience to God. I believe that if sincere Christians will put these things into practice, their relationship with Jesus will grow exponentially. Let's take a look at each one in more detail.

MEDITATION ON THE WORD

The primary way in which God speaks to His children is through His Word. Therefore if we want a close relationship with God, we are going to have to be the kind of Christians who regularly meditate on the Word of God. First of all, we have to decide to make time for reading God's Word. It is unrealistic to expect that we will spend hours and hours reading the Bible every day. Most of us have families, a job, and many other responsibilities. We can, however, make time for devotional reading of at least thirty minutes each day.

In addition to devotional reading, we need to set aside some time regularly for pure studying purposes. Every Christian should know the Bible's teachings and precepts on the major issues of life. One cannot know the mind and heart of God and not know His Word. God will speak to us through the Bible if we will take the time to read it and listen for that still small voice. Several benefits are ours when we read God's Word.

First of all, by reading and meditating on the Word of God, we actually grow our faith. Romans 10:17 states, "Faith comes from hearing, and hearing by the Word of Christ." As we feed our souls on a steady diet of the truths of the Bible, God imparts a supernatural portion of faith and expectancy into us to believe His claims.

Second, it is the Word of God that develops discernment in the life of the believer. Hebrews 5:14 mentions this important role: "But solid food (the Word of God) is for the mature, who because of practice have their senses trained to discern good and evil." When Christians continually spend time in the Word of God, they begin to become familiar with God's nature, purposes, and methodology.

As they interact with others in religious or secular settings, they develop an ability to almost immediately know if actions and attitudes are of the Spirit or of the flesh. This is certainly needed when the gifts of the Spirit are being practiced as well.

The Word of God is the anchor in the Christian's life. We should cherish it, meditate upon it, and let it guide us in all our endeavors.

PRAYER

Prayer is vital to keeping our relationship with God fresh and growing. Many Christians have a very carnal prayer life that mainly consists of asking God to bless their family and meet their laundry list of needs. Conversely, our prayers should be Spirit-led prayers in which God determines much of what we bring before Him.

Again, this is a skill and type of praying that must be learned. We have to learn to pray this way just like we have to learn to hear the voice of God. We have to guard our prayer time, for the enemy will see to it that this does not become a habit in our lives. Satan realizes that if we ever get really connected to God by establishing a strong prayer life, then we become Christians who are dangerous to him.

Paul tells us in 1 Thessalonians 5:17 that we are to "pray without ceasing." We ought to be in communication with our heavenly Father throughout each day. We ought to talk with Him when we first get up, while at work, even while we are at the grocery store. If we will get in the habit of bringing all our business before the Lord, we will discover that He has lots to say to us about everything. Begin to discipline yourself to inquire of the Lord's will in all things as you go about your day. Throughout the day praise Him and tell Him how much you love Him. Get in the habit of being half in tune with this world and half in tune with God at the same time. After practicing this for a while it will become second nature.

We all need to get into the spiritual habit Paul called praying "without ceasing." It will reap huge rewards for us in terms of intimacy with the Lord. Surprise God this week by conversing with Him at times other than your structured settings. You'll be surprised by what you hear when you have these little talks throughout the day. The closer you are to God and the more you are around Him, the more you overhear.

SEPARATION FROM THE WORLD

Sin affects every area of the Christian's life, and the gifts of the Spirit are no exception. When we allow sin to enter our lives, we can begin to lose the anointing of God. God seeks to work through clean vessels (2 Timothy 2:21) and He will not continually allow us to be used of Him if we have habitual sin in our lives.

I am shocked today at the low standards by which so many Christians live. Oftentimes we think the same way, talk the same way, and live the same way as our unsaved friends and neighbors who do not know Christ. As the apostle James tells us, "Brothers, these things ought not so to be" (James 3:10, KJV).

Ultimately, the one thing that most hinders our relationship with God is the sin in our life. If we want to grow spiritually, we must continually allow God to sanctify us through the Holy Spirit. This means that God will constantly be speaking to us about the sin in our life and drawing us to repentance and change. There should be activities, thoughts, and attitudes that we don't feel comfortable with today that we tolerated at one time earlier in our Christian life. This pattern should continue throughout our lives as we grow in our sensitivity to the Lord.

A good illustration of this concept can be seen in the life of Samson. Samson was the strongest man who ever lived. Judges 15:15 records that once Samson single-handedly killed 1,000 Philistines with the jawbone of a donkey. Scripture also records that Samson had a character problem. He was prone to sexual impropriety.

He lusted after and married a foreign woman, which God had forbidden the Israelites to do. He also solicited prostitutes on occasion. In one instance Samson was spending the evening with a prostitute and the next day "the Spirit of God came upon him" and he delivered Israel from a Philistine attack. The Lord allowed this to go on for some time, but eventually, because Samson would not change his behavior, God allowed him to fall and to lose his supernatural strength as well.

Jesus compared the condition of the human heart to differing types of soil in Matthew 13:1-23. This is one of my favorite illustrations of our Lord because it so accurately illustrates how we live our lives spiritually. When I think of that parable, a garden always comes to mind. A garden must constantly be tended to or else the weeds will destroy it. It is not a question of whether weeds will grow; it is a matter of plucking them out when they come.

There is a universal law in science known as entropy. The law of entropy states that everything eventually moves from order to chaos, and that everything eventually breaks down. This applies to everything from molecules to mansions to men. An ancient castle left alone on a tract of land will eventually deteriorate. After about age twenty-six, the body begins to slowly deteriorate over the next forty to fifty years until it eventually breaks down and dies. The sun is not gaining energy, it is slowly dying out. Drop a glass on the floor and the pieces disperse all over the floor in a random manner. Scientists agree that entropy affects every aspect of life, except creation of course, in which we are told the earth started off from an explosion that moved from total randomness to intricate complexity!

The law of entropy applies to the spiritual world as well. Without a volitional act of our will, our natural spiritual inclination will be to sin against God. Our spiritual lives, like a garden, must constantly be tended in order to yield fruit. The sin in our lives is like those weeds. We have to constantly pluck out the weeds or they will grow into our garden and kill it. Like Samson, we may entertain sin for a season, but if it is not dealt with, it will eventually destroy not only our spiritual gift, but us as well.

Fellowship With the Church

The Christian faith does not lend itself well to individualism. God has designed us to function properly only when we live together in community. There is a direct correlation between the state of our fellowship with a local church and our state of fellowship with God. Invariably the two go hand in hand.

The Lord made us to live together in a mutual give-and-take relationship with others in the body of Christ. At all times we both minister to others and receive ministry from others. That is the way God designed it to be, and we cannot alter that formula without inviting consequences. Therefore, another key discipline to live by is to always be a part of a local fellowship of believers. When we stay yoked together, there is accountability to maintain our Christian walk. Let's face it, our flesh would love to go its own way and do its own thing. When we are in relationship with other Christians who love us and pray for us and regularly check up on us, we don't have to fight the flesh all alone. We have brothers and sisters in the body of Christ who intercede on our behalf and help us overcome the enemy when we are weak.

When we are in relation with others, God uses those individuals to speak into our lives and to develop us in a deeper way. When we are a part of a local church, we are able to receive instruction, edification, and impartation from others. When we isolate ourselves from other Christians and from the local church, we are being set up by the enemy to fall. Lone Ranger Christians are backslidden Christians.

Obedience

This last item of the five I listed is ultimately the most important. Obedience is one of those keys to the Christian faith that you can bank on. But what I am talking about here is a lifestyle of obedience. What I am talking about is a mindset that says, "Lord, the issue is settled. You are my Master and whatever you say goes for me and my house." Sadly, this is not the mindset of many Christians.

I decided long ago that I was going to try to live my life completely submissive to the will of God, and it has done nothing but wonders for me in every area of my life. I have noticed that when Christians honestly try to live out this value, it makes them powerful in every area, including their spiritual giftings. When we live this way, we don't have to constantly ask God to work in us and through us. It just happens automatically.

I've found that God gives us three things when we surrender to Him. He gives us His presence, His provision, and His power. I know from personal history that when I live an obedient lifestyle unto God I can feel a tangible presence upon me. And when I am obedient to Him the provision is always there as well. I rarely ask the Lord for anything material. I find that the closer I get to Him the more satisfied I am with just being His child and fellowshipping in His presence. The few times I do ask for something I usually get it, and very quickly.

And I have also noticed that when I live this way I seem to have His power on my life as well. I have prayed for people when I have not been in good spiritual condition and nothing has happened. But when I am close to God and properly submitted to Him, there is power in my prayers and things happen when I pray. Haven't you noticed the same thing in your life as well? When you live a life of obedience to God, your whole life is a success. And when you live in obedience to Him, your spiritual gifts continue to develop and grow stronger all the days of your life.

EXERCISE YOUR GIFTS

The parable of the talents in Matthew 25:14-30 reveals to us an important spiritual truth. The Lord expects progress from His servants. When God gives His child a spiritual gift, He expects that Christian to not only receive the gift, but to use it to further His kingdom. In this parable in Matthew chapter 25 the workers were rewarded and given more talents based on their use and productivity of what they had already received.

This is a simple yet powerful biblical truth. If we want to grow stronger in our particular spiritual gift, we must commit to using that gift on a regular basis. Look for ways to express your gift in your ministry with others. Volunteer and get involved in ministries in your church that utilize your giftings. In prayer always ask God to open doors for you to use your gifts to bless others.

If you will ask Him for this, you will see Him opening doors of ministry for you all the time. God wants us to use these gifts; that's why He gave them to us. As we use our gifts we begin to strengthen them and they grow within us. And I'm convinced that most Christians are nowhere near their potential. If not careful, any Christian can backslide and neglect their giftings. Apparently even Timothy once began to neglect his spiritual gifts and the apostle Paul had to speak into his life and exhort him to "Stir up the gift of God which is in thee" (2 Timothy 1:6, KJV).

As you begin to look for ways to use your spiritual giftings, God will begin to open doors for you. However, don't despise the day of small beginnings. It may be awhile before you are given a place of ministry in the church, so be faithful to use your giftings where opportunity presents itself.

I discovered as a teenager that one of my gifts was exhortation. I began to notice that people who were discouraged or hurting seemed to always be attracted to me. I would impart new hope to them and would see them strengthened as I ministered to them. I don't know how many private counseling sessions I held for my peers in high school, but let's just say this, it was a lot. It was a while later before God opened doors in local churches where I could use this gift to bless larger crowds via preaching opportunities. Until then, I just faithfully used that gift at work, at school, or sometimes in the checkout lines at grocery stores. By the way, I still use my gifts in these places. We need to always remember to use these gifts outside of the four walls of the church where they can do this world some good!

Submerge Yourself in an Atmosphere of Faith

In developing our gifts we must seek to be around those who will accept our gifts and encourage us to develop them. There is no guarantee that your church will accept all of the gifts as being valid today. As we mentioned in chapter 2, some of the gifts are more readily accepted than others. Certain denominations have very strong opinions about the spiritual gifts.

If you belong to a church that does not accept the gift of tongues or prophecy as being for today, you will more than likely not be able to practice that gift publicly or be able to develop in it. If your church does not believe that God gives some Christians the gift of healing, then your request to pray over the sick on Sunday mornings will probably not be well received. If you simply repressed that gift and no longer tried to exercise it, then you would be in danger of wasting an endowment that God has given you. In such cases what should a Christian do?

The first thing you should do is pray and seek God's will in the matter. God may use you as the instrument in helping your church become open to the gifts. However, God may not be interested in changing that feature of your particular church right now. God's priorities for any particular church may not be the same as your priorities for that church.

The worst thing you could do would be to bring division to your church. After talking with your pastor about this issue, he may still refuse to allow you to exercise your gift in the church. If that is the case, you are to be submissive to your pastor regardless of whether you think he is wrong in the matter. The pastor is God's shepherd over the local congregation and he is to be respected and obeyed (Hebrews 13:17). It would be better for you to respectfully leave your current church and to find another than to cause division and talk negatively about your pastor.

Hopefully the church you belong to wants all Christians to develop their gifts no matter which ones they may have. Being in a church where the gifts are practiced will build your faith. As you see them in operation, you witness their power and it encourages you to develop your own. You do not want to surround yourself with Christians who will stifle your gifts or try to downplay their importance.

FIND A SPIRITUAL MENTOR

The whole concept of mentoring is one that is currently in vogue in the church today. Much is being written on the subject and there is plenty of good material available for those who are interested in being a mentor or being mentored by someone. Mentoring involves forming an intentional growth relationship with someone who is more developed in a particular area than you are.

A mentor is someone who can help you develop a deeper Christian walk. This person could be a family member, a mature Christian friend, or your pastor. You and this person meet together regularly for prayer and discussion, and you also minister alongside them as you are learning to develop your spiritual gifts.

This is the training modality used by Jesus to train His twelve apostles. For three years the Twelve traveled and ministered with the Lord Jesus. He would take them aside after each of their ministry meetings and ask them questions, testing their hearts and their understanding of what had just taken place. Jesus intentionally gave the Twelve more access to Himself because they were His protégés who would be leading His church after His ascension.

Finding a mentor will help you develop your spiritual gifts. If possible try to find a mentor who has the same primary spiritual gift and ministry calling as you do. After I felt God's call to pastoral ministry as a sixteen-year-old, I immediately sought out a mentor. God used my own pastor. He also recognized God's call on my life and began a mentoring relationship with me. I consider him one of my fathers in the faith.

As a sixteen-year-old young Christian, I accompanied my pastor on home and hospital visitations. Through his guidance I learned how to pray over people, prepare and preach sermons, and a host of other skills that I would need as a pastor one day. I consider those three or four years with him to have been just as valuable to me as the seminary training I later received. Pray that God will send you mentors.

Learn All You Can About Spiritual Gifts

A very wise man once told me, "Read a book on building bridges and you'll know more about bridge building than 97 percent of the people on the planet." That's good advice. If you want to mature in your spiritual giftings you must learn all you can about spiritual gifts. Begin by reading several other books on this topic besides this one. Appendix IV at the back of this book lists some excellent books to start with.

Also go back and study intently the biblical passages that discuss the gifts. Particularly study 1 Corinthians 12 – 14, this is the apostle Paul's definitive teaching on the subject. It would also be beneficial to read the biographies of great Christians who shared your spiritual gift. You will derive inspiration and faith from reading about these great men and women of God. If you are gifted in intercession, read books on Rees Howells. If you're gifted in faith, read about George Mueller or Smith Wigglesworth.

Rest assured in the Word of God that promises us, "Faithful is he that calleth you, who also will do it" (1 Thessalonians 5:24, KJV). God will fulfill all He has called you to do. Stay faithful to Him and rest assured that all will be accomplished in the fullness of time. Remember to always cultivate your relationship with Jesus. Exercise your giftings as God provides opportunity. Surround yourself with people who will build up your faith. And finally, in addition to learning all you can about your spiritual gifts, pray that God will send someone into your life to personally help you in developing your gift.

A FINAL WORD

I hope you've enjoyed digging deeper into what the Bible teaches about the fascinating truth of spiritual gifts. If you already know what your unique gifts are, then my prayer for you is that you will grow stronger and more anointed in those gifts every year of your life. May you bear much fruit for the kingdom and for our Lord. If you are presently not sure which gifts the Lord has given you, then allow me to pray for you right now. Agree with me in prayer as we petition the Father:

Father, thank you that all good things come from you. Lord, I want to lift up your servants right now who read this book. Lord, they're asking that you will confirm their spiritual gifts to them; that you'd show them how Your Spirit has uniquely gifted them for ministry in the body of Christ. Lord, I pray that even in this current season of their lives that you would clearly reveal to them what their gifts are and that you'd even confirm them through others as well. Open doors for them to minister mightily in the name of Jesus, and may Your anointing be heavy upon them. Thank you Father, for honoring our request. For it's in the name of the Lord Jesus Christ, and for His glory, that we ask this. Amen.

To the extent that we as the body of Christ discover our gifts, use them, and work together in unity, is the extent that the church of today will be all she was designed by God to be. We are a family. We are an army. But we are also a body. A body made up of many members with varied roles. A body that should lovingly care for all its members, to show the world how real love is supposed to operate. A body, in its individual parts is nice and adequate, but when working in unity, is supernatural and undefeatable.

All of us who are called into God's kingdom are given among other things three precious gifts: A permanent deposit of the very Spirit of God that raised Christ Jesus; an individual calling from our Father with special gifts enabling us to fulfill that calling; and a set amount of days until we are called home to give an accounting of what we did with the first two.

It is time that we meditate anew on the command of our Lord in Luke 19:13, "Occupy until I come" (KJV). Let's get busy doing the Master's work, and let's be amazed at His grace and power throughout the process. And let none of us from here on out ever have to dread the day when we will give an account of our gifts and what we did with them. Let us find new and creative ways to bless and minister to others, to win souls into the kingdom, and to make

God proud of us. Remember, your life is God's gift to you…what you do with it is your gift to Him.

Chapter Notes

Chapter 1

[1] Many scholars believe that Mary was a young girl, possibly in her teens, when she gave birth to the Messiah.

[2] Andy Butcher, "Churches Neglect Teaching on Spiritual Gifts," *Charisma News Service*, www.CBN.com, February 12, 2002.

Chapter 2

[1] Albert Shulman, *The Religious Heritage of America* (San Diego: A.S. Barnes & Co., 1981), p. 214.

[2] Ibid., p. 282.

[3] Ibid., p. 248.

[4] The great outpouring of the Holy Spirit, which occurred in 1901 and continues today, is viewed by scholars as consisting of three waves. The first wave were the Pentecostals with their emphasis on holiness and a separate baptism of the Spirit as evidenced by speaking in tongues. Leaders in this movement today would be men such as Oral Roberts or Bill Hamon. The second wave was the charismatic renewal movement of the 1960s and 70s. They formed no denominations of their own, rather they stayed in mainstream churches as a force for renewal within. Their emphasis

was less on holiness and more on spiritual gifts in particular and freedom of worship. They are divided over whether tongues are the sign of Spirit baptism. A notable leader from this camp today would be Pat Robertson. The Third Wave consisted of conservative evangelicals like Southern Baptists, Nazarenes, etc. who later in the 1980s and 90s came to be convinced that miraculous spiritual gifts were for today. Third Wave Christians do not believe one must speak in tongues to be Spirit filled, and they retain their traditional stances on many other issues as well. Leading advocates of this camp today would be Jack Deere and C. Peter Wagner. It was Wagner who coined the phrase "Third Wave."

[5] Jack Deere, *Surprised by the Power of the Spirit* (Grand Rapids: Zondervan, 1993), p. 55.

Chapter 3

[1] Of course I do not mean to imply here that there are sins we can actually get away with and not be held accountable to God for. I am simply attempting to make the point that the more mature we are in our walk with God, the more He expects of us in much the same way that a parent expects more of their fourteen year old than they do their four year old.

Chapter 4

[1] See Romans 11:25 and 1 Thessalonians 4:13. For Paul to use this phrase while discussing spiritual gifts highly implies, in my opinion, that the apostle considered this issue a foundational doctrine that he desperately wanted the church to understand.

[2] Don & Katie Fortune, *Discover Your God Given Gifts* (Grand Rapids: Chosen Books, 1987), pp. 15-17. Although I disagree with the authors on this one point, this is overall an excellent book on the seven gifts of Romans 12.

[3] C. Peter Wagner, *Your Spiritual Gifts Can Help Your Church Grow* (Ventura: Regal Books, 1994), p. 46.

[4] The one exception obviously being Acts chapter 2. Here we have the apostles and the 120 waiting for the Spirit to fall upon the

infant church. Until Acts chapter 2 the Holy Spirit had not yet fully "indwelled" the small number of Christians that were on the earth just after the ascension of Christ. After the Day of Pentecost the normative pattern found in Acts is the reception of the Spirit in close proximity to one's acceptance of Christ as Lord and Savior.

[5] There is much disagreement amongst different groups regarding this troublesome passage. Charismatics trying to teach a second blessing doctrine point to the phrase "for He [Holy Spirit] had not yet fallen upon any of them" (v.16) to mean that Luke was describing that the Samaritans had not yet been baptized in the Holy Spirit, but did receive the initial indwelling of the Spirit at conversion due to Romans 8:9. Many evangelicals argue that these Samaritans were not saved at all; they had only mentally assented to Philip's preaching. Upon receiving ministry from Peter and John they then fully accepted the gospel claims and were then saved and indwelled by the Spirit. I personally believe the Samaritans were saved by Philip's preaching, were water baptized, and yet did not receive the indwelling of the Holy Spirit that normally occurs at salvation. Why? The Samaritans were of mixed Jewish-Gentile descent. They practiced their own homegrown form of Judaism and even had their own version of the Hebrew Bible that differed from that of the Jews. They refused to worship in Jerusalem (John 4:20-22) and were rebuked by Jesus for their incorrect and unorthodox beliefs. Historically, the Samaritans never accepted the authority of the priests in Jerusalem and continued to practice their syncretic faith. I believe that once and for all God was sending them a message by withholding the Spirit from them. Truly salvation was "of the Jews." The message the Lord was sending was that the authority for this outpouring is from the apostles in Jerusalem. Receiving the Spirit by the laying on of the apostle's hands was a powerful symbolic picture about where the real power and authority in this movement resided. This was, in my

opinion, an exception to the rule. God temporarily withheld the Holy Spirit from a group of individuals who accepted Christ and were baptized. He's God. He can do that, you know.

[6] This is another controversial passage in Acts. Some believe these disciples of John the Baptist were saved individuals who then received a second blessing evidenced by tongues. I personally do not believe they were saved. It seems to me that Paul gives them a summary gospel message and explains to them that Christ was the promised Lamb that John the Baptist preached about. Upon hearing that, these disciples accepted what Paul said and they were baptized for the first time properly, in Jesus' name. They then received the Holy Spirit at their new birth (as normally occurs) and were gifted with the gifts of tongues and prophecy. I would not be dogmatic here, but it does seem to me that these individuals were "saved" via Paul's preaching.

Chapter 5

[1] Christian A. Schwarz, *Natural Church Development: A Guide to Eight Essential Qualities of Healthy Churches* (Carol Stream: Churchsmart Resources, 1998), p. 24.

Chapter 6

[1] J.D. Douglas, ed. *The New Bible Dictionary* (London: The Inter-Varsity Fellowship, 1962), p. 48.

[2] Ibid., p. 48.

[3] Jon Ruthven, "The Foundational Gifts of Ephesians 2:20," *Journal of Pentecostal Theology*, (Vol. 10, No. 2, April 2002), p. 41.

[4] Albert Hebert, *Raised from the Dead: True Stories of 400 Resurrection Miracles* (Rockford: Tan Books & Publishers, Inc., 1986), p. 191.

[5] William R. Moody, *The Life of D.L. Moody* (New York: Fleming H. Revell Co., 1900), p. 48.

[6] James F. Findlay, Jr., *Dwight L. Moody American Evangelist* (Chicago: The University of Chicago Press, 1969), p. 59.

[7] Moody, p. 47.

[8] Helen Kooiman Hosier, *100 Christian Women Who Changed the 20th Century* (Grand Rapids: Fleming H. Revell, 2000), p. 82.

Chapter 7

[1] Leslie Brickman, *Preparing the 21st Century Church* (Fairfax, VA: Xulon Press, 2002), p. 143.

[2] C. Peter Wagner, *Your Spiritual Gifts Can Help Your Church Grow* (Ventura: Regal Books, 1994), p. 70.

[3] Francis McGaw, *Praying Hyde* (Minneapolis: Bethany House Publishers, 1970), p. 43.

[4] Ibid., p. 50.

[5] Ibid., pp. 53-54.

[6] Ibid., p. 29.

[7] Pat Robertson, with Jamie Buckingham, *Shout it from the Housetops* (South Plainfield, NJ: Bridge Publishing, Inc., 1972), p. 103.

[8] D. Michael Henderson, *John Wesley's Class Meetings: A Model for Making Disciples* (Nappanee, IN: Evangel Publishing House, 1997), p. 94.

[9] Faith Coxe Bailey, *George Mueller* (Chicago: Moody Press, 1958), p. 157.

[10] Basil Miller, *George Mueller: The Man of Faith* (Grand Rapids: Zondervan Publishing House, 1941), p. 127.

[11] David Porter, *Mother Teresa: The Early Years* (Grand Rapids: William B. Eerdmans Publishing Co., 1986), p. 56.

[12] "Mother Teresa," *The New Encyclopedia Britannica Vol. 11* (Chicago: Encyclopedia Britannica, Inc., 1998), p. 643.

Chapter 8

[1] J. Theodore Mueller, *Great Missionaries to Africa* (Grand Rapids: Zondervan, 1941), p. 136.

[2] Ibid., p. 144.

[3] Nicol MacNicol and Vishal Mangalwadi, *What Liberates A Woman? The Story of Pandita Ramabai A Builder of Modern India* (New

Delhi: Nivedit Good Books Distributors Pvt. Ltd., 1996), p. 111.

[4] J. Rodman Williams, *Renewal Theology Vol. II: Salvation, the Holy Spirit, and Christian Living* (Grand Rapids: Zondervan, 1996), p. 356. Here Williams refers to a word of knowledge as "essentially an inspired word of teaching or instruction that occurs within the context of the gathered community."

[5] Helen Kooiman Hosier, *100 Christian Women Who Changed the 20th Century* (Grand Rapids: Fleming H. Revell, 2000), p. 114.

Chapter 9

[1] Eusebius, G. A. Williamson, trans., *The History of the Church* (New York: Penguin Books, 1983), p. 268.

[2] Thomas P. Halton et al., ed., Michael Slusser, trans., *The Fathers of the Church Vol. 98: St. Gregory Thaumaturgus – Life and Works* (Washington, D.C.: The Catholic University of America Press, 1998), pp. 62-64.

[3] Ibid., pp. 66-68.

[4] Ibid., pp. 56-58.

[5] Ibid., p. 3.

[6] Colin C. Whittaker, *Seven Pentecostal Pioneers* (Springfield: Gospel Publishing House, 1983), pp. 59-60.

[7] Charles H. Spurgeon, "The Holy Spirit: Who He Is and What He Does," compiled by Jack Gritz, ed., *The Baptist Messenger*, the Baptist General Convention of the State of Oklahoma, August 12, 1976, pp. 14-16.

[8] Charles H. Spurgeon, *C. H. Spurgeon Autobiography Vol. II: The Full Harvest*, compiled by Susannah Spurgeon and Joseph Harrald (Carlilse, PA: The Banner of Truth Trust, 1973), p. 59.

[9] Ibid., p. 60.

[10] Charles H. Spurgeon, *The Autobiography of Charles H. Spurgeon*, compiled by Susannah Spurgeon and his private secretary (Philadelphia: American Baptist Publication Society, 1900), p. 227.

[11] Personal interview with author, March 18, 2003.

[12] Vinson Synan, *Voices of Pentecost: Testimonies of Lives Touched by the Holy Spirit* (Ann Arbor, Michigan: Servant Publications, 2003), p. 149.

[13] Gary Lane, "Carrying the Cross in Pakistan: Terror at Bahawalpur," *The Voice of the Martyrs,* February 2002, p. 3. If this story touched your heart like it did mine, perhaps you would consider making a financial contribution to the Families of Martyrs Fund. These donations go to help support the children and spouses of the brave men and women who have given the ultimate sacrifice in their service to our Lord. Checks can be mailed to: The Voice of the Martyrs, P.O. Box 443, Bartlesville, OK, 74005. You can check out their organization online at www.persecution.com.

[14] David B. Barrett and Todd M. Johnson, *World Christian Trends* A.D. *30-* A.D. *2200* (Pasadena: William Carey Library, 2001), p. 32.

HELPS AND APPENDICES

Glossary

cessationism – The belief that the miraculous gifts of the Spirit, such as healing, tongues, miracles, etc., have ceased and are no longer given by God to the church.

cessationist – One who believes the tenets of cessationism.

charisma – The Greek word for "gift" (plural form is *charismata*). This is the primary word used in the New Testament to describe spiritual gifts. It is derived from the root word *charis*, which means "grace." Thus spiritual gifts are divinely given "gifts of grace."

charismaticism – The belief that all spiritual gifts listed in Scripture are valid today and are still being given by God to the church.

charismatic – One who believes the tenets of charismaticism.

constitutional view – The belief that God gifts individual Christians with particular spiritual gifts that they possess for a lifetime.

foundational gifts – The five spiritual gifts listed in Ephesians 4:11 that are foundational to the health and maturity of the church. They consist of apostles, prophets, evangelists, pastors, and teachers.

gift drift – The tendency to drift toward and be attracted to ministries that utilize one's giftings. The phenomenon of gift drift is an early indicator of one's giftedness. The idea of "giftedness drift" originated with J. Robert Clinton.

gift mix – The unique combination of spiritual gifts that each Christian possesses.

gift projection – A phrase coined by C. Peter Wagner to describe the error of thinking that every Christian should have the same emphasis in ministry as you do. Gift projection also involves one Christian looking down on another because that other Christian does not have the motivation or ability to engage in the same ministry activities that they do.

glossolalia – From the Greek *glossa*, "tongue," and *lalia*, "speaking." The theological term used for speaking in ecstatic utterances like those described by the apostle Paul in 1 Corinthians 14:2.

hermeneutics – The science of biblical interpretation; the process of using interpretive rules and logic to arrive at the accurate meaning of a biblical passage.

heteroglossolalia – From the Greek *heteros*, "other, different" and *lalia*, "speaking." The theological term used to describe speaking in one's own language and yet being heard by another in their language, which is different from that of the speaker.

manifestational view – The belief that Christians do not actually possess specific spiritual gifts, but rather manifest different gifts at different times throughout their lives as need arises.

ministry gifts – The spiritual gifts that are given to do the practical ministry of the church. These consist of all the gifts other than the "foundational" gifts and the "sign" gifts.

motivational view – The belief that God gives some of the gifts as permanent possessions and that others are given only as need arises. This view states that every Christian has one or more of the seven gifts listed in Romans 12:6-8 in the form of a resident ability retained for life. The gifts in 1 Corinthians 12:8-10 are seen as manifestational in nature, and are given by the Holy Spirit only as need arises. Finally, the gifts listed in Ephesians 4:11 are not spiritual gifts per se, but are "gifts of people" given to lead the church.

natural talents – Natural God-given talents and abilities that all people possess from birth. These may take the form of abilities for intellect, athletics, music, speech, etc. that both Christians and non-Christians possess. These should not be confused with spiritual gifts that are associated only with Christians.

sign gifts – The spiritual gifts that serve as signs or proofs that the kingdom of God has been established and is advancing upon the earth. These gifts demonstrate the power of God to the lost world and include the gifts of healing, miracles, prophecy, deliverance, tongues, and martyrdom.

spiritual gifts – Supernatural endowments and abilities selectively given to every Christian by the Holy Spirit for the purposes of personal ministry and for the advancement of the kingdom of God.

xenoglossolalia – From the Greek *xeno*, "stranger, foreigner," and *lalia*, "speaking." The theological term used for speaking in a foreign language one has never learned. Many scholars view the tongues mentioned in Acts 2:1-12 as an example of this.

Appendix I

Definitions of Spiritual Gifts

Apostleship: The unique, God-given ability to exercise strategic leadership and spiritual authority over large segments of the body of Christ for the purpose of greatly increasing the church's impact in its work for the kingdom of God. Ephesians 4:11, 2 Corinthians 12:12

Prophet: The unique, God-given ability to receive special revelations from God and to serve as a messenger, delivering those communications to those whom God directs. Ephesians 4:11, Acts 21:9-12

Evangelism: The unique, God-given ability to cause others to be aware of their need for Christ and to then present the gospel in such a way that others believe it and accept it. Ephesians 4:11, 2 Timothy 4:5

Pastoring: The unique, God-given ability to nurture, protect, and to help bring to maturity, a group of Christians. Ephesians 4:11, 1 Timothy 3:1

Teaching: The unique, God-given ability to discover God's truths and to communicate them in such a way that others can understand them and grow spiritually. Ephesians 4:11, Acts 18:24-26

Faith: The unique, God-given ability to discern God's will for a particular matter and to fervently pray and work toward accomplishing that end while inspiring others to do the same. 1 Corinthians 12:9, Numbers 13:30

Exhortation: The unique, God-given ability to encourage, strengthen, and admonish others for the purpose of helping them to reach their God-given potential. Romans 12:8, Acts 9:26-27

Serving: The unique, God-given ability to be aware of the physical and practical needs of others and to meet those needs in a way that blesses them. Romans 12:7, John 12:3

Helps: The unique, God-given ability to partner and come alongside others for the purpose of greatly increasing the other person's ministry effectiveness. 1 Corinthians 12:28, Acts 13:4-5

Craftsmanship: The unique, God-given ability to work skillfully and creatively to design, build, or create things that are useful and inspirational in the work of the kingdom. Exodus 31:3-5, Exodus 35:30-35

Hospitality: The unique, God-given ability to open one's home to others and to create such an environment of warmth and acceptance that genuine ministry occurs. 1 Peter 4:9-10, Acts 16:14-15

Discernment: The unique, God-given ability to detect whether the actions and intentions of others are from a heavenly, a human, or a demonic influence. 1 Corinthians 12:10, Acts 16:16-18

Leadership: The unique, God-given ability to perceive God's ideals for a matter and to then organize, inspire, and lead others in the completion of that endeavor. Romans 12:8, Acts 15:13-20

Administration: The unique, God-given ability to administrate and organize people and resources in order to achieve maximum efficiency in the work of the kingdom. 1 Corinthians 12:28, Acts 6:1-6

Interpretation of Tongues: The unique, God-given ability to interpret and translate a message in tongues into an understandable language that others can receive and benefit from. 1 Corinthians 12:10, 1 Corinthians 14:26

Interpretation of Dreams: The unique, God-given ability to decode the symbolism and explain the meaning of dreams and/or visions that others receive from God. Daniel 1:17, Genesis 41:12

Missionary: The unique, God-given ability to effectively minister in a foreign culture for the purposes of establishing and/or strengthening the church within that cultural group. Acts 13:1-5, Acts 22:21

Intercession: The unique, God-given ability to perceive the heart of God for nations, individuals, or specific situations and to pray fervently and strategically until God's will comes to pass. Luke 2:37, Acts 12:5

Giving: The unique, God-given ability to give unselfishly of one's resources (time, money, affections, etc.) to ensure that the work of the church and the needs of others are taken care of. Romans 12:8, Matthew 27:57-60

Simplicity: The unique, God-given ability to voluntarily divest oneself of most material comforts so as to simplify one's lifestyle for more effective ministry. 1 Corinthians 13:3, Acts 2:44-45

Mercy: The unique, God-given ability to comfort and restore others who are experiencing a physical, spiritual, or emotional hardship. Romans 12:8, Luke 10:33-35

Knowledge: The unique, God-given ability to perceive the truths of God and the mysteries of the faith and to share these insights for the edification of the church. 1 Corinthians 12:8, Acts 18:24-26

Wisdom: The unique, God-given ability to discover principles and precepts in the Word of God and to accurately apply them to everyday living so that oneself and others live skillfully and are blessed by God. 1 Corinthians 12:8, Acts 15:13-20

Worship: The unique, God-given ability to usher in the presence of God during a time of worship for the purpose of drawing others into an intimate encounter with God. 1 Corinthians 14:15, 1 Samuel 16:23

Miracles: The unique, God-given ability to perform supernatural acts which supersede natural law for the purpose of causing others to recognize the power and glory of God. 1 Corinthians 12:10, Acts 19:11-12

Prophecy: The unique, God-given ability to receive an inspired message from God that is then shared with others to bring encouragement, edification, or correction. 1 Corinthians 12:10, Luke 2:25-35

Deliverance: The unique, God-given ability to perceive and confront demonic forces and to bring freedom to those trapped in demonic bondage. Mark 16:17, Luke 10:17

Tongues: The unique, God-given ability to communicate with God in a special, heavenly language for the purpose of praise, intercession, and spiritual edification. 1 Corinthians 12:10, Acts 19:6

Healing: The unique, God-given ability to cure and restore those who suffer from physical and/or emotional ailments. 1 Corinthians 12:9, Acts 3:1-8

Martyrdom: The unique, God-given ability to endure suffering and persecution for the cause of Christ and yet maintain a spirit of joy and thankfulness for the purposes of witnessing to the oppressors and inspiring the church at large. John 21:18-19, Acts 21:13

APPENDIX II

Carraway Spiritual Gifts Inventory

© 2005 by Bryan Carraway

The following 150-question inventory is meant to help steer you in the right direction as to your possible spiritual gifts. This test alone is not the final word on the matter. It is, however, a good starting place and is often very accurate in helping people confirm which gifts they possess. For the results to be accurate, you must answer each question on the basis of your past experiences. Do not answer the questions based on how you feel you *should* answer them or based on what sounds more "spiritual." These questions are designed to test both your inward motivations and your life experiences. Answer each question by circling one of the following numerical responses…

0 This **Never** describes me or I have no experience with this.
1 This **Rarely** describes me.
2 This **Sometimes** describes me.
3 This **Usually** describes me.
4 This **Almost Always** describes me.

Read each question and circle the single most appropriate response. After you finish, plot the circled numbers next to the question numbers on the scoring sheet. Add those five numerical values across each row to determine your total score for each gift.

N R S U A

1. I have an instinct for knowing the best way to accomplish a given project and I have been used by God to create a step-by-step plan for accomplishing a task. 0 1 2 ③ 4

2. I have a strong love for the people of God, both in the local and universal church. I'm willing to make whatever personal sacrifices are necessary to see the church come into the fullness of God's will. 0 1 ② 3 4

3. I enjoy working with my hands to create or design things which bless people spiritually. 0 1 ② 3 4

4. I have been used by the Lord to cast demons out of people. ⓪ ① 2 3 4

5. I can sense much about the spiritual state and inward motivations of others. My impressions on these things are later proved to be true. ⓪ 1 2 3 4

6. I engage people in conversation about their need for Christ. Many times I'm able to lead those people to accept Jesus as their Lord. ⓪ 1 2 3 4

7. People often come to me with their problems because I am approachable and they seem to sense that I can be trusted. 0 1 2 ③ 4

N   R   S   U   A

8. I don't have trouble believing and acting on the promises of God.   0   1   2   3   4

9. I give more than 10% of my yearly income to the work of the Lord.   0   1   2   3   4

10. I have prayed for people with sickness or disease and God has healed them.   0   1   2   3   4

11. I get more fulfillment in helping someone else do something great for God than in my own ministry achievements.   0   1   2   3   4

12. When guests visit my home I take extra care to make sure they feel welcome and comfortable. I want my home to project a safe and loving environment.   0   1   2   3   4

13. I have discovered that I pray much more often and intensively than most other Christians that I know.   0   1   2   3   4

14. While others comment about how strange or confusing their dreams are, I always seem to find a message or a meaning in my dreams.   0   1   2   3   4

15. When I hear Christians praying in tongues I can discern the general content of the prayers. I know whether it is a prayer of praise, intercession, or spiritual warfare.   0   1   2   3   4

16. Other Christians have told me that I bring out truths from the Bible that they have never realized before.   0   1   2   3   4

	N	R	S	U	A
17. I have an ability to influence others to my way of thinking.	0	1	2	3	4
18. I have thought about what an honor it would be if I had to die for the Lord Jesus.	0	1	2	3	4
19. I have a burden for people who are hurting physically or emotionally and I minister the love of God to them.	0	1	2	3	4
20. God has performed amazing supernatural feats through me.	0	1	2	3	4
21. I have a special love and concern in my heart for foreign nations and peoples.	0	1	2	3	4
22. I have a desire to be directly involved in the discipling of other Christians.	0	1	2	3	4
23. I am persuasive when I speak. When I speak about spiritual things people believe that what I am telling them is of God.	0	1	2	3	4
24. The Lord often speaks to me through impressions, dreams, or visions.	0	1	2	3	4
25. I have a heart to meet the practical needs of people that other Christians don't seem to notice.	0	1	2	3	4
26. I feel I can serve God more wholeheartedly if I am not distracted by lots of material possessions.	0	1	2	3	4
27. When I teach a lesson from the Bible others respond well and are able to understand and grow spiritually from it.	0	1	2	3	4

	N	R	S	U	A

28. I have a desire to speak in tongues so that I may enrich my prayer life. ⓪ 1 2 3 4

29. I have an ability to see how scriptural principles and teachings can be applied in people's lives today. 0 1 ② 3 4

30. It deeply grieves me when I am in a worship service and I notice that the congregation is unresponsive and is not entering into the presence of God. 0 1 2 3 ④

31. When working on a project, I enjoy the detailed work of creating an overall plan, deciding how to best use our resources, and dividing up responsibilities between group members. 0 1 2 ③ 4

32. God has given me translocal authority and influence. Entire groups of churches look to me as a spiritual leader and submit themselves to my counsel and oversight. ⓪ 1 2 3 4

33. When I build or create things for the church others comment to me about how beautiful or unique my projects are. ⓪ ① 2 3 4

34. I have ministered to someone who was afflicted by a demonic spirit. They later told me that after I ministered to them they finally felt rid of the spirit and experienced spiritual freedom. ⓪ 1 2 3 4

                            N R S U A

35. I can easily distinguish between the Spirit of God and the spirit of the evil one. I can do this with individuals or when I am with a group of people.   0 1 (2) 3 4

36. When I meet someone the first thing I think about is whether they have accepted Jesus as their Lord and Savior.   (0) 1 2 3 4

37. God uses me to bring encouragement to those who are feeling defeated or distressed.   0 1 (2) 3 4

38. Once God gives me an assurance about something I don't waver. I persevere in prayer until it comes to pass.   0 1 2 (3) 4

39. I don't mind giving of my time, resources, or money if I know it will bless someone or help them better accomplish their work for the Lord.   0 1 2 (3) 4

40. When I pray for people who are afflicted with an illness or disease God gives me supernatural faith to believe that the person will be healed.   (0) 1 2 3 4

41. I feel a great sense of accomplishment and fulfillment when I have assisted a brother or sister in Christ in completing a ministry task that God assigned to them.   0 1 2 (3) 4

42. I'm usually among the first to approach visitors at my church. I always greet them warmly and help put them at ease.   0 (1) 2 3 4

	N	R	S	U	A

43. When I tell someone, "I'll be praying for you," I pray for that person regularly until I know the situation has been remedied or until I feel God releases me from that burden. 0 1 ②3 4

44. When people are talking about their dreams in front of me, I can figure out what God is trying to tell them before they can. 0 1 2 3 4

45. I have been used to give an interpretation of a message in tongues that was given in a corporate church service. 0 1 2 3 4

46. There are times in my life when God illuminates my understanding of some aspect of His will and I have provided direction by sharing this with other Christians. 0 1 2 3 4

47. God has put within my heart a desire to lead others into great works for His kingdom. 0 1 2 3 4

48. When hardship or persecution comes into my life I do not complain or have feelings of resentment toward God. 0 1 ②3 4

49. When I am in a group, I can intuitively sense if someone is hurting inside, and compassion wells up within me for that person. 0 1 2 3 4

50. I desire and pray to see God do powerful supernatural acts like He did in the Bible so that the lost world will see His power and be in awe of Him. 0 1 2 3 4

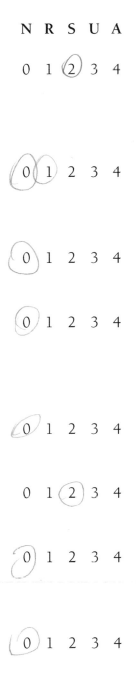

N R S U A

51. It bothers me deeply that the gospel has not penetrated every nation and people group. I want to help change this.   0 1 (2) 3 4

52. God leads me to form lengthy time commitments to other Christians for the purposes of helping them to mature in their walk with God.   (0) (1) 2 3 4

53. God has spoken to me in a clear manner and directed me to share specific information with another person that ministered to an exact need that they had.   (0) 1 2 3 4

54. The Lord reveals things to me about the future that concerns individuals, churches, or even nations.   (0) 1 2 3 4

55. When I am at a group function and I notice that something needs to be done, I just do it; no one has to ask me.   0 1 2 (3) 4

56. God uses me to minister and meet the needs of people who are poor and/or neglected.   0 (1) 2 3 4

57. Other Christians have told me that I have an ability to make the teachings of the Bible clear and interesting.   (0) 1 2 3 4

58. I have the ability to pray in tongues and when I do I feel strengthened and renewed spiritually.   (0) 1 2 3 4

N R S U A

59. Others tell me that I give wise advice   0 1 2 3 4
and that they have been greatly helped
by the counsel I have given them.

60. God seems to touch people in notice-   0 1 2 3 4
able, visible ways when I sing or lead
worship.

61. Management comes easy to me. I can   0 1 2 3 4
put together the right people with the
right tasks to see a job completed ef-
ficiently.

62. The Lord gives me amazing insights   0 1 2 3 4
into the spiritual forces at work against
the church. I use this information to
bring both correction and direction
to the church so that we will be more
effective for God.

63. God seems to have given me an abil-   0 1 2 3 4
ity to create beautiful works that bless
other Christians when they see them.

64. Demonic spirits have supernaturally   0 1 2 3 4
revealed themselves to me and ha-
rassed me or threatened me.

65. My motto is "everything in the name   0 1 2 3 4
of Jesus is not necessarily of Jesus."
I'm cautious about some teachings or
spiritual experiences that others have
embraced.

66. I regularly witness about Christ and   0 1 2 3 4
give my personal testimony to family
members, unsaved friends and co-
workers, and even strangers.

	N	R	S	U	A

67. I have a desire to impart faith and hope in other Christians in order to help them understand that God has given them abilities and has a call on their life. 0 1 (2) 3 4

68. I have believed God to do something that others thought highly unlikely or even impossible, and then He has done it. 0 (1) 2 3 4

69. I find great satisfaction in giving to people in need and knowing that God uses me to be a blessing to others. 0 1 (2) 3 4

70. I feel a special compassion for people who are suffering because of a physical infirmity or sickness. (0) 1 2 3 4

71. The Lord lays on my heart specific things to do for others that will ease their burden in their service to God. (0) 1 2 3 4

72. In my church I tend to be among the first to volunteer to open up my home for missionaries or other guests that need a place to stay. 0 1 (2) 3 4

73. I have a burden to pray for individuals, situations, or the universal church. 0 (1) 2 3 4

74. When I have attempted to give an interpretation to other Christians' dreams, they have excitedly responded that my interpretation was of the Lord and that their spirit bore witness to it. (0) 1 2 3 4

	N	R	S	U	A

75. In a small-group setting, I have told the group what I felt God was having us pray about when we prayed in tongues. Later other Christians confirmed this and told me that they felt the same thing.   0 1 2 3 4

76. I seem to be able to discover biblical principles or truths about God that others don't notice or realize.   0 1 2 3 4

77. God often gives me a vision of what He wants to do in a specific situation, and when I share it with other Christians they get excited and want to be a part of it.   0 1 2 3 4

78. I feel like the unjust suffering that I have endured in my life has brought me closer to God, so I have thanked Him for it.   0 1 2 3 4

79. In my church I tend to be among the first to get involved in ministry opportunities directed toward those who are suffering a physical or emotional hardship.   0 1 2 3 4

80. Powerful supernatural manifestations have occurred in others' lives when I have asked God to intervene on their behalf.   0 1 2 3 4

81. I can relate well with people of diverse cultures, religions, and worldviews.   0 1 2 3 4

	N	R	S	U	A

82. I have noticed that I have a paternal/ maternal instinct in regard to other Christians. I want to warn and try to protect them from things that could harm them spiritually.   0   1   2   3   4

83. I feel a strong anointing on me when I speak or preach to a group about the things of God. Later, others tell me they sensed that anointing as well.   0   1   2   3   4

84. I regularly receive prophetic revelations from the Lord and when I share them with others they take heed to my message.   0   1   2   3   4

85. I find great satisfaction in serving the physical or practical needs of others.   0   1   2   3   4

86. I voluntarily live below my means financially because I would rather use my extra money and resources to help those less fortunate than myself.   0   1   2   3   4

87. I love to do in-depth studies of the Bible's teachings and then present my findings to others so they will grow in their faith.   0   1   2   3   4

88. I have noticed that my gift of tongues has developed. I notice new sounds and words and a new intensity when I pray as compared to when I first began to exercise this gift.   0   1   2   3   4

89. I don't struggle with making difficult decisions. I know which biblical principles to apply to each decision, which   0   1   2   3   4

N R S U A

ensures that I choose the right course of action.

90. After I sing or lead a group in worship, people come to me afterwards and tell me that they sensed the presence of God in a powerful way.   0   1   (2)   3   4

91. It really bothers me when I see a church or ministry program that is disorganized and poorly managed. I want to help with the future planning and administration so that it can be successful the next time.   0   1   (2)   3   4

92. The Lord Jesus Christ has personally appeared to me and commissioned me as an apostle in His church. (For "yes" mark 4, for "no" mark 0)   (0)   1   2   3   4

93. I tend to be among the first to volunteer in my church for projects that require one to build or decorate something.   0   (1)   2   3   4

94. I have a desire to see people freed from demonic strongholds.   (0)   1   2   3   4

95. I've learned to trust my intuition and feelings about other people because I am usually right.   0   1   (2)   3   4

96. I seem to have an ability to adapt and find common ground with people of different personality types and diverse backgrounds.   0   1   (2)   3   4

97. Others have told me that my advice and ministry to them helped them   (0)   1   2   3   4

N R S U A

grow in some aspect of their personal or spiritual life.

98. It disturbs me when I see Christians living below their privileges in Christ. I want to stir them up to believe God for great things.   0 1 2 3 4

99. Others describe me as a generous person who always gives to the work of the Lord.   0 1 2 3 4

100. Others have told me that they have been healed of their affliction after I have prayed for them.   0 1 2 3 4

101. I have noticed that God will often draw me to particular persons because He wants me to invest myself and my talents in helping them become more of what God wants them to be.   0 1 2 3 4

102. Other people have commented that I am a very warm or hospitable person.   0 1 2 3 4

103. I see specific answers to my prayers on a regular basis.   0 1 2 3 4

104. God speaks to me in dreams or visions and I have come to depend on them as a source of guidance and revelation.   0 1 2 3 4

105. When I hear an utterance delivered in tongues, I pray that God will grant me the interpretation of that tongue so that the whole congregation can hear the message God has for us.   0 1 2 3 4

	N	R	S	U	A

106. The Holy Spirit gives me special insight into the interworking relationships between God, the world, and the church, and I have seen people blessed when I share these insights with them.
N R S U A — 0 1 2 3 4

107. While I was in charge, I have made a tough decision because I thought it was the right course of action. I did this even though I could have made a different decision which would have been more popular with the group.
0 1 2 3 4

108. I would not be persuaded from ministering long term in an area of the world just because there was a greater chance of being killed there for my faith in Christ.
0 1 2 3 4

109. When Christians fall into sin, I don't judge them. I would rather comfort and restore them than give them a rebuke.
0 1 2 3 4

110. I believe that one of the greatest ways that God receives glory and praise is when people see Him perform a miracle.
0 1 2 3 4

111. When I minister to people outside of my own cultural or ethnic group, they respond favorably to me.
0 1 2 3 4

112. I am very much a "people person" and I love to invest myself in the lives of others.
0 1 2 3 4

	N	R	S	U	A

113. God supernaturally reveals the future to me about situations or people that is later proved to be true. — **0** 1 2 3 4

114. It deeply grieves me when I see God's laws ignored and when I see Christians tolerate the sin in their lives. I feel called to speak out against these things. — **0** 1 2 3 4

115. In my church I tend to be among the first to get involved in projects that require manual labor or me serving others. — 0 1 **2** 3 4

116. I have a special place in my heart for the poor and needy and I do everything I can to minister to them and help them. — 0 **1** 2 3 4

117. I can organize and classify the Bible's teachings in a way that helps people learn more effectively. — **0** 1 2 3 4

118. I pray in tongues regularly during my quiet times with the Lord. I do not just pray in tongues when I am around others who are doing so. — **0** 1 2 3 4

119. I can easily predict the end result of personal decisions that others make before they can. — 0 1 **2** 3 4

120. God has given me abilities that relate to worship such as singing, dancing, playing an instrument, or writing music. — 0 **1** 2 3 4

		N	R	S	U	A
121.	I can see the "big picture" of a complex task and can easily create a strategy that will best accomplish that task.	0	1	2	③	4
122.	God has displayed miraculous signs and wonders through me and throughout my ministry.	⓪	1	2	3	4
123.	I actively look for ways to make my church more physically attractive. A church should look impressive and have a distinct "spiritual décor" to it.	⓪	1	2	3	4
124.	I think that most of the problems in the church and in individual Christians could be solved if we were more aware of how evil spiritual forces gain entry into our lives.	0	1	2	③	4
125.	I have actually seen or strongly sensed the presence of, angels and/or demons.	0	1	②	3	4
126.	I am often burdened for the salvation of specific people and I begin to pray and intercede on their behalf, asking God to save their souls.	0	①	2	3	4
127.	I offer solutions or issue spiritual challenges to other Christians in a way that motivates them to act.	⓪	1	2	3	4
128.	Others have told me that I strengthened their faith during a time of crisis or trouble.	⓪	1	2	3	4
129.	I don't have a hard time giving money away when the Lord prompts me to do so.	0	1	2	3	④

	N	R	S	U	A

130. God has specifically directed me to pray for someone with a sickness or physical condition and after I prayed there was a noticeable improvement in their condition.　0 (1) 2 3 4

131. I don't mind being behind the scenes and helping out with the routine or mundane tasks as long as I know I'm really helping someone in their ministry.　0 1 2 (3) 4

132. I enjoy using my home as a ministry base where I can minister to those whom God brings across my path.　0 1 (2) 3 4

133. God gives me revelation and insight into the spiritual world so that I can pray accurately and strategically about the concerns that He lays on my heart.　(0) 1 2 3 4

134. The Lord uses me to interpret the spiritual dreams of others.　(0) 1 2 3 4

135. When someone gives a message in tongues in a public church service, I want God to give me the interpretation of that message so the congregation will be blessed and in awe of God.　(0) 1 2 3 4

136. The Lord has bypassed my intellectual knowledge of a spiritual issue and has used me to speak a message about it that came straight from Him.　(0) 1 2 3 4

	N	R	S	U	A

137. God has used me to rally other Christians around a common goal, and I have successfully guided the group to complete that goal. — 0 1 2 ③ 4

138. I have endured physical abuse and injury because of my stand for Christ. When this occurred, I considered it an honor to suffer for the sake of the gospel. — ⓪ 1 2 3 4

139. I minister to people who are neglected, broken, and often overlooked by others. — 0 ① 2 3 4

140. In a time of great need God has used me to perform a miracle that was an answer to everyone's prayers. — ⓪ 1 2 3 4

141. I would be willing to relocate, learn a foreign language, and give up many of my present comforts if I could help reach an unreached nation or people group with the gospel. — 0 ① 2 3 4

142. I have been used of God to impart new vision in others and to help develop new ministry skills. — ⓪ 1 2 3 4

143. The Lord has given me an inspired message and directed me to deliver it to someone for their edification. — ⓪ 1 2 3 4

144. I have become aware that God uses me to speak into the lives of others for their edification. I have been used at times to warn, instruct, confirm, or encourage others in their walk with God. — 0 ① 2 3 4

	N	R	S	U	A
145. I don't mind doing menial tasks if I feel it will really bless someone.	0	1	2	(3)	4
146. I feel God has called me to invest my life in the less fortunate of society and to show them the love of Jesus.	0	(1)	2	3	4
147. I have a high regard for the Word of God. It disturbs me when people teach false doctrine and use Scripture out of context.	0	1	2	3	(4)
148. When I am ministering or praying for people, God will often give me insight into what needs to be prayed or said to them after I have first prayed for them in tongues.	(0)	1	2	3	4
149. I have warned others about certain people or situations that may not be God's will for them. My counsel has proved helpful and saved them from the pain of making a mistake.	0	(1)	2	3	4
150. I can perceive what God wants to do in a worship service and can exhort and prepare people to receive from Him.	(0)	1	2	3	4

Scoring the Carraway Spiritual Gifts Inventory

© 2005 by Bryan Carraway

Place the number you scored on each question next to its matching number and then add the five values across to arrive at your total score for that corresponding gift. Your top two or three scores should serve as a good starting point for further investigation as to your possible giftings.

1. 7	31. 7	61. 5	91. 2	121. 5	14	Administration	✓
2. 2	32. 0	62. 0	92. 0	122. 0	2	Apostleship	
3. 2	33. 1	63. 0	93. 1	123. 0	4	Craftsmanship	
4. 1	34. 0	64. 0	94. 0	124. 3	4	Deliverance	
5. 0	35. 2	65. 4	95. 2	125. 2	10	Discernment	0
6. 0	36. 0	66. 2	96. 2	126. 1	5	Evangelism	
7. 3	37. 2	67. 2	97. 0	127. 0	7	Exhortation	
8. 4	38. 3	68. 1	98. 3	128. 0	11	Faith	0
9. 4	39. 3	69. 2	99. 1	129. 4	14	Giving	✓
10. 1	40. 0	70. 0	100. 0	130. 1	2	Healing	
11. 4	41. 3	71. 0	101. 1	131. 3	11	Helps	
12. 3	42. 1	72. 2	102. 0	132. 2	8	Hospitality	
13. 1	43. 2	73. 1	103. 2	133. 0	6	Intercession	
14. 2	44. 1	74. 0	104. 0	134. 0	3	Int. of Dreams	
15. 0	45. 0	75. 0	105. 0	135. 0	0	Int. of Tongues	
16. 1	46. 0	76. 0	106. 0	136. 0	1	Knowledge	
17. 3	47. 0	77. 0	107. 4	137. 3	10	Leadership	0
18. 1	48. 2	78. 2	108. 3	138. 0	8	Martyrdom	
19. 1	49. 0	79. 2	109. 3	139. 1	5	Mercy	
20. 0	50. 0	80. 0	110. 3	140. 0	3	Miracles	
21. 2	51. 2	81. 3	111. 1	141. 1	9	Missionary	
22. 2	52. 1	82. 2	112. 1	142. 6	6	Pastoring	

23. 7	53. 0	83. 0	113. 0	143. 0	2	Prophecy	
24. 1	54. 0	84. 0	114. 0	144. 1	2	Prophet	
25. 0	55. 3	85. 2	115. 2	145. 3	10	Serving	0
26. 0	56. 1	86. 3	116. 1	146. 1	6	Simplicity	
27. 1	57. 0	87. 2	117. 0	147. 4	7	Teaching	
28. 0	58. 0	88. 0	118. 0	148. 0	0	Tongues	
29. 2	59. 2	89. 3	119. 2	149. 1	10	Wisdom	0
30. 4	60. 0	90. 2	120. 1	150. 0	7	Worship	

A score of 15-20: This is probably one of your spiritual gifts.

A score of 12-14: This may be one of your spiritual gifts; further confirmation is needed.

A score of 0-11: This is probably not one of your spiritual gifts.

Reflection Questions for Group Study

Chapter 1: The Pattern of God

1. The statement is made early on that "God always accomplishes His purposes through people." Why do you think God chooses to work this way?

2. This chapter provided examples in the Old and New Testament of God partnering with people to accomplish great tasks. Do you think God still wants to work through people today like He did in the Bible? If so, what kinds of things do you think the Lord wants to use people to do?

Chapter 2: The Continued Debate: Cessationism vs. Charismaticism

1. Describe the theological system known as cessationism. What verses from Scripture are used to support this belief? Do you believe this position is valid? Why or why not?

2. Charismatic Christians are sometimes said to formulate their beliefs based on their experiences rather than the Word of God. Should personal experiences play any role

at all in coming to our beliefs about God or how He works in the lives of people? Does Scripture ever portray biblical characters as validating their beliefs about God or how He works based on their unique experiences? (See 2 Kings 6:15-17, Job 42:1-6, John 9:18-25, Acts 10:44-48.)

3. Equally intelligent, godly Christians can disagree over certain doctrines in the Bible. How do you believe that God would have us relate to and treat those who hold a different view than we do on the gifts of the Spirit?

Chapter 3: New Testament Teaching on the Gifts

1. What's the difference between a spiritual gift and a natural talent?

2. What does the apostle Paul say the purpose of spiritual gifts is in 1 Corinthians 12:7? What does the apostle Peter say the purpose of spiritual gifts is in 1 Peter 4:10?

3. If persons do not have a certain spiritual gift, are they exempt from performing a role associated with that gift? For example, are Christians without the gift of serving expected to serve a neighbor they see in need? Are Christians without the gift of evangelism still expected to share their faith? Where is the balance between flowing in your particular gifts and still performing some of the functions of other gifts that you may not have? Discuss this with the group.

4. How are the gifts of the Spirit different from the fruit of the Spirit?

Chapter 4: A Closer Look at 1 Corinthians 12-14

1. What are some negative consequences that occur when Christians don't know their spiritual gifts?

2. What is gift projection? Have you ever experienced someone projecting their gift on you? Share this experience with the group.

3. What are the top two or three points that the apostle Paul is trying to make in 1 Corinthians 12:12-31 about how Christians are to relate to one another based on their different gifts?

Chapter 5: The Classification and Implementation of the Gifts

1. What is the five-fold purpose of the church as revealed in Acts 2:42-47? Is there a link between this five-fold purpose and the different spiritual gifts available to the church? How do they work together to fulfill God's perfect plan?

2. Do you think a church that doesn't emphasize or teach much on spiritual gifts can be just as successful as one that does emphasize them? Whose responsibility is it to do most of the ministry in the community, the pastoral staff or the members of the local church?

3. What percentage of the members of your church do you estimate can name their spiritual gifts? Does your church have a plan in place for helping its members to discover their gifts? If not, what can you do to help change that?

Chapter 6: The Foundational Gifts

1. What does the apostle Paul say are the purposes of the five foundational gifts in Ephesians 4:11-12?

2. Do you believe the gift of apostleship is still being given today? Do you believe the gift of apostleship is the same as it was in the New Testament? Is the gift still needed today? Why or why not?

3. Have you ever been ministered to by someone with a prophetic gift? How did it make you feel? What do you think would happen if your lost friends or family members could experience someone ministering through a prophetic gift? What did the apostle Paul say was one benefit of non-believers experiencing a worship service in which a prophetic word was shared (see 1 Corinthians 14:24-25)?

4. What is one way that you can show appreciation to your pastors for all that they do in nurturing and caring for the members of your church? Is everyone who has the gift of pastoring necessarily called to pastor an entire congregation full time?

Chapter 7: The Ministry Gifts, Part I

1. Do you know anyone with the gift of intercession? Do you think churches should organize those with intercessory gifts for formal, corporate times of prayer? List the ways a church would benefit from doing this.

2. How are the gifts of leadership and administration similar? How are they different? Should people lead ministries in the church if they don't have the gift of leadership? Why or why not?

3. How are the gifts of giving and simplicity similar? How are they different?

Chapter 8: The Ministry Gifts, Part II

1. What kinds of ways can churches make full use of those with the gifts of serving and helps? What types of ministries would allow them to best utilize their gifts?

2. What kinds of ministries and programs in the church should be staffed by Christians with the gift of mercy? Is your church fully utilizing these folks?

3. Do you know people in your church who are known for their wisdom? How can churches use Christians with that gift for the maximum good of the congregation? What type of ministries do you think they would be excellently suited for?

Chapter 9: The Sign Gifts

1. What's the purpose of the sign gifts? Why are they called this?
2. Which of the six sign gifts do you believe is most needed in your church at this time? Do you believe there could be people in your congregation who could have one of these gifts and may not know it? Is there anything a church could do to ensure that the sign gifts are represented in their church? Are there things churches do that cause these gifts to not be expressed in their services? Discuss these issues with the group.
3. Does your church have a ministry in place for those suffering from demonic strongholds? If not, how might a church institute such a ministry? What kinds of guidelines and parameters would need to be set up to protect the church and its reputation if such a ministry was instituted?

Chapter 10: Discovering Your Spiritual Gifts

1. Do you believe you have a good idea as to which spiritual gifts the Holy Spirit has given you? Do you exhibit the traits and passions associated with those particular gifts? Are you usually successful when you attempt the functions associated with those particular gifts? Have other members in the body of Christ confirmed those gifts in you? If you feel confident at this point, list the gifts you believe the

Holy Spirit has given you. What do you consider to be your primary gifts? What are your secondary gifts?

2. Are you currently involved in a ministry at your church that uses your gifts? If so, list that ministry or ministries. If you are not sure what your gifts are yet, would you commit to God that you will use them in His service as soon as you do confirm your giftings?

Chapter 11: Maturing in Your Spiritual Gifts

1. Have you ever been closer to Jesus in times past as compared to today? If so, what are some things you can begin to do today to have a closer relationship with Him?
2. Have you ever held back in exercising your gifts because of fear? If so, read 2 Timothy 1:6-7 and spend some time in prayer asking God to help you overcome this so that you can flow in your gifts unhindered.
3. Do you have a spiritual mentor who has helped you develop in your gifts? If so, share with the group how this person has helped you to develop your God-given potential. Have you considered mentoring someone less spiritually mature than yourself? If not, consider seeking the Lord on someone you could invest in.

Suggested Reading for Further Study

For those desiring more study on the gifts of the Spirit, I recommend the following books that should get you started in the right direction.

Are Miraculous Gifts for Today? Four Views – Wayne Grudem, ed. Four well-respected scholars debate this issue from four viewpoints: Cessationist, Open But Cautious, Third Wave, and Pentecostal/Charismatic. A little technical and scholarly in places, but otherwise a very informative read. (Zondervan, 1996)

Surprised by the Power of the Spirit – Jack Deere. Not a book on spiritual gifts per se, but rather the personal testimony of a former cessationist and professor at Dallas Theological Seminary who came to later believe in the gifts of the Spirit. This polemical work does devote much time to showing why biblically, God desires for all the gifts to continue until the return of Christ. Masterfully written, his thesis is hard to refute. (Zondervan, 1993)

Your Spiritual Gifts Can Help Your Church Grow – C. Peter Wagner. A classic, popular work on the gifts first released in 1979 but revised in 1994. Written from the constitutional view, the book covers some 27 gifts and is written with a special emphasis on how implementing the gifts contributes to growing a healthy, well-balanced local church. (Regal Books 1994)

Showing the Spirit: A Theological Exposition of 1 Corinthians 12-14 – D.A. Carson. A detailed scholarly look at Paul's teaching on the *charismata*. Carson covers such issues as the baptism of the Spirit, the diversity of the gifts, and the role of tongues and prophecy. A very balanced work from a scholar who arrives at his answers from a careful interpretation of the Scriptures, not a dogmatic adherence to any group or denomination. (Baker Book House, 1987)

Index

To order additional copies of

SPIRITUAL
GIFTS

Have your credit card ready and call:

1-877-421-READ (7323)

or please visit our web site at
www.pleasantword.com

Also available at:
www.amazon.com
and
www.barnesandnoble.com

Printed in the United States
137698LV00003B/111/A